Journal for Architecture and Literature

Writing place

#8+9 SPECIAL ISSUE

Writing Urban Places

New Narratives for the European City

Edited by

Klaske Havik

Susana Oliveira

Jorge Mejía Hernández

Holly Dale

nai010 publishers

writing urban places

cost
EUROPEAN COOPERATION IN SCIENCE & TECHNOLOGY

Funded by the European Union

CONTENT

Writing place

writing urban places

INTRODUCTION

Klaske Havik and Susana Oliveira

> ***'Cities were always like books to me, each street a page, each building a sentence, and the people, the characters who populated the pages, bringing the story to life with their hopes and dreams.'***
> Carlos Ruiz Zafón, *The Shadow of the Wind*

The special issue of *Writingplace Journal*, *Writing Urban Places: New Narratives on the European City*, marks the culmination of an international research network that delved into the intricate interplay between communities, urban spaces and narratives. At its core, this endeavour introduced an inventive approach aimed at deepening our comprehension of urban communities, their dynamics and their rootedness, all through the lens of narrative methodologies. As chairs of this network, we are thrilled to present a collaborative publication that reflects and reimagines the ways we perceive urban spaces and narratives. This collection gives an account of the dynamics of this network of academics, which consists of over 175 individuals from 35 different European countries and a variety of disciplinary backgrounds. As such, the issue offers a conclusion to the *Writing Urban Places* COST Action while also, hopefully, providing a springboard for further reflections and discussions on urban narratives, and the role these could play in spatial developments in the European city.

Central to this network is the acknowledgment of the value embedded in local urban narratives. These narratives, brimming with insights into the sociospatial behaviours, perceptions and aspirations of citizens, serve as a wellspring of knowledge. This initiative endeavoured to articulate a range of literary techniques that harmonize with various spatial disciplines. By weaving together scholarly investigations from the realms of literary studies, urban planning, architecture and other related practices, the project sought to align its findings with the progressive urban revitalization policies that are currently unfolding in medium-sized European cities. *Writing Urban Places* drew from a legacy of rigorous investigation within diverse preoccupations – including those of our network members, whose work on the meeting point between architecture and literature has been the point of departure for this initiative.[1] By uniting the realms of literary studies with the domains of urban planning and architecture, this network hoped to offer another reading of the contemporary city, and to highlight the nuances of local urban cultures in a European context. Through a range of activities – which will be addressed in detail in this volume – the network aimed to bring together various concepts related to urban narratives, to examine reading and writing techniques for urban narratives, and to apply, test and evaluate these techniques in concrete urban realities of a diverse series of European mid-size cities. By these means, we hoped to gain a nuanced, locally relevant understanding of urban settings that would consider the viewpoint of residents and users – local communities with their own relationship to places and their own customs, memories and dreams about their surroundings. Our premise was that such a perspective could be incorporated into spatial policies and urban and architectural design, and eventually help shape cities in more locally specific and socially meaningful ways.

The first part of this volume presents the outcomes and reflections of the four working groups in which this network was organized: communication, theory, methodology and fieldwork. While this basic structure led our activities, the four teams worked together within a thematic framework, which provided a starting point for our investigation into this vast field of urban narratives. This *Writing Urban Places* framework was built upon three themes: meaningfulness, appropriation and integration.[2] The dimension of *meaningfulness* endeavours to equip local communities and professionals with the tools to enhance their comprehension of their built environment. By tapping into narratives that illuminate the significance of urban spaces, this facet enriches our understanding of the spaces we inhabit. At the heart of the second theme, *appropriation*, lies the idea of empowering communities to project their emotions and experiences onto their physical surroundings. By doing so, communities establish a profound connection with their urban environment, fostering a sense of ownership and agency. The third theme, *integration,* is centred on the capacity of narrative strategies to create common ground among communities. Based on the principles of meaningfulness and appropriation, spatial strategies derived from the study of local narratives may bridge divides and cultivate shared spaces within the urban fabric. In the working groups, these themes were addressed in theoretical and methodological discussions, and were further explored through a series of case studies in European cities.

The series of reflections by the working groups opens with the article 'Placing Urban Writing', by Jorge Mejía Hernández and Onorina Botezat, leaders of the working group dedicated to communication. Pondering on the role of stories as a means of exchange, their contribution brings forward the hypothesis that narrative means could bring together the aspects needed to strive for such meaningful, appropriable and integrative built environments, and goes on to question with whom the knowledge that is present in such narratives could be shared, and how. The realization that all participants in the network are not only scholars in their distinct fields, but also users and inhabitants of urban places who have their own stories related to their environment, opens up a potential for stories to be shared on different levels: both academically, and towards a general public. Conversations with network members about their personal urban experiences led to a reflection on narrative techniques, such as sense, sequence and proportion, and their importance for the development of urban places.

The core objects of our study were European medium-sized cities, as we provisionally called them, with their blend of historical significance, contemporary innovation and community intimacy. Cities that may be overlooked in urban studies and in literature, but still accommodate many local narratives that are less widespread and internationally known. The contribution by working group 2, led by Sonja Novak, Angeliki Sioli and Giuseppe Resta,[3] critically addresses this notion of the 'mid-size' city, and proposes the term 'intermediate' instead. The chapter introduces, through descriptions by different members of the working group, a series of conditions of intermediate cities, such as 'the parochial realm', 'perceptual coherence', 'walkable distances' and 'fragmentability'.

Writing Urban Places envisioned a process that paired investigation with implementation. Working group 3, bridging theoretical exploration and fieldwork, conducted an exploration of narrative techniques articulated within spatial and literary practices. The contribution by Carlos Machado e Moura and Dalia Milián Bernal[4] narrates the process towards a repository of methods, a collaborative project that took multiple forms, and resulted in the Repository book,[5] presenting a range of methods and assignments to reveal, understand and construct urban narratives. The article shares how, along this process, the understanding of two key terms used by this working group, narrative and method, was deepened and further elaborated. The authors conclude by sharing their observation that many of the methods proposed and discussed in relation to urban narrative dealt with the complex and rich dimensions of human experience, related to places and communities.

The specificity of the different urban places studied by this network was addressed through fieldwork, as conceptualized, discussed and conducted by working group 4, led by Slobodan Velevski and Luís Santiago Baptista. Through a series of fieldwork events, carried out in the second part of our Action, we uncovered the nuanced dimensions of urban community environments – from sociocultural practices to the intricacies of situatedness within the urban fabric. The article 'Fieldwork for Writing Urban Places' discusses fieldwork as a research experience and an experimental spatial practice, and embeds this multifaceted understanding in an overview of fieldwork practices.

This reflection on fieldwork forms the introduction to the next series of articles that delve into the reality of a number of intermediate cities in Europe. The itinerary of activities among European locations – Almada, Limerick, Porto, Tallinn, Osijek, Tampere, Çannakalle, Skopje, Delft, Kamaza and Tirana – transcends the boundaries of academic discourse. Through fieldwork events, training schools and on-site meetings carried out in these cities, they became places of investigation as well as places of our network's collective experience – a physical common ground. The accounts from these cities, collected in this publication, is a celebration of the collective curiosity and wit that emerge when individuals from diverse backgrounds come together to contemplate, reflect upon and act on urban experience. Each author's voice – and the reader will encounter them in different narrative formats: poetical, literary, graphic, photographic and cinematic – adds a layer of richness to our understanding of these cities, revealing insights that are as affectionate as they are analytical.

The accounts of urban experience offered here may be seen as evidence of the power of collective exploration, the vitality of storytelling and the significance of places that forge connections between the past, present and future. We extend our gratitude to the contributors, colleagues and friends who have shared their expertise, experiences and passions, making this project a reality. It was truly a surprising effect, that this project caught the attention of and captivated such a diverse group of people, of different ages, backgrounds, countries and circumstances – who reacted with enthusiasm and creativity to many of the challenges of this project. We envisage that the results of these researches and the convergence of the long, turbulent and creative lifetime of our network, its experiences, events, publications and, above all, people, will build a ground and a framework to think and plan for the future. This collection is an invitation to the young scholars in the network to initiate spin-offs and new projects. The knowledge and energy that we've been producing together can be used to inform future projects and initiatives, which can help further build and shape cities.

Finally, this publication is not merely a conclusion to a research network; we hope it stands as proof of the potential of narratives to shape our urban environments, enrich our experiences and foster cohesion within the communities that inhabit them.

1 The team of proposers consisted of scholars in architecture and literature who had already been working on the topic extensively. Two conferences were crucial in establishing collaborations that led to the *Writing Urban Places* COST Action. Susana Oliveira organized, with Pedro Gadanho, the first conference on architecture and fiction *Once Upon a Place*, in Lisbon in 2010. At Delft University of Technology, Klaske Havik organized, with Jorge Mejía Hernández, Mark Proosten and Mike Schäfer, the conference *Writingplace, Literary Methods in Architectural Research and Education*, in Delft in 2013. See: Susana Oliveira and Pedro Gadanho (eds), *Once Upon a Place: Architecture and Fiction* (Lisbon: Editora Caleidoscópio, 2013); and Klaske Havik et al. (eds), *Writingplace: Investigations in Architecture and Literature* (Rotterdam: nai010, 2016). For an extensive list of publications on the topic by the network members, please refer to the bibliography page of the network's website: writingurbanplaces.eu/library/bibliography/.

2 These three lines of investigation were proposed by Jorge Mejía Hernández. See also the introduction to these themes in the chapter 'Placing Urban Writings' by Jorge Mejía Hernández and Onorina Botezat in this issue. See also: Sonja Novak, Susana Oliveira, Angeliki Sioli and Klaske Havik (eds.) Writingplace#6 *City Narratives as Places of Meaningfulness, Appropriation and Integration.* (Rotterdam: nai010, 2022).

3 In the first period of the Action, working group 2 was led by Svava Riesto and Henriette Steiner. In 2020, Sonja Novak and Angeliki Sioli took over their task, later joined by Giuseppe Resta.

4 In the first period of the Action, working group 3 was led by Lorin Niculae and Mark Proosten. In the course of the Action, Carlos Machado e Moura replaced Mark Proosten; in a later stage, when Lorin Niculae had to withdraw, Dalia Milián Bernal joined as group leader.

5 Carlos Machado e Moura, Dalia Milián Bernal et al. (eds.), *Repository: 49 Methods and Assignments for Writing Urban Places* (Rotterdam: nai010, 2023).

ACKNOWLEDGMENTS

The *Writing Urban Places* COST Action Network has grown over the past 4.5 years to include almost 200 participants – scholars, architects, urban designers, researchers, artists and authors – from 35 European countries. Many of these participants have contributed to the network in one way or another at some point during its existence. The impressive body of work we have produced, and of which this special issue is only a sample, reflects the knowledge, expertise, experience, creativity and collaborative capacity of the participants in *Writing Urban Places*, to whom we are immeasurably grateful. Without the effort and work of all the dedicated contributors, this special issue would not exist. Thank you also to all those who gave us permission to use their images, drawings, photographs, travelogues and quotes, which now illuminate these pages.

While the present publication gathers contributions from a group of participants, as previous *Writingplace* journal issues did, the network could not have been built and kept alive without the input and collaboration of many. First and foremost, our gratitude goes to our excellent Core group, with whom we have developed all our activities, engaged in lively discussions during our many meetings, face-to-face and many more online, and whose energy and dedication endured even through the challenges of the Covid pandemic: Jorge Mejía, Onorina Botezat, Sonja Novak, Angeliki Sioli, Giuseppe Resta, Carlos Machado e Moura, Dalia Milián Bernal, Slobodan Velevski, Luís Santiago Baptista, Kinga Kimic and Marcel Pikhart.

We would also like to thank Svava Riesto and Henriette Steiner from Copenhagen, who were the first to lead Working Group 2 and who, together with Kris Pint, were the initiators of the *Vademecum*, the first publication of the network. Likewise, our gratitude goes to Lorin Niculae and Mark Proosten, Action co-proponents and Working Group 3 leaders in the first phase of the COST Action. We had great support from project assistants Holly Dale and Willie Vogel, who kept us on track with meetings, publications, back office, executive production and social media. And a special thanks to Salma Ibrahim, our grantee manager at Delft University of Technology, who has been indispensable as a behind-the-scenes organizer, kindly making it all possible.

From the COST association, our gratitude especially goes to our scientific officer, Mickael Pero, for his keen enthusiasm and interest in our work, and for his continuous support. Thanks to Olga Gorzcyca, our administrative officer, and Karima BenSalah for valuable reflections on communication, and to Lorna Stokes for her enthusiastic response to our Action.

This publication was kindly made possible by nai010 publishers, who have always been receptive to our suggestions and have supported many of our publications. We are grateful to our proof-reader, D'Laine Camp, for her patience and critical reading of all the contributions to this special issue – and the previous ones. Finally, the success of this network cannot be separated from its consistent visual appearance. Our sincere thanks go to graphic designer Sanne Dijkstra, who has been responsible for the design of our website, publications and all visual and graphic materials, giving this network such a unique and distinctive character.

Having an idea and turning it into a book is as hard as it is exciting. Turning it into several books, webinars, films, drawings, workshops, meetings, training schools and conferences within a huge international network has been as challenging as it has been rewarding. We would like to personally thank all the people we have had the opportunity to meet, work with, talk to, discuss, collaborate with and witness their creative growth – thank you for being the inspiration, power and substance of our network.

Placing Urban Writings
Narrative Technology and Possible Futures for the European City

Jorge Mejía Hernández and Onorina Botezat
WORKING GROUP 1

Stories and Cities

How can stories be used for the development of cities? Over the past four years, we have looked into this question from different perspectives as a multidisciplinary network of researchers from nearly all European countries. The objectives of our network were formulated as follows:

> *Writing Urban Places proposes an innovative investigation and implementation of a process for developing human understanding of communities, their society, and their situatedness, by narrative methods. It focuses particularly on the potential of narrative methods for urban development in European medium-sized cities.*[1]

This programme was carried out through several activities, organized by four independent working groups, focused respectively on the communicative, theoretical, methodological and operative aspects of the topic. Our focus on communications required that we zero in on the question of exchange.[2] To study how stories can be used for urban development, we started by recognizing them as a particular form of exchange. From this perspective, we could establish a clear relationship between the two main aspects of our study, where stories are means (of exchange) towards an end, which is urban development.

Rather than studying them separately, we became interested in knowing how the means and ends relate to each other. Among other possibilities, we found that a useful methodology to study interrelated means and ends is implicit in philosopher of science Marx Wartofsky's definition of models. Normally, we think of models as

> *. . . imitations, diagrams, scale versions, or pictures of something already existing. However, they can be more than this, as in prototypes, plans, hypothetical constructions of various sorts which serve as guides to action . . . Models are the highly specialized part of our technological equipment whose specific function is to create the future . . . In this sense, models are embodiments of purpose and, at the same time, instruments for carrying out such purposes.*[3]

Wartofsky's inscription of models within our future-making technologies required that we make a clear distinction between narrative techniques and narrative technology. Put simply, narrative techniques can be understood as the different ways in which stories can be told (that is, the discrete instruments and methods used by storytellers to craft and communicate experiences and events). Narrative technology, on the other hand, refers to the branch of knowledge that deals with all those techniques jointly. For instance, while Jean-Paul Sartre's *The Reprieve* develops a cinematographic technique to move seamlessly between characters and actions, the novel itself is part of a larger technology of the novel as a distinct narrative form.[4]

Besides allowing us to realize that narration operates simultaneously at the technical and technological levels, Wartofsky's definition of models also seemed particularly relevant to our work because it allowed us to keep the 'human understanding of communities' we strove for clear from determinism. A deterministic approach to urban development presumes that citizens have little effect on the future of their city, which is believed to be shaped elsewhere, by someone else, or in advance. On the contrary, Wartofsky's models intend to

> *characterize the normal process of creating the future, by bringing it down from the scale of cosmic crisis to that of daily and local necessity. I do not think there is a millennial solution to the future; but I do think that the pattern of our ordinary planning and striving prefigures whatever larger structures there are in terms of which long-range creation of the future can take place.*[5]

From this vantage point, we could see the singular hopes and actions of many different individuals as alternatives to prophecy or utopia, which Wartofsky refers to as 'larger structures in which long-range futures take place'.[6] Contrary to utopias, where means are made subservient to ends (or neglected altogether), Wartofsky's models make possible futures (*telos*) inseparable from the instruments and methods (techniques) required to get there.[7] Seeing them as models required us to reflect on how the cities we imagined have been made or should be made in the future.

Accordingly, the telos for our work was defined in relation to an undesirable (albeit changeable) situation that reflected strongly on different cities and an available resource that seemed useful to confront that situation. The resurgence in Europe of dissociative movements brought back a politics of cosmic crises (with their equally cosmic solutions, naturally). At the urban level, over the past decades, many local and national governments have used such politics to enforce across-the-board master plans and impose different types of uniformity on their cities.[8] The many negative results of such master plans include the decrease in the quantity or quality of public space, the displacement of affordable housing from central to peripheral areas, the decimation of productive economies for the sake of a supposed planetary benefit, a new wave of programmatic functionalization or clear-cut zoning, and what is usually referred to as 'overtourism'.[9]

In contrast to these and other ill effects of one-party planning, previous research on the interrelations that exist between architecture and literature afforded us three leads to study the past, present and possible futures of the European city.[10] Based on that research, we hypothesized that the good quality of life in many of those cities is the result of the inhabitants' ability to recognize meaning in their built environment, but also to appropriate it piecemeal by projecting their own ambitions and hopes onto it. Furthermore, it appeared to us that it is essentially through said meaning and appropriation of their surroundings that those inhabitants are able to integrate with each other productively while preserving their singularity.[11]

These three conditions – meaningfulness, appropriation and integration – are not easily attainable when urban planning is conceived as a top-down, centralized or univocal response to a cosmic crisis. On the other hand, we realized that all three conditions are essential to great stories. Writing about Henry Miller, George Orwell invites us to:

> *. . . read him for five pages, ten pages, and you feel the peculiar relief that comes not so much from understanding as from being understood [emphasis original]. 'He knows all about me,' you feel; 'he wrote this specially for me.' It is as though you could hear a voice speaking to you . . . with no humbug in it, no moral purpose, merely an implicit assumption that we are all alike. For the moment you have got away from the lies and simplifications, the stylized, marionette-like quality of ordinary fiction, even quite good fiction, and are dealing with the recognizable experiences of human beings [emphasis added].*[12]

Indeed, stories – especially the better ones – have a distinct ability to convey meaning, foster empathy (that is, the ability to 'put oneself in someone's shoes') and encourage mutual understanding among strangers. But can similar relations be established between inhabitants and buildings, or between the different parties involved in the construction of the city? And if so, how?

Possible Futures

Architecture and the other disciplines that specialize in the production of buildings are by nature polytechnic. Even the simplest construction requires diverse technologies, such as those needed to defy gravity, protect from adverse climatic conditions, provide electrical power and running water, or communicate status or beliefs through style.[13] Likewise, even the simplest of stories operate at different levels, based on the choice and use of specific narrative techniques.[14] On these grounds we set out to study the ways in which narrative technology can be used to develop meaningful, appropriable, and integrative built environments.

We are aware that the mere claim that one aims for meaningful, appropriable and integrative cities remains a vague and probably banal proposition, unless joint sense is made of these qualities and criteria are established to evaluate them. In other words, a theory was required to explain the city and justify a course of action for its future development in relation to the principles we defined for our work.

To some extent, the telos of our network is founded on an architectural theory that melds piecemeal engineering with the ecological sciences. Regarding the first, we can refer to the article 'L'Ambiente Come Artefatto' (Environment as Artefact) that was published in the Italian architecture journal *Casabella* in 1971, which recognizes cities as:

> *. . . organizations of form that are the (often unforeseen) result of many human actions, as environments that must sustain a wide range of (often unforeseen) human actions. Such an organization of form, in contrast*

> *to an object that is the result of a deliberate design, has been termed an 'artifact'.*[15]

The diversity of those many human actions is further considered through an ecological framework, the description of which can be found in the introduction to the book *On Streets*, published in 1978:

> *The notion of territoriality, transferred from ethology, has played an increasingly prominent role in human ecology, and in more narrowly defined studies of architecture. As in A.E. Parr's definition of territory, 'space which an individual or close-knit group will defend,' the concept necessarily involves a principle of competitive exclusion. Ethologists, however, have pointed to two extreme types of territory or 'niche specificity.' 'In one the animal . . . requires to be spatially separate from its closest allies and competitors . . . In the other the various species are structurally specialized to use different resources; they do not need to have behavioral mechanisms fixing them in place and in fact cross each other's paths.' Ecological sympatry, the sharing of the same region by different kinds of organism [sic], is thus a concomitant of the description of territories.*[16]

Both fragments converge in a theory that explains the city as the sum of many ordinary plans, conceived by different people in order to deal with their daily and local necessities. That theory also defines the principles on which the practice of that city is based: a series of sympatric relations between diverse (even antagonistic) individuals, who contribute and use disparate resources. Together, ordinary planning and sympatry justify a course of action for the future development of cities, which is to foster and protect urban resilience, understood as the city's ability to adapt to changing situations.

Urban resilience can be grasped and explained by different means, such as the texts where we've read about this theory, or the different drawings and three-dimensional scale-models architects use to practice this or any other theory in design. Like these, and the many other forms of communication people use to make cities, stories have a number of advantages and disadvantages. Here we will focus on a single one of those advantages, namely, their ability to convey evidence of previous and potential understandings. Aldous Huxley offers us a good distinction between knowledge and understanding in the following terms:

> *Knowledge is always in terms of concepts and can be passed on by means of words or other symbols. Understanding is not conceptual, and therefore cannot be passed on. It is an immediate experience, and immediate experience can only be talked about (very inadequately), never shared. Nobody can actually feel another's pain or grief, another's love or joy or hunger. And similarly nobody can experience another's understanding of a given event or situation. There can, of course, be knowledge of such an understanding, and this knowledge may be passed on in speech or writing, or by means of other symbols. Such communicable knowledge is useful as a reminder that there have been specific understandings in the past, and that understanding is at all times possible.*[17]

Normally, the means we use to communicate our plans for the built environment fit Huxley's definition of knowledge. Drawings, models, technical texts and other instruments of architecture help us abstract aspects of buildings and cities and pass them on to others unambiguously. Building beyond a minimum degree of complexity would be unimaginable without this ability. However, our experience of the environments we project and build is first and foremost direct, and therefore fits Huxley's definition of understanding, meaning that it cannot be passed on to others. An important part of what buildings and places say to us, the ways in which we make them ours, and how we associate with others by doing so, is also direct. While there are aspects of the three goals we set for ourselves that can be known, it is clear that others remain within the realm of understanding.

As Huxley notes, stories cannot pass on direct experience. Mindless of how well-crafted a story might be, it will never allow us to actually feel the amazement of others as they are bathed by the cleansed light in a Gothic cathedral, their fear of walking down a dark alley in the bad part of town, or the joy of sharing food and drinks with loved ones on a sunny terrace. What stories can do, especially when they are of the excellent kind, is to record as clearly and convincingly as possible that those understandings have indeed taken or could take place and remain possible, and by doing so remind us that our ordinary plans and the environments we generate will inevitably lead to new and hopefully desirable understandings. In other words, stories of (or about) the city, or 'urban narratives', allow us to record previous and promote new understandings of life in cities. But how does that happen? And, most importantly, what effect could that distinct capacity of stories have in relation to the kind of city we are striving for?

Urban Narratives

Trying to understand what it is about stories that allows us to imagine ourselves in situations that are unknown to us, as well as to empathize with the strangers who partook in those events, we collected a handful of urban narratives from within our network. A first step in this direction had already been taken on 12 May 2021. Under lockdown, our working group organized an online seminar on the topic of communication. The title of the seminar was 'Integration through Discourse', followed by the double question 'How do we communicate, and why?'[18]

Our goal then was to reflect on our own discourse through a public conversation carried out by different people focused on a known topic.[19] During a four-hour long programme, we tried to examine the different instruments and methods that made our discourse possible, but also asked ourselves if those instruments and methods made sense in relation to our network's telos. Among other positive results, the event revealed an urgent question. Before asking how and why we communicate, shouldn't we first know *who* we should be communicating with?

Truth be told, the seminar showed that we were mostly talking to ourselves. With a single exception, all participants were academics, which had evident effects on the selection of topics, but also on the way the conversation was carried out. In some cases, there was actually no conversation, but lecturing. We thus recognized that the fulfilment of our telos required exchanges with different kinds of citizens and the institutions that represent them. Reflecting on her book *Open Architecture*, historian Esra Akcan shows how the voices of citizens, scholars and institutions can be productively interwoven:

> *By paying attention to immigrant appropriations of domestic and urban spaces, we can register architectural design as something that constantly evolves in time, and acquires new forms and meanings with the contribution of resident architects. By honouring the residents' stories equally with those of the architects, we can admit that architectural history does not end when a building leaves the hand of the professional architect.*[20]

Besides reaching out to local media (such as regional newspapers, radio stations and TV channels) as a means to engage with a larger, non-academic public, we also appealed to some of our colleagues, not as experts but as citizens (or as residents, in Akcan's terms). Beyond the specific knowledge every scholar has developed, it is also clear that they inevitably understand the city directly, in ways that cannot be codified into disciplines. So what does the city look like, from that perspective?[21]

Esteban says:
I come from Medellín, which has this awful image related to violence and drugs. Since I've been in Paris, Medellín has evolved in my mind. Every time I return, I explore it again, as I have become a foreigner in my own city. I discover the new city that was born during my years here, in France; a new Medellín that was born in my mind. I don't want to say that it's a nostalgic experience, it's just something I appreciate in a different way. Paris is a very dense city, and it's always changing. There's always something to discover, not only in the centre. I've become a fan of the suburbs, because it's there where you can find real differences, real changes, real conflicts, not in a pejorative way but rather as movement. I started exploring the suburbs as a hobby and then realized that, by doing so, Paris grew on me. Every time I cross the ring that divides city centre from periphery, I feel elsewhere, and I know I'm going to discover something new every time.

Jeremy says:
I've lived in Strasbourg for over a decade, but I was born in New York City and raised in Hudson Valley, in a small city called Middletown, one of 50 – if not more – Middletowns that exist in America. I grew up thinking of Middletown as quite unremarkable. Very recently I've been having memories of being a boy, not yet a teenager but a boy, and crossing a certain part of that landscape on bicycle, on foot, on rollerblades. There used to be a railroad track behind my best friend's house, a little service rail that was supposed to carry freight to some tiny factory. We were following that line across town. It was reminiscent of the movie *Stand by Me*, without the dead bodies, although we really wanted to find one at that age. My attempt to be independent in a small city in upstate New York was about getting out of my immediate neighbourhood and going to the two or three other neighbourhoods across town. In hindsight, it was maybe a kilometre, but at the time it seemed huge. Two years ago, I moved to the edge of Strasbourg and when I go for a run I leave Strasbourg, I cross the city line into some German-sounding villages that are to the northwest. At the same time, I'm also at

a 12-minute bicycle ride from the Central Station and my work. In many ways it's bigger than Middletown, but it feels like a very small city, especially because I made my way to Strasbourg through Brooklyn and Edinburgh and other places that were more intensely populated. Strasbourg feels like a village that kept on eating Alsatian food and so has taken on an obese size. I can make a comparison to my accumulated memories of Brooklyn becoming less and less a place of interest. The field of possibility shrinks every time I go back. There's no residual space to inhabit there as a thinker, as a maker, as a creator, unless you happen to be wildly wealthy.

Karima says:
I was born in Brussels and when I had the age to travel, I was really eager to go to London, where I worked and lived for about ten years. Then I decided to come back and it was great, because after living all those years in a busy town, I could step back and rediscover my city. Lots of things had changed. I decided to live in Ixelles, where it is busy, but not too much, where you can do things within walking distance, really close to the woods. I didn't have a terrace or garden in my previous places, so I really enjoyed the feeling of living in the country without living in the country, and at the same time not having to take lots of public transport for long journeys like I used to do in London. Now we live in the country, not far from town. We commute by train for an hour, maybe an hour-and-a-half, it depends. The kids are big, so, now, we're free to improvise and stay after work in the city for theatre, drinks with friends, exhibitions. My father was a farmer originally and it's kind of ironic that he left Morocco to settle his family in Brussels, and that after experiencing the big city, now, I'm also back in nature, yet not completely cut off from what the town has to offer. Brussels is well-sized, it's kind of human-sized. You can do things, you can discover other quarters without having to organize yourself or plan in advance. There are 19 *communes* in Brussels, like little boroughs, and each of them functions like a village. The other thing about Brussels is the quality of life. Here you can still have access to things you can't have in big cities, where you would have to have a lot of money

to be in the centre. Here you can still have a little garden without having to be on a huge corporate wage. And even though it's not like it used to be 20 years ago, you can still find a mix between different communities, with students mixed with old, retired people.

Mennatullah says:
I was born and raised in different parts of Cairo. Other than Jakarta, I've never visited a more intense city than Cairo. I love living in big cities! I studied in Stuttgart, which most Germans would consider a big city, but for me it was very small. For further studies, I only wanted bigger cities, it was an important factor. I like the differences between the different parts of a big city. In each neighbourhood, you can feel the lack of homogeneity. Sometimes it's mind-blowing, it's too much, especially after living some time elsewhere. Sometimes it's hard to comprehend all that's going on, but at the same time you can live in your own bubble, without really having to see what's happening outside. Now I live between different cities. Coming from Cairo, it's like juggling with different parts of the city, but now with different parts of the world.

Mickael says:
I was born in Maubeuge, which is a tiny little town in France, next to the Belgian border. I recall it being nice but cold, green, and having friends. I came to Brussels at a very young age, to live in a neighbourhood outside the city centre. It was also green, very pleasant, and I remember commuting to school on a bus, again with friends. The neighbourhood was Watermael-Boisfort, in the southern part of Brussels, which is known to be more of a village-like neighbourhood. It's not as hectic as the centre of Brussels. Neighbourhoods in Brussels have a very strong identity, also at the administrative level. Management is done at the level of the *communes*, as they are called, not at the level of the whole city. We are still a bit medieval. Neighbourhoods that used to be little cities still keep a lot of power in local politics. It causes a lot of friction because coordination and public infra-

structure become big issues, but at the same time it creates a lot of dialogue. Consensus takes a lot of time. For an outsider it might seem chaotic, but I find this the perfect environment for creativity to step in. Behind all the chaos, and the impression that it's not a fully modern city, I see a place where new ideas can actually be imagined. Brussels is also changing constantly. People criticize the fact that it's always under construction. Everything takes a long time due to the difficult planning, which could be seen as a lack of efficiency, but it can also be seen as a very open city that is ready to hear many opinions before actually engaging in something concrete.

Narrative Technology

Brussels, Medellín, Cairo, Paris, London and New York do not fit the range of mid-sized cities that we initially tried to focus on, especially if you think of them on a map, the number of their inhabitants, the intensity of their public transport networks, or their GDP. The above stories, though, allow us to revise our initial focus on a particular kind of city, and recognize that size is always relative. As we can see in these stories, the bigness of cities can be acknowledged and confronted through different means. For instance, large territories, dense inhabitation, and busy movement can be fragmented into much smaller pieces, which Mickael and Karima refer to as villages, and Mennatullah calls bubbles. Could this fragmentation explain how all narrators seem to find meaning and achieve different degrees of appropriation of the cities they told us about?

In relation to our telos, stories would indeed make it feasible to attain this kind of fragmentation, which was also implicit in our original goals as a network.

> *By recognising the value of local urban narratives – stories rich in information regarding citizens' socio-spatial practices, perceptions and expectations – the Action aims to articulate a set of concrete literary devices within a host of spatial disciplines; bringing together scientific*

> *research in the fields of literary studies, urban planning and architecture; and positioning this knowledge vis-à-vis progressive redevelopment policies carried out in medium-sized cities in Europe.*[22]

Indeed, our focus on the experience of local and concrete citizens of the city would denote that, far from deterministic readings of the past (or utopian visions of the future), stories could allow us to appraise human experience piecemeal. According to Orwell, this individual, piecemeal experience is actually the *sine qua non* of literary prose.

> *Literature as we know it is an individual thing, demanding mental honesty and a minimum of censorship. And this is even truer of prose than of verse ... The atmosphere of orthodoxy is always damaging to prose, and above all it is completely ruinous to the novel, the most anarchical of all forms of literature ... The novel ... is a product of the free mind, of the autonomous individual.*[23]

We can certainly see this fragmentation at work in the five narratives above, where urban life is described as a series of discrete, yet ever-changing realities, even when it takes place within a vast and basically ungraspable territory. Time braids itself into long and short cycles and uneven rhythms, like when Jeremy shifts seamlessly from the railroad tracks of Middletown to the borders of Strasbourg, decades apart. Furthermore, all conflicts and contradictions that are inherent to social life in big and small cities are described as opportunities for constructive disagreement, carefully crafted opinions and consensual compromises based on trust – all conditions for sympatry. As Mickael notes: 'It is not sure where Brussels is going, but it's going ahead! This is what I love about Brussels, and what I sometimes miss in other towns that seem a bit too sure of what they are.'

The openness and doubt that are common to these stories appear to shield us from the allure of total planning. Esteban, for instance, would be much less likely to rediscover the suburbs of Paris every other day if, instead of a messy clustering of vibrant neighbourhoods, those suburbs looked more like the ideal cities of the Renaissance, or the totalitarian dreams of a socialist dictator. But unless we somehow articulate the indeterminacy and ambiguity recognized as value in his narration, ineffectuality could just as well ensue. In other words, Esteban could find it just as hard to discover anything of interest or value if Paris or Medellín were vast brownfields, suggesting that meaningless, in-appropriable, or disintegrative cities and stories can result as much from too much planning as from weak structure.

In urban terms, we usually refer to lack of structure as sprawl, with rambling as its narrative counterpart. It does not seem far-fetched to presume therefore that the technology we are looking for in both stories and cities – those 'literary devices within a host of spatial disciplines' mentioned above – should be able to position our telos as far as possible from the extremes of total planning or sprawl, full prescription, or rambling.

To see how stories can help us adopt this well-calibrated position we can start by identifying one of their fundamental capacities. Contrary to rambling, they must make *sense*, or allow us to *understand* the experiences or events they relate to. From its origin, the term we use to refer to this particular quality (the Latin *sēnsus*: sensation, feeling, understanding) conveys a distinct technical feature of stories. Stories can arouse our feelings and sensations as much as they can render comprehensible what is being communicated. Neither rambling nor univocal text (think of an instruction manual) are able to fulfil both conditions of sense simultaneously.[24]

Like stories, meaningful and appropriable built environments must also make sense, by being comprehensible and being able to arouse our feelings and sensations. Our equation of sprawl to rambling suggests that below a degree of consistency or coherence, built space turns unintelligible. Too much prescription, on the other hand, leads to environments that fail to stimulate our minds and senses. In addition, to a great degree, stories make sense because they structure events and experiences as a *sequence.* This simply means that they establish a particular order that can be followed by our mind as much as by our senses. Some sequences are linear while others meander intricately, some extend broadly while others barely cover instants. In all cases, though, a narrative sequence imposes a temporal restraint on reality that certainly favours our understanding.

Again, it isn't difficult to establish parallels between this technical capacity of stories and the built environments we are striving for. Human actions necessarily unfold in rhythms and time-lapses that are often neglected or oversimplified by extensive or comprehensive planning. Absent these sensitive timeframes, too much planning results in predictable outcomes and boring sequences, characteristic of both humdrum stories and cities. On the contrary, fecund architectures and texts manage to unfold time in ways that remain clear but are not entirely predictable, disclosing and revealing events at a pace that remains within the limits of our understanding, while keeping us alert and curious. Karima, for instance, is able to weave her story of decades (ten years in London, ten years after returning from London) into the longer process of her father's move from rural Morocco and the much more regular meetings with friends for drinks after work.

The last technical capacity of stories we will mention here is their ability to *proportion* reality. One can attribute extension in space or time to basically any object or event in and of itself, but as soon as two or more objects or events come in contact with each other, the relationship they establish is necessarily proportional. It is not by chance that the act of relating is synonymous with narrating or storytelling.

Relating means telling or giving an account of events or circumstances, but it also means bringing them into an association or connection. In great stories and beautiful cities, those connections achieve a degree of harmony that is often referred to as proportionate. In other words, the different objects, experiences or events that narrators and constructors alike bring together in their work, remain within a particular range (beyond which they would become futile, unbelievable or shocking). Attempts to make beauty completely relative, and therefore ethereal, ignore the robust proportional systems that underlie some of humankind's most cherished aesthetic achievements.[25] Mention of commuting, walking, biking, running and rollerblading in the above narratives offers us a sense of how the city is proportioned in different ways, depending on the instruments we use to proportion it.

While proportional systems establish ratios among two or more objects of different magnitudes, when one of the interrelated objects is deliberately fixed, proportion turns into something else. From the Latin *scālae*, meaning ladders or stairs, *scale* is usually understood as a progression in quantity or a degree based on a fixed variable, such as the even height of each step in a flight of stairs.[26] Architectural drawings and models, for example, start from a fixed unit of measure, such as the metre or the foot, to re-present real or conceived objects.

Clearly, all the abovementioned technical features of stories are essential to our telos because they jointly refer to a fixed magnitude. For stories to be understandable, their sense, sequence and proportion must remain within the quantities and qualities that are distinct to creatures of similar anatomy, perception and intellect. Granted that stories are made by and for human beings, they remain bound to a *human scale*, which is what allows us to appraise the events or experiences they relate in proportion to ourselves. And while we can abstract reality and systematize it (know it, in Huxley's terms) in relation to magnitudes way beyond ourselves (utopian, deterministic, totalitarian, and therefore in-, sub- or super-human scales), we also inevitably remain bound to the scale imposed on that same reality by our bodies, and the direct experience that they offer us.

In response to our initial question ('How can stories be used for the development of cities?'), Karima's observation that 'Brussels is well-sized (because) it's kind of human-sized' is revealing. Unlike other future-making technologies that operate at the scale of the cosmic crisis, urban narratives, through their different techniques, are useful for the development of meaningful, appropriable and integrative cities, simply because they offer us the distinct technology of scale required to recognize, foster and protect past, present and future human understandings. And because they allow us to continue conceiving and practicing them in fundamentally human magnitudes (piecemeal, ordinary, local and diverse), urban narratives should always have a key place among the technological equipment we use to analyse our past and project our present into the future of our cities.

References

Stanford Anderson, 'L'Ambiente Come Artefatto: Considerazione Metodologiche', *Casabella* 359-360 (1971)

Stanford Anderson, 'People in the Physical Environment: The Urban Ecology of Streets', in: Stanford Anderson (ed.), *On Streets* (Cambridge, MA and London: MIT Press, 1986)

Aldous Huxley, 'Knowledge and Understanding', in: Aldous Huxley, *Tomorrow and Tomorrow and Tomorrow* (New York: Harper & Bros., 1952), 33-68

Marx W. Wartofsky, 'Telos and Technique: Models as Modes of Action', in: Stanford Anderson (ed.), *Planning for Diversity and Choice: Possible Futures and Their Relation to the Man Controlled Environment* (Cambridge, MA: MIT Press, 1968)

1 About the Action, *Writing Urban Places*, writingurbanplaces.eu/about/.

2 Within the internal part of the network, we participated in Working Group 1 'Science Communications', which was 'responsible for the overall communication and output of the initiative, via the dissemination of the status and results of the projects and the deliverables of the different WG's through the website and beyond the network. This implies dealing with the output of the project, in terms of reports, academic journal, website and conference proceedings, guaranteeing internal and external communications.' *WG1 – Science Communication*, Writing Urban Places, writingurbanplaces.eu/about/team/wg-1-science-communication/.

3 Marx W. Wartofsky, 'Telos and Technique: Models as Modes of Action', in: Stanford Anderson (ed.), *Planning for Diversity and Choice: Possible Futures and Their Relation to the Man Controlled Environment* (Cambridge, MA: MIT Press, 1968), 261.

4 Richard Menke, 'Review: The Technology of the Novel: Writing and Narrative in British Fiction, by Tony E. Jackson', *Victorian Studies* 53/1 (2010), 158-160; Jean-Paul Sartre, *The Reprieve*, trans. Eric Sutton (New York: Vintage Books, 1978).

5 Ibid., 260.

6 Ibid.

7 Referring to the Marxist utopianism's disregard for technique, Frederick Crews notes: 'Instead of the anticipated triumph of a specific class which was alleged to be the unified subject-object of history, we now get the merest hints of a soporific Marcusean paradise for all – and no proposed means of arriving there.' Frederick Crews, 'Dialectical Immaterialism', in: Frederick Crews, *Skeptical Engagements* (New York and Oxford: Oxford University Press, 1986), 153.

8 Among the most interesting cases of such total planning is the city of Skopje, which adopted a large-scale 'metabolist' plan after the devastation caused by the 1963 earthquake, and more recently has been subjected to another attempt to achieve an overarching stylistic uniformity through the plan popularly known as 'Skopje 2014'.

9 World Tourism Organization (UNWTO); Centre of Expertise Leisure, Tourism & Hospitality; NHTV Breda University of Applied Sciences; and NHL Stenden University of Applied Sciences (eds.), 'Overtourism'? Understanding and Managing Urban Tourism Growth beyond Perceptions' (Madrid: UNWTO, 2018).

10 Pedro Gadanho and Susana Oliveira (eds.), *Once Upon a Place: Architecture & Fiction* (Lisbon: Caleidoscopio, 2013); and Klaske Havik et al. (eds.), *Writingplace: Investigations in Architecture and Literature* (Rotterdam: nai010 publishers, 2016).

11 In relation to this network, these three categories were first proposed in: Jorge Mejía Hernández, 'Technical Annex 2017 (edit)', e-mail, 6 September 2017.

12 George Orwell, 'Inside the Whale', in: George Orwell, *Selected Essays* (Harmondsworth: Penguin, 1960), 12.

13 Giancarlo Motta and Antonia Pizzigoni, *La Máquina de Proyecto* (Bogotá: Universidad Nacional de Colombia, 2008).

14 For an excellent example of said narrative techniques at work, see Esteban Restrepo Restrepo, 'The Readjusted Arabesque: Narrating Architecture in Literary Text, the Case of Kafka's Bridge', *Writingplace Journal* 5 (2021), 8-29.

15 Stanford Anderson, 'L'Ambiente Come Artefatto: Considerazione Metodologiche', *Casabella* 359-360 (1971), 71-73. The term artifact, in quotations, refers to F.A. Hayek, 'The Results of Human Action but not of Human Design', in: F.A. Hayek, *Studies in Philosophy, Politics and Economics* (London: Routledge and Kegan Paul, 1967), 96-105.

16 Stanford Anderson, 'People in the Physical Environment: The Urban Ecology of Streets', in: Stanford Anderson (ed.), *On Streets* (Cambridge, MA and London: MIT Press, 1986), 3; Notes refer to A.E. Parr, 'In Search of Theory VI', *Arts and Architecture* (September 1965), 2-3 and G.E. Hutchinson, *The Ecological Theater and the Evolutionary Play* (New Haven: Yale University Press, 1965), 55.

17 Aldous Huxley, 'Knowledge and Understanding', in: Aldous Huxley, *Tomorrow and Tomorrow and Tomorrow* (New York: Harper & Bros., 1952), 33-68.

18 For the call of this event, see *Online Seminar: Integration through Discourse: How do We Communicate, and Why?*, Writing Urban Places, writingurbanplaces.eu/online-seminar-integration-through-discourse-how-do-we-communicate-and-why/. Recordings of the whole seminar are available at Communication, Writing Urban Places, youtube.com/playlist?list=PLXlMnpOPXf1d7CqhmgMQpcQc4NBlxC_KJ.

19 We specifically refer to public discourse in order to make a clear distinction with private conversation and other aspects of intimate individual life. While the effects of information technology on this distinction are certainly challenging for the preservation of privacy, and thus open new and extremely interesting discussions about the role and nature of narrative techniques and technologies today, the scope of this text does not allow us to elaborate further on this matter.

20 Esra Akcan, 'Writing Open Architecture as a Book on Human Rights (and Against Nation-States)', *Footprint* 31 (2021), 15.

21 All stories below were collected in two online conversations with COST Senior Communications Officer Karima Ben Salah and Science Officer Mickael Pero (held on 26 October 2022) and with action members Esteban Restrepo, Jeremy Hawkins, and Mennatullah Hendawy (held on 20 December 2022). All excerpts have been used with their permission.

22 *About the Action*, op. cit. (note 1).

23 Orwell, 'Inside the Whale', op. cit. (note 12), 39.

24 For interesting cases of pseudo-technical text that is in fact rambling, see: Alan Sokal and Jean Bricmont, *Fashionable Nonsense* (New York: Picador, 1996).

25 Richard Padovan, Proportion: *Science, Philosophy, Architecture* (Oxon and New York: Routledge, 1999).

26 See: Julio Cortázar, 'Instrucciones para Subir una Escalera', in: Julio Cortázar, *Historias de Cronopios y Famas* (Bogotá: Punto de Lectura, 2005 [1962]).

Intermediate European Cities Conditions Between Metropolis and Town

Angeliki Sioli, Sonja Novak and Giuseppe Resta
WORKING GROUP 2

Our Urban Condition

In 2007, for the first time in history, more people in the world lived in urban areas than in rural areas; by 2021, this figure had risen to 56.61 per cent of the world's population, and it is expected to rise to 68 per cent by 2050.[1] Cities of all scales have become increasingly strong magnets for people in the context of the twenty-first century. This comes as no surprise when we look at Europe in particular. The big capitals of all major European countries have long attracted hordes of people not only from within Europe, but from all over the world. Their historical, cultural, architectural, professional and infrastructural affordances have fascinated people from all walks of life for years. Novelists, poets, filmmakers and storytellers have given us mesmerizing depictions of the popular and prevalent or hidden and surprising aspects of these cities. For example, Leopold Bloom, James Joyce's famous protagonist, revealed intimate aspects of Dublin's streets and public life to readers all around the globe. The fact that the whole nation celebrates the famous Bloomsday as a national holiday on 16 June demonstrates the power of narrative to capture the multiple and diverse identities of a place, but also its seductive capacity to add to and enhance those identities.[2]

In the Shadow of the European Metropolis

While the metropolises and capitals of Europe have fascinated us for a long time now, numerous smaller cities bloom beautifully in their shadow. Limerick and Cork in Ireland carry the marks of the unique historical developments of the country and have produced wonderful stories and narratives of their own.[3] The Hague in the Netherlands is not only home to the Dutch parliament as well as to many international organizations such as the International Court of Justice, but exhibits a fascinating cultural and artistic life that extends beyond the boundaries of its territory.[4] Osijek in Croatia is host to a multicultural population, a vibrant university student life, and the biggest zoological garden in the country. The article 'Mapping the Fictional and the Physical City: Spatiotemporal and Cultural Identity of Osijek, Croatia', also included in this publication, further discusses the multiple literary narratives in which the city features as a strong protagonist. Volos in Greece flourishes as a magnet for winter tourism, lying at the feet of the impressive mount Pelion, with contemporary novels and narratives containing the ancient mythological traces of the Argonaut Campaign and interpreting these in light of recent urban developments.[5]

The affordances and rhythms of everyday life in these smaller, but no less significant, cities are undoubtedly different from those of the metropolises and capitals as well as from the towns and villages of Europe. To say that the rhythm is slower or smoother and that the affordances are fewer or less up to date in comparison with the metropolises, is a generalization that fails to see the true potential of these places. If that was the case, these cities would not have survived over centuries of existence, becoming what issue 89 of the journal *OASE*, titled *Medium: Images of the Mid-Size City*, called the model of a resilient city, one with power in light of today's urban challenges.[6] The articles of that issue explore how the mid-size city as a place with an 'unexciting character' and a 'tempered urban experience' can currently be the object of urbanism and architecture. In addition to the adjective 'mid-size', some other denominations are put up for discussion, such as 'secondary', 'other', 'lesser known' and 'peripheral', placing the mid-size urban environments somewhere between the excitement of a big city and convivial suburbia, which is known for its tranquillity, greenery and security.[7] More specifically, the mid-size city is seen as

> *a city with a specific historical and geographical ancestry that finds a new purpose in a European city archipelago, at times operating on its own within this new configuration, at times in networks. This makes the model of this European 'generic city' a resilient model, re-inventing itself precisely in light of contemporary urban problems . . . the power of the concept to project divergent – at times seemingly irreconcilable – meanings and desires onto the contemporary city . . . The mid-size city, but also 'mid-size urbanity' can serve as a useful lens in describing a broad section of the European continent, and in developing a design outlook freed from the overstrained reference framework of the metropolis, without lapsing into an oppressive discourse about small-town identity.*[8]

Unconvinced of its 'unexciting character' and strongly believing that the future of the European urban condition lies in these very mid-size European cities, in 2019 the COST Action *Writing Urban Places: New Narratives of the European City* embarked on a study of such cities around Europe, with a focus on narrative methods. By recognizing the value of local urban narratives, the COST Action brought together research in the fields of literary studies, urban planning and architecture, positioning this knowledge vis-à-vis progressive redevelopment policies carried out in mid-size cities in Europe.[9] The aim was to discover the stories and narratives (official and unofficial) of these cities and understand their deeper urban characteristics.

Questioning the 'Mid-Size'

Our starting point was that the term 'mid-size' (which we started questioning very early on) refers to European cities, which are neither metropolises nor towns. They are separate entities lying somewhere in-between, but they cannot simply be defined by parameters of size and scale alone, such as the size of their population and number of inhabitants, the size of their territory, etcetera. Such quantitative parameters fail to capture their special urban and cultural character, a versatility so characteristic of the European context, which is built on diversity. At first glance, even the simple task of listing 'mid-size' cities was revealed as anything but simple. Capital cities such as Skopje, Ljubljana and Tallinn, for example, could in terms of population numbers be described as 'mid-size', but in their national context they do not fit this characterization, as they are both administrative capitals and the largest cities in their respective countries. On the other hand, explored through the perspective of their stories and narratives, these same European capitals seem much closer to cities like Limerick, Osijek or Volos. The way they are represented in literary narratives and the myths or stories about their foundation and origins as well as their physical, spatial and architectural characteristics are the reason for this paradox.[10] If we adopt one quantitative parameter, the resulting pool of cities will be contradictory by nature, including capital cities, such as those in the Balkans, with an international resonance and infrastructure, but which at the same time have preserved a scale of walkable distances, integration with their natural surroundings, and architectural coherence in their central areas. For this reason, this paradoxical condition in which some European capitals undoubtedly fit the category of 'mid-size' cities can be explained, according to Mladen Stilinović, by the fact that, historically and culturally speaking, there have been regions identified as lacking a metropolitan culture, thus comprised of only 'mid-size' cities, with even capitals being 'mid-size' urban formations.[11] Stilinović illustrates this in the example of the Balkans, but this can also be perceived in some eastern parts of Europe. Hence, what makes a parametrical definition impossible is also the trigger we used to stimulate a debate on how to render the mid-size condition alternatively.

As mentioned, some of the possible ways to define these cities can be developed if we agree that mid-size does not need to be defined in terms of quantity of population, geographical size or scope, but that there is a vast variety of qualities and variables that can be observed in mid-size cities. Thus, we decided that we should not aim for a definition, but for a set of conditions that should remain flexible and that are actually relational; they can both point towards what these cities are, but also to what they are not.

Urban Conditions under Discussion

In discussions within the wide interdisciplinary community of researchers that the COST Action 'Writing Urban Places' incorporates, such issues kept opening up new directions instead of narrowing down our path towards an encompassing definition of the term. Instead, we embraced the idea of offering a broad overview of these cities from different perspectives – narratological, sociological, architectural, urbanist, anthropological, etcetera – identifying and naming conditions that differentiate these cities from metropolises on the one hand, and from small towns on the other. Through collaborative discussions both in person and via online platforms such as Zoom, the Action's members suggested conditions based on the four following overall categories:

1. The inhabitants' or visitors' perception, experience, and feeling of the overall atmosphere of the city, such as wandering the city and being in-between complete anonymity and familiarity with others, owning the city over time, 'intimacy' and/or 'territorial awareness', 'care', 'belonging' and 'security'.

2. The tangible infrastructure, such as the availability of modes of transport characteristic to these cities (there is no metro, but there are

trams and buses, for example), accessibility to the airport(s), spatial urban figures like by-passes, markets, a river, etcetera, businesses (the existence of a certain number of specific amenities, such as a cinema), having only one main square and several small ones.

3. Their centrality or, in other words, the position of and within the city, such as the city as the centre of a region, the city as having an important historical centre, perceptual coherence in the positioning by its inhabitants, fragmentability or the lack thereof.

4. Their distinct capacities to deal with challenges or crises, such as community resilience, urban branding, the capacity to receive, being effective and affective, allowing the involvement in decision-making of a large number of inhabitants to a certain degree, dealing with the Covid-19 pandemic, and many others.

Indeed, if applied to specific cities and the fieldwork cases featured in various articles of this special issue, these categories of conditions are characteristic of the lived experience of the different stakeholders and diverse communities inhabiting these unique cities: Osijek's provinciality in relation to its broader context while having a regional centrality, its infrastructure, and its connection with nature rather than detachment from it; Çanakkale's peripheral role among other Turkish cities, but its cultural prominence as the place of Homer's grand epics and the historical value of the First World War Gallipoli campaign for the formation of the republic;[12] Skopje's struggle to form a coherent metropolitan system and emerge as a credible European player alongside its stunning brutalist heritage and the widespread creative initiatives that animate the urban environment. A strong suggestion that emerges from these conversations and fieldwork experiences was that the term 'intermediate', as being or occurring at the middle place, stage or degree, or between extremes,[13] is more appropriate than 'mid-size' to describe the nature and character of the cities under examination. Consequently, we proceeded with suggesting this alternative term and created an online platform on Padlet to define it further.

While working on this definition, we noticed that by looking at the case studies that we investigated as a network, one could make the argument that what we call the intermediate European city seems to carry some strong characteristics of pre-industrial times, such as a clearly legible historical centre or easy access on foot. However, the conditions we identified could also be observed in more recent urban developments as the Ruhr area (also referred to as the Ruhr district) in Germany. This polycentric urban area consists of 13 intermediate cities, as we argue, that since the nineteenth century have developed together within a diverse and extensive industrial landscape. Some of these cities have long-standing historical origins, while others have emerged more recently. Each city is its own administrative centre and within its boundaries the conditions of an intermediate European city are abundant.[14] These separate, intermediate cities together create what contemporary research calls a horizontal metropolis: a larger urban conglomeration that attempts to 'upgrade the city-territory' in order to achieve 'spatial and social justice through equal accessibility and mobility across their landscape', as Sylvie Tram Nguyen explains in her contribution to the 'vademecum' of minor terms, initiated and produced by the COST Action 'Writing Urban Places'.[15] With all of this in mind, our working hypothesis was that intermediate European cities can function as separate urban entities or can work collaboratively to form larger metropolitan areas.

Seven Selected Conditions

Below, we present seven illustrative conditions, as captured by the voice of seven members of the COST Action, defining the cities we have explored, investigated and worked on over the last four years. These terms vary in focus and perspective as some approach the intermediate European city from the lenses of an experiential perspective, while others look at it more from a bird's-eye view, defining it in relation to its immediate surroundings as well as in comparison with bigger metropolises. The first condition, a contribution by Michael G. Kelly, clarifies in concrete terms the argument that relates to the size and scale of these intermediate European cities. It explains why size is not an appropriate parameter to define the intermediate character of the cities under investigation and offers a reading of scale as a commodity instead of as a measuring unit. Moving from size and scale to the gravitational pull that a city may have, Kris Pint explains the gravity that an intermediate city possesses in attracting population, infrastructure and potential. In relation to these overall conditions, Saskia de Wit talks about 'perceptual coherence'. De Wit describes the intermediate European city in relation to its immediate surroundings and the physical and formal elements that make it a distinct and easily recognizable entity. Adding to the conditions that make intermediate European cities a distinctive entity, Mustafa Zeki Çirakli proposes a reading of these societies as 'open-ended images'. Contrary to the imposing symbolic images that European metropolises carry (Paris as the 'city of light', for example), intermediate cities are open-ended relational images that allow the inhabitant or visitor to become an active creator of such an image through their everyday encounters with them. Diving further into the experiential aspect of intermediate cities, Matej Nikšić focuses our attention on the walkability of these urban environments. Walking is easier in an intermediate European city than in a metropolis, but also richer and more layered than in a town. Sernaz Aslan proposes the condition of the 'parochial realm', discussing the experiential sense of commonality within the urban community, with its positive and negative features. Moving further into the experiential content of the city, Amer Obied looks at a condition we may prefer to overlook, namely conflict. He argues that the intermediate European city is not capable of sustaining conflict, maintaining instead a unified front unlike the larger urban entities.

The selected conditions, offered here *in lieu* of a conventional conclusion, showcase both the uniqueness and extraordinary potential of the intermediate European city. A place moderate and balanced in nature, avoiding extremes and hyperboles, the intermediate European city emerges as the level-headed counterpart of the metropolises. It suggests the 'middle way' for a meaningful urban existence and for integrated urban narratives, which promote a diversity encompassed by care, a space of freedom surrounded by boundaries, and a future anchored in the shared stories of the communities. With this article we do not wish to argue that the intermediate city is solely a European condition. We would not be surprised if a study of North American or Asian contexts revealed similar urban conditions, at least in specific regions or areas. Our network, being composed of mainly European researchers, focusing on mainly European countries, and being able to visit European cities only, did not wish to expand this hypothesis to geographical contexts outside our direct accessibility, experience and understanding. With this in mind, we offer the reader the following seven conditions of the early twenty-first century European intermediate city.

1. Scale as commodity by Michael G. Kelly

The ambiguity of the designation of a European city as intermediate – in which the object is primarily a function of what it is *not* (neither a metropolis nor a town) – exacerbates the *othered* quality of these cities. This othering can be one of sheer size (though simple recourse to population numbers or surface area as an identifying criteria is problematic), one of economic or political power within the evolving structures and parameters of the state's dialogue with capitalist transformation, but is perhaps most interestingly one of how the intermediate European urban entity becomes the expression of a set of equilibria internal to the 'urban' scale. Linked to – but not necessarily a beneficiary of – the connection between this 'urban' scale and the 'new scalar hierarchies of state institutional organization and state regulatory activity',[16] the intermediate city is potentially both an indirect symptom of and a partial antidote to the evolving urban condition more typically described and critiqued in relation to major cities. To cite one well-known analysis in this regard, Marc Augé's *Non-lieux* (1992) discusses a contemporary 'super-modernity' in terms of the emergence or predominance of seemingly frictionless (non-)places, structuring spaces of transition that are typically urban or peri-urban.[17] These are contrasted with the idea of the *lieu anthropologique* (anthropological place) – the residual figure of the city that offers an experience of 'place' to its inhabitants – in which 'place' is the space where experiences and perspectives interact and modify each other, and where, potentially, quality and meaning are generated in the individual lives that they host. The 'super-modern' condition that gives rise to the figure of the non-place is consistent with the 'new scalar hierarchies' outlined by Brenner: in each, the city spatially embodies and enacts a logic of the contemporary economic, political or technological reality.[18] In this respect, the intermediate city can be seen as a figure of equilibrium, as it develops on the margins of the 'problem', both as a (secondary) site of these changes and as a potential victim of the core or privileged intensities of the larger city. Bound up in change, the pace of change within this 'epi' or 'subsidiary' phenomenon may be moderated or attenuated in relation to the core of the 'urban' scale. Whether individual intermediate cities are net beneficiaries or casualties of the process depends on a range of individual properties, and in this respect urban destinies vary considerably.[19] Faced with the spectrum of such destinies, it is interesting to reflect on how this 'epi' quality is itself subject to the processes of super-modernity, that is, becoming a transferable, alienable or marketable signifier.[20]

The embourgeoisement or gentrification of certain intermediate European cities, as net beneficiaries of a concern for 'quality of life' and individual optimization in a process of ongoing transformation, could thus be seen as pointing to a destiny of 'scale' as *commodity*, where intermediate becomes imaginarily synonymous with a theme of human scale, proximity and reciprocity in a nonetheless 'urban' environment. This is a fungible notion of the safe or ideal distance from the fuller logic of the urban scale as bound up with the demands and logic of capital flows. Commodity, too, in the Francophone etymological sense of comfort and convenience, refers to the still anthropological space of the city as offering the moral affordances of the *non-lieu*, a protection from the very logic that produced it.[21] In this respect, those 'mid-sized' cities that emerge as net 'losers' in the evolutionary processes of national or state territories – bearing the stigmata of decline, disinvestment and depopulation – are inverted confirmations of the same idea: the fungibility of the mid-size designation here means insufficiency of size, distance from power and lack of prestige, distinction or desirability in the spatial and social 'commodity market' to which the optimally skilled, employable or mobile subject has access.

2. Gravity by Kris Pint

It is always a broader geographical and cultural context that qualifies a European city as intermediate in relation to other cities in the same region or country. The term 'urban gravity' is used in demographical and transportation studies to determine the attractiveness of specific areas in analysing urban density. We want to argue that within a specific region, an intermediate city possesses a modest gravitational pull. The presence of another city can prevent it from fully developing into a 'big' city, because it cannot compete with the cultural and economic attractiveness of this nearby city. But at the same time, the intermediate city nonetheless creates enough gravity to prevent it from turning into a mere satellite city or commuter town. The 'gravitational pull' of a city is hard to quantify and operates on different levels. Obviously, there is socioeconomical gravity, both reflected in but also enhanced by the city's position, its population and its accessibility within a specific network of transportation. But more intangible forms of 'gravity' also play an important role. There is the cultural scene of a city, the way it is represented in culture, especially popular fiction such as movies or TV-series that help to give a city a specific identity. There is also a form of historical 'gravity', based on the city's role in (inter)national history. This is visible not only in actual historical buildings (often used for city branding), but more generally in the self-identity of its inhabitants, creating a stubborn sense of place that resists merging into a larger metropole. History also shows how 'gravity' can shift over time: an intermediate city may have been an important regional and even international centre in the past, before its role was gradually overtaken by other cities. In Belgium, Bruges is a good example of this: the city was once a medieval metropolis, one of the biggest in Europe, but over the centuries it became an intermediate city, compared, for instance, with the now much larger Belgian cities of Antwerp, Brussels or Liège.

3. Perceptual Coherence by Saskia de Wit

Perceptual coherence addresses the physical-spatial aspect, the material realm of the city. That is, its physical-spatial characteristics – its appearance – make it perceivable as a coherent ensemble, different from its surroundings.[22] The grammar of the form, of the context and of the world of perception can be unravelled as three dimensions of perceptual coherence; perception cannot be viewed apart from form, form not apart from its physical context.[23] Intermediate European cities can be understood as a particular and specific part of space, with internal characteristics, giving the city its own order. This order distinguishes the city from the next place, a periphery as the transitional zone between centre and surrounding landscape that is perceptually rich enough to add to the definition of the city, as well as externally connected to other places. On the one hand, they are components of a larger, hybrid and complex metropolitan landscape, which is a profound mix of city and landscape, nature and culture, spaces and flows. On the other they can be perceived as a unity with a distinction between centre and periphery, in terms of perception both by inhabitants (based on their deeper knowledge) and by visitors (at first glance). It is the unifying centre that distinguishes intermediate European cities from a metropolis, which has in essence a hybrid appearance consisting of different districts with their own centres, fringe areas and peripheries, and where inhabitants identify more with the centre of their district than with the formal city centre. Whereas on the other end of the spectrum, as a perceptual unity, it is not as singular as a small town, and the relation between centre, periphery and surrounding landscape is more layered and multidimensional than in small towns.

4. Open-ended Image by Mustafa Zeki Çıraklı
Drawing on literary terms and narratological notions, the characteristic of the particular 'image' or universal 'silhouette' (symbol) of an urban environment can be considered among the conditions of an intermediate European city. From a geographical perspective, places are social and spatial territories with relational boundaries that refer to how individuals perceive, imagine, experience and interact with the city. However, a place with a universal image and symbolic value may dominate or suppress the subjective, experiential and imaginative potential of a personal encounter. An intermediate city does not have a universal and fixed symbolic silhouette that governs the imagination of the citizens, inhabitants, residents or visitors. An image, by definition, is fluent, flexible and open-ended in a state of becoming, not a fixed and solid symbol (or symbolic silhouette). This open-ended image of a place is a particular narratological construction and an experiential accumulation, whereas the silhouette of a city is of symbolic value and universally circulates a figurative meaning. So, an open-ended image of a place is more subjective and experiential, while a universal silhouette of a city holds a collectively shared meaning and function. In the former, the inhabitant or the visitor is an active participant in the unique encounter with the city; in the latter, the participant is expected to be part of the prevailing silhouette with a grand narrative behind it. Narratives of intermediate cities, therefore, represent spatial, experiential, perceptive and fluid images of these cities in a narratological, psychological, phenomenological and aesthetic sense, and surpass any symbolic (universal) or collective metaphorical signification.

5. Walkable Distances by Matej Nikšić
Distance is a quantitative or qualitative measurement of the space between two locations. It can be a matter of objective measurement based on predefined measuring units, or a matter of subjective evaluation based on one's perception.[24] Walkable distances used to be essential for survival in the traditional city,[25] and it was not until the introduction of the widespread use of motor vehicles that walking truly became a matter of choice rather than

necessity.[26] Similarly, nowadays, types of urban development in accordance (or not) with walkable distances is a matter of choice, too. While in big cities the high-capacity transportation network is a key infrastructure for the functioning of the city as a whole, in intermediate European cities, walkable distances still play a significant role, not only in providing urban commodities to their users, but also as the basis for the specific environmental experience and lifestyle associated with these cities. By embedding the idea of walkable distances in their urban (re)development mindset, intermediate European cities are more likely to promote human-centred urban design and pay greater attention to the variety of specific needs of different user groups (senior citizens, families with young children, disabled people, etcetera). When addressing walkable distances, however, it is not only the distance that needs to be taken into account, but also what is on offer at the final destination that can be reached on foot, as well as the experiential pleasantness of the path that has to be taken to reach the destination.[27] The intermediate European city will normally offer many walkable final destinations (more than a small city), while also providing a perceptual experience to the walker that will be nicer than in a big city.

6. The Parochial Realm by Sernaz Arslan

In her article 'The Morality of Urban Public Life: The Emergence and Continuation of a Debate', Lyn H. Lofland distinguishes between three different realms: the private, the public and the parochial. She defines realms as social territories, each characterized by a distinctive relational form that refers to how individuals interact with one another.[28] Accordingly, the parochial realm is characterized by a sense of commonality among acquaintances and neighbours who are involved in the interpersonal networks that are located within communities. In contrast, the public realm is marked by a stranger, or categorical, relational form. It signifies the non-private parts of urban areas, occupied by individuals who are personally unknown or only categorically known to each other. Lofland's conceptualization of urban space is important for two reasons. First, she emphasizes the sociospatiality of the city. For her, the city is characterized by a diversity of social spaces. The city includes the tribe, the village and the small town, which are dominated by private and parochial spheres. What is unique about the city is that it also includes public spaces that tend to be inhabited by strangers or people who know each other only in terms of professional or other non-personal identity categories. Thus, everyday life in the (big) city offers a distinctive variety of places and interactions that go beyond private and parochial spaces. Second, by differentiating between types of urban spaces, she provides a better understanding of sociospatial structures, boundaries and dynamics that are manifested in interpersonal relations. But what about the mid-size city?

The parochial realm could be a parameter to define the mid-size European city. On the one hand, it has positive connotations; like urban belonging, care, sense of a community, neighbouring practices. On the other it creates certain constraints, which are connected with known social positions, roles and smaller communities where residents know each other. It lacks the anonymity of urban space and anonymity among 'strangers' – hence freedom – provided by the metropolis. It is worth investigating whether the rules, meanings, expectations, physical structures associated with urban space, and community are relatively fixed, explicit and less fluid or loose in the mid-size European city.

7. Against Fragmentability by Amer Obied

One hidden side of European cities is their (dis)ability to maintain unity. Plato's *Republic* tells us how any city is, in fact, two: one for the rich and one for the poor. These two appear to coexist geographically, overlap in urban structure, but differ in accessibility to resources. While wanderers could always travel from the city of the poor to the city of the rich and vice-versa, they might find it extremely difficult to stay in the opposite city. During peacetime, the city presumes unity. During conflicts, however, the city shatters. Examining large, divided cities shows their capacity to split geography, resources and infrastructure if and when a polarizing conflict occurs. These poles (usually ideological or religious) aggregate fragments to form emergent cities. Berlin, Nicosia, Belfast, Jerusalem, Beirut and, recently, Aleppo are examples of once or currently fragmented cities. Is 'fragmentability' characteristic of metropolises? Evidence seems to suggest it is. Heterogeneity, an abundance of resources, a large population, and a vast geographical and urban footprint are all contributing factors to inciting, prolonging and sustaining division. The resulting two cities (or even more than two, if we extend Plato's thinking to contemporary urban phenomena) are of course strongly contrasting in character and, unlike Plato's cities, are sharply demarcated to prevent potential overlap and unwanted porosity. It is interesting to look at how many points and lines of demarcation come to exist in the built urban infrastructure itself. Intermediate European cities, on the other hand, have different dynamics for conflicting groups; more often than not, one group prevails in winning or controlling the city as a whole, rather than dividing the territory. This is mainly due to homogeneity and scarcity of resources. In other words, while it is possible for intermediate cities to accommodate conflict, they cannot sustain it. Or rather, they cannot afford to be divided, because neither part can survive without the other.[29]

1 Statistics Times, 'World Urban Population', statisticstimes.com/demographics/world-urban-population.php, accessed 12 December 2022.

2 Bloomsday is a national holiday in Ireland, but is also celebrated informally in many places around the world every year.

3 As most remarkable examples we can mention: Frank McCourt's *Angela's Ashes: A Memoir* (1996), a literary masterpiece capturing the social life and urban conditions of Limerick during the Great Depression; Sheila Connolly's *County Cork Mysteries Series* (2014-2017), three detective novels unfolding in Cork; and *Glorious Heresies* (2015) by Lisa McInerney, which captures the underbelly of the city of Cork with its drug and mafia networks.

4 Such as, for instance, the Royal Conservatory, the Royal Art Academy, and the Nederlands Dans Theater (Dutch Dance Theatre), the latter of which is known for its contemporary dance performances across Europe and around the world.

5 The most characteristic example would be the 2019 novel *Zaharias Skrip* by Dimitirs Karakitsos.

6 Bruno Notteboom, Klaske Havik and Michiel Dehaene, 'The Mid-Size City as a European Urban Condition and Strategy', *OASE* 89, *Medium: Images of the Mid-Sized City* (2013).

7 Ibid., 2-9.

8 Ibid., 9.

9 COST Action CA18126 'Writing Urban Places. New Narratives of the European City', 'Memorandum of Understanding', 2.

10 Such local stories include Tallinn in the myths of the Old Man from Ülemiste Lake or in the medieval story about the market square of MartBread; Skopje's legend of creation by a hero's spear or its Old Bazaar District; Ljubljana as the city of dragons founded by Jason. As for literary narratives, there are not as many as for European metropolises and big cities, which is exactly what makes them lesser known, much like the cities we can undoubtedly define as 'mid-size'. Nevertheless, there are some examples of novels set in these urban contexts. For Ljubljana, see: *Minuet for Guitar* by Vitomil Zupan and *Crumbs* by Miha Mazzini; for Skopje, *The Time of the Goats* by Luna Starova or *A Spare Life* by Lidija Dimkovska; and for Tallin, Indrek Hargla's medieval Tallinn in his series of crime novels.

11 Mladen Stilinović, 'Bitola: Shifting Images of a Western Balkan City', *OASE* 89, *Medium: Images of the Mid-Sized City* (2013), 40-48.

12 Çanakkale, like Istanbul, sits across continents with some districts on the European continent and others on the Asian one.

13 Merriam-Webster, 'intermediate', merriam-webster.com/dictionary/intermediate, accessed 12 December 2022.

14 For more information on the Ruhr area, see: Norman J.G. Pounds, 'The Ruhr Area: A Problem in Definition', *Geography* 36/3 (1951), 165-178.

15 Sylvie Tram Nguyen, 'Horizontal Metropolis', in: Klaske Havik et al. (eds.), *Vademecum: 77 Minor Terms for Writing Urban Places* (Rotterdam: nai010 publishers, 2020), 82-83.

16 Neil Brenner, *New State Spaces: Urban Governance and the Rescaling of Statehood* (Oxford: Oxford University Press, 2004), 3.

17 Marc Augé, *Non-lieux: Introduction à une anthropologie de la surmodernité* (Paris: Seuil, 2004).

18 Brenner, *New State Spaces*, op. cit. (note 16).

19 Emeline Cazi, 'Les Français vivent de plus en plus dans les zones urbaines; les periphéries attirent davantage', *Le Monde*, 27 October 2020.

20 Achille Warnant, *Les Villes moyennes sont de retour* (Paris: Fondation Jean Jaurès, 2020).

21 Thus, to take a French example of the ambivalent relationship between this 'commodity' and the context in which it is produced, we see that smaller urban centres linked to the metropolis (Paris) by high-speed train (TGV) are most likely to benefit from this rebalancing, although it is important to note that this 'benefit' is not equally shared (often accompanied, for example, by increased difficulties in obtaining affordable housing for those who do not share in the metropolitan aura). Again, it is clear that government (and indeed EU) planning and infrastructure interventions can have a decisive impact on the value attached to individual cases of urban characteristics such as 'mid-size'. The EU-supported development of the motorway network in Ireland between several regional urban centres and Dublin, and to a lesser extent between these centres (Galway-Limerick, for example, but not yet Limerick-Cork), is arguably another example of this revised viability of the 'mid-sized' European city, albeit one that ideologically favours private over public transport, in this case.

22 Joseph A. May, *Kant's Concept of Geography and Its Relation to Recent Geographical Thought* (Toronto: University of Toronto Press, 1970).

23 Saskia I. de Wit, *Hidden Landscapes: The Metropolitan Garden as a Multi-sensory Expression of Place* (Amsterdam: Architectura & Natura Press, 2018).

24 Jonathan R. Zadra, Arthur L. Weltman and Dennis R. Proffitt, 'Walkable distances are bioenergetically scaled', *Journal of Experimental Psychology: Human Perception and Performance* 42.1 (2016): 39.

25 Rebecca Solnit, *Wanderlust: A history of walking* (Penguin, 2001).
Joseph Amato, *On foot: A history of walking* (NYU Press, 2004).

26 Gerard Duc, Oliver Perroux, Hans-Ulrich Schiedt and Francois Walter (eds.), *Transport and Mobility History. Between Modal Competition and Coordination* (Editions Alphil., 2014).

27 Ann Forsyth, 'What is a walkable place? The walkability debate in urban design', *Urban design international* 20 (2015): 274-292.

28 Lyn H. Lofland, 'The Morality of Urban Public Life: The Emergence and Continuation of a Debate', *Places* 6/1 (1989), 18-23.

29 For more on the issue, see: Jon Calame and Esther Charlesworth, *Divided Cities: Belfast, Beirut, Jerusalem, Mostar, and Nicosia* (Philadelphia: University of Pennsylvania Press, 2009); and the novel *The Fever in Urbicande* by Benoît Peeters and François Schuiten.

Unearthing Urban Narratives Towards a Repository of Methods

Dalia Milián Bernal and Carlos Machado e Moura
WORKING GROUP 3

Unearthing Narratives

Dealing with urban narratives sometimes requires a certain degree of imagination, as many are not directly available in a clear written form, or even linked to a specific text. It requires tools and approaches to discover and render them legible, an approach almost similar to forensics or archaeology. Indeed, while history is built upon the text, archaeological interpretation begins as the material is being excavated, working directly with debris. Naturally, one could ask if unwritten stories can be considered a form of narrative. But the interaction between urban space and people always implies a certain degree of narrativity – either explicit or implicit – one strongly related to the meanings and knowledge of a given place and the spatial experiences of that same place. Knowing that many of these narratives and stories provide opportunities to decipher the complex system of relationships between urban spaces and its users, it is also true that finding these narratives and attaching a written interpretation to them might sometimes require considerable creativity, especially when addressing materials or places that are not present anymore to be read and interpreted.

This is where the discovery of certain urban places by means of constructing narratives seems to share ground with the processes of archaeology. Learning directly from objects and places, from instruments of transmission of knowledge that may have been lost, from materials often not available at every moment and every place, certainly not in the pervasive manner that digital tools now offer us. Doing this kind of research implies looking at the methods – including the means, instruments and techniques, alongside their limitations – to understand how the transmission of knowledge operates. And how, unlike history, it sometimes requires looking in different directions, realizing things that have changed or disappeared. The methods used to find existing narratives, to read them and to construct new ones, are crucial to overcome the distances imposed by different times, disparate places, distinct cultures and ideas, rendering necessary a certain level of openness and, sometimes, performativity.

On the Quest for Methods

To unearth urban narratives, our working group has aimed to locate, collect, organize and share the methods that help read, understand and construct narratives in the first place. A quest for methods has required an intense engagement with the members of the network across all working groups brought together by means of different tools, activities and projects. In time, all of these actions and components merged and morphed into an iterative space we call the Repository of Methods: a project that has no specific form – it takes many forms – and is 'in permanent expansion, discussion and auto-generation'.[1]

One of the first tangible projects in the process of co-constructing this Repository of Methods took the form of an issue of *Writingplace, Journal for Architecture and Literature*, entitled 'Narrative Methods for Writing Urban Places' (Fig. 1). The issue gathered six articles that 'relate to urban and architectural narratives, understood as the spoken or written accounts of connected events that take place in . . . buildings and cities'.[2] A second

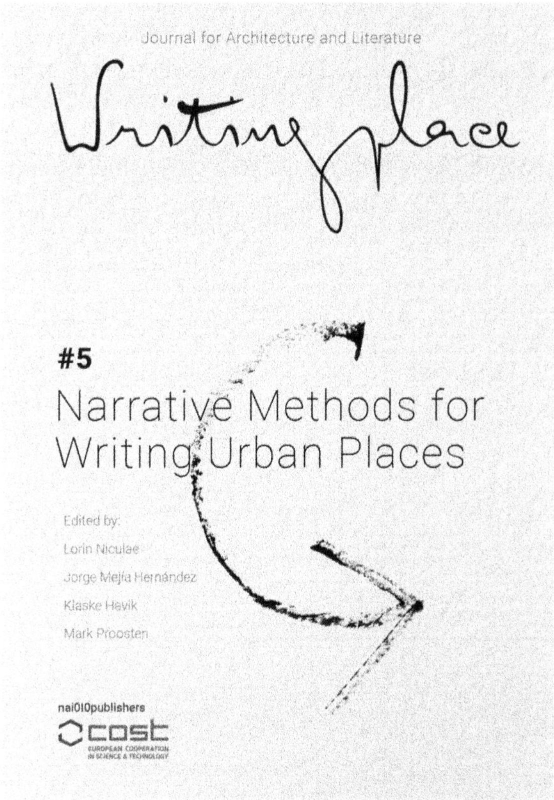

Fig. 1. Cover of Writingplace 5: *Narrative Methods for WritingUrban Places* (2021). Design: Studio Sanne Dijkstra

Fig. 2. A digital platform on Padlet for a fast and wild brainstorming of terms, ideas, and references. Available at writingurbanplaces.eu/library/links/

undertaking assumed the shape of a digital environment where anyone in the network could, in a fast, dynamic – and almost wild – way, contribute to mapping the diverse range of methods that our multidisciplinary community was employing to capture, experience, engage with, analyse and even transform the material and immaterial dimensions of urban places. This mapping unfolded on Padlet – a digital online instrument where participants could easily add a method followed by a short description.[3] (Fig. 2). The methods gathered in the Padlet became the basis for a PechaKucha-style webinar held in April 2021, titled 'Reading, Writing and Activating Urban Places: Methods and Assignments'.[4] (Fig. 3). The 21 participants in the webinar were invited to rapidly present a method, describe it, explain how it had been mobilized in practice and propose an assignment.

Two essential issues were raised in this webinar. First and foremost, the preparation of this event triggered a process of grouping and categorizing the different types of methods gathered thus far under the categories of *reading, writing* and *activating*. Secondly, it introduced assignments to accompany the methods. While not featuring prominently in the presentations, assignments were instrumental in rendering straightforward that part of our task that consists of transforming this Repository of Methods into an open space that can be entered and searched, and its contents put into action outside its delimiting but permeable boundaries. Thus, the function of the assignments is to help 'interpret, complete and continue the methods . . . but also encourage constant dialogue between (methods), contributors and users, through a series of easy-making and immediate experiments and practices within the urban space'.[5] All of these outputs – *Writingplace* 5, the Padlet, the webinar and the booklet collecting the presentations, along with all the discussions that surrounded them – became the foundation of *Repository: 49 Methods and Assignments for Writing Urban Places*: a momentary manifestation of a constantly morphing space that took the form of a book.[6] (Figs. 4-5).

Fig. 3. PechaKucha-style webinar 'Reading, Writing and Activating Urban Places', April 7 2021. Design: Carlos Machado e Moura.

Fig. 4. A multitude of different methods rendered recognizable, comparable, and exportable to other contexts.

Fig. 5. *Repository: 49 Methods and Assignments for Writing Urban Places* (nai010 publishers, 2023), a momentary manifestation of a constantly morphing space that took the form of a book. Photo: Arto Ilkka Jalonen.

Fig. 6. Esteban Restrepo Restrepo reading an assignment at the *Repository* (2023) book launch in Tampere, April 2023. Photo: Arto Ilkka Jalonen.

The architecture of that book was such that it made it possible to render each of the different methods – the title with a verb, a short description and an assignment in the form of clear sequential steps – easily recognizable and comparable. Intended to be taken into the field and used by anyone interested in urban places, including students, scholars and professionals from all sorts of disciplines and the broader urban community, it even includes blank spaces for the users to fill with their own notes and a postcard to share experiences with others across cities and beyond the lifecycle of this network (Fig. 4).

As this project continues to expand and generate new outputs, and starts to be used in different disciplinary arenas, a critical task we must confront is defining the terms we utilize. Only after many iterations has it become clear that our mission has not been to locate or develop 'narrative methods' for Writing Urban Places, a term utilized in the network's general statement.[7] Instead, as noted above, it is to find, gather and share 'methods' to unearth, understand and construct those urban 'narratives'. Thus, the methods contained in the different formats of the Repository of Methods are not intrinsically narrative. But *what* could we then try to unearth (and *why*?) and *how* do we intend to do so?

On Narratives and Methods

Defining 'narrative' in a multidisciplinary context, like this network, requires a certain degree of ambiguity (and open-mindedness). Etymologically, it derives from the Latin *narrat-* ('related', 'told'), *narrare* ('to tell') or the late Latin *narrativus* ('telling a story').[8] However, depending on the discipline in which it is employed, narratives may be understood and used differently. Literary urban scholar Lieven Ameel defines 'narrative', following James Phelan, as a 'rhetorical act: somebody telling somebody else on some occasion and for some purpose(s) that something happened'.[9] In their practical field guide for narratives in urban design, Ameel, Jens Martin Gurr and Barbara Buchenau define 'narrative' as being 'when somebody at a particular occasion tells somebody else a real or fictional story'.[10] In a similar vein of thought, sociologist Catherine Riessman defines 'narrative' as 'everyday oral storytelling (in which) a speaker connects events into a sequence that is consequential for later action and for the meanings that the speaker wants listeners to take away from the story. Events perceived by the speaker as important are selected, organized, connected and evaluated as meaningful for a particular audience'.[11] Geographers, like Marie-Laure Ryan, Kenneth Foote and Maoz Azaryahu define 'narrative' as 'a temporal art involving the sequencing of events'.[12] Narrative scholars, such as Jo Woodwiss, Kate Smith and Kelly Lockwood argue that 'narratives are a communicative event, not a thing' and scrutinize the idea that narratives are solely an *oral* form of storytelling.[13] In their view, narrative 'tellings' are (oral, visual, written . . .) texts that involve 'writerly' (authorial) and 'readerly' (co-participant, audience) dynamics.[14] These notions resonate productively with multiple discussions about the role of the author and text involving various authors, from Roland Barthes to Michel Foucault and Jacques Derrida.[15] Also, with the contrasting understandings of the narrative in architecture, ranging from its acknowledgment as a representational system that communicates – and even that this is its primary mode of operation, imbued with symbolical or political discourses – to the attempts to replace this capacity with a focus on the fundamental conditions of its physical nature.

Often, the terms 'narrative' and 'story' are used interchangeably and their distinctions are not always made explicit, thus complicating the task of defining 'narrative'. Ameel, Gurr and Buchenau argue that defining 'narrative' also requires determining what a story is.[16] They define a story as having, 'first, human or human-like characters doing something; secondly, a change of situation; thirdly, an association with mental states'.[17] A story, Kim argues, 'is a detailed organization of narrative events arranged in a structure based on time although the events are not necessarily in chronological order'.[18] Story structures usually have a beginning, a middle and an end. However, narratives may include, but are not reducible to, stories.[19]

For example, Jeremy Allan Hawkins's contribution to *Repository*, 'Collaging Community Narratives', problematizes definitions of 'narrative' that consider it a 'temporal art' and argues that the polyphony of a textual collage is 'seemingly ill-suited to immersive storytelling' but can be accommodated under broader understandings of 'narrative'.[20]

But are these 'tellings' and 'communicative events' solely human? What can non-human others, like trees or inert material, buildings or visual matters, 'tell', or can they be part of such communicative acts and events? As Mark Wigley put it: 'Architecture is nothing but discourse about building, but something about building supposedly precedes discourse . . . a kind of quasi-philosophical claim about the status of objects that is built into our endless conversation about buildings.'[21] Indeed, while almost philosophical in nature, these questions were latent throughout the process of editing the *Repository*, which included nearly as many varied voices from different disciplines as its methods. For example, in a Latourian approach, Saskia de Wit, a landscape architect, invites readers of the *Repository* to engage in a sort of communicative event or act with the 'innumerable other-than-human beings' that also inhabit our cities.[22]

Like that of De Wit, several other contributions to the Repository of Methods problematize the argument that non-human others or the built environment 'cannot literally tell a story'.[23] Ameel et al. argue that they 'can have narrativity', which they define as 'the ability to evoke stories'.[24] The built environment is an intrinsic element of inquiry that brings together scholars and practitioners from a multiplicity of disciplines in *Writing Urban Places*. Few would deny that architecture communicates and, in that sense, is a language or like a language with its own signs – classifiable according to Ferdinand de Saussure's semiology or Charles Sanders Peirce's semiotics, as Umberto Eco clearly synthesized.[25] Still, digital technologies and alternative approaches to the built environment presently introduce new dimensions and emphasize the communicational ability, either by the use of digital devices in our current 'smart cities', able to read and respond to our online footprint, or through 'forensic architecture', an emergent academic field that refers to the production and presentation of architectural evidence in legal forums, including courts, and for advocacy purposes.[26]

Besides providing a definition of the term 'narrative', this chapter aim to illustrate the complexity of the Repository of Methods and the way its multiple manifestations problematized and broadened the existing definitions of 'narrative'. Besides searching definitions of 'narrative', is it equally relevant to ponder what exactly narratives do, particularly in the context of *Writing Urban Places*? *Narrat-*, *narrare*, *narrativus*, Kim notes, 'are akin to Latin *gnārus* ('knowing'), derived from the ancient Sanskrit *gnā* 'to know')'.[27] Thus, it is a 'form of knowledge that catches the two sides of narrative: telling as well as knowing'.[28] In this spirit, anthropologist Clifford Geertz coined the famous definition of culture as the sum of 'the stories we tell ourselves about ourselves'.[29] Thus, as theorist and philosopher Benedetto Croce stated: 'Where there is no narrative, there is no history.'[30] In the context of *Writing Urban Places*, we believe that narratives offer a situated, experiential and subjective way of *telling* and *knowing* urban places. The question that follows is: *How* can we unearth such narratives to construct (new) knowledge about urban places?

Methods

We thus enter the realm of methods, and query what exactly can be considered *legitimate* methods to find, understand and construct urban narratives. Etymologically speaking, the word 'method' derives from the Latin *methodus*, 'way of teaching or going', from the Greek *methodos*, 'pursuit or following after', from *meta*, 'in pursuit or quest of' + *hodos*, 'a way or manner' and also 'a travelling, journey'.[31] Any dictionary includes several definitions of 'method' and depending on our disciplinary alignments, the word may evoke different emotions and judgements of what a method legitimately is and how it is to be employed. For the Repository of Methods, we decided to embrace one of the broadest definitions: method is 'a (particular) way of doing something'.[32] So, a method works primarily as a roadmap for what it is to follow.

In the introduction to the *Repository*, we argue that 'the *ways* we choose to inquire about the world around us are strongly influenced by who we are and where we stand'.[33] Therefore, adopting a broad definition of 'method' has been an intentional move because the Repository of Methods, in its many forms, is a project built by a multiplicity of ontological, epistemological and theoretical perspectives and positions. Nonetheless, these multiple perspectives cohabit in a realm that recognizes narratives as a form of knowledge and that knowledge can be constructed from a situated, experiential and subjective position.[34] Thus, while not (entirely) narrative in nature nor even deriving (wholly) from literary studies and regardless of their theoretical underpinnings – either ontologically or epistemologically speaking – all of the methods we collected throughout this journey function as a roadmap to unearth narrative knowledge about urban places. A process that, as noted by the editors of *Writingplace* 5, is 'seemingly unattainable by other means'; a view that is echoed in several chapters of this book.[35] See, for instance, the chapters on Tampere and Çanakkale.

The Repository of Methods contains *ways* and *roadmaps* that employ a far larger degree of experimentation and creativity than commonly established methods. Some 'tailor' academically conventional approaches, such as ethnography or interviewing ('Tailoring Ethnography and Weaving Stories').[36] Others capture (mini-)narratives in unexpected or idling moments – when sitting on a bus or waiting in a line, for instance (see 'Eavesdropping').[37] Others find inspiration in creative literary works to invent methods that invite other engagements – sometimes playful or seemingly absurd – with urban places (see 'Uncannying the Ordinary . . . with Cortazar').[38] In other words, the Repository of Methods, in its diverse forms, offers a rich palette of methods to draw from to approach urban places. Furthermore, it recognizes that those places are experienced in multiple ways all the time, and that taking the everyday and the ordinary seriously as sources of knowledge is perhaps one of the major advantages that narratives can provide.

The question that follows is where, then, can we find such narratives? Throughout our quest for methods, we stumbled upon expected and unexpected venues where narrative knowledge can be found. 'Graffiti and street art,' Clara Sarmento tells us, 'are produced to be discodified.'[39] She argues that 'there are two possible layers of meaning in graffiti and street artwork: the internal narrative (the story told) and the external narrative, i.e. the social context that produces the image and sustains the framework of its interpretation when visualized.' Hers is just an example of where one might unexpectedly find narratives.[40] What is more, in her contribution, she explains what kind of knowledge they may render and puts forth a method to engage with graffiti by mapping digital routes of graffiti and street art. In 'Reading the City', Onorina Botezat locates narratives in literature and urban texts. She argues that 'urban narration can play different roles, from a simple description to a central part of the plot'.[41]

Other contributions, instead of looking for narratives, aim to produce them. For example, one of Luc Pauwel's contributions, 'Re-Acting with Images', 'involves asking respondents to produce visual output (such as photographs, videos, drawings and installations) in connection with a specific research question'.[42] In 'Scaling Stories', Klaske Havik proposes a method that 'explores urban places by means of storytelling' operating at different scales.[43] For each scale, 'participants first identify a local protagonist' they will either interview or walk with and document this process 'by means of a map, a series of photographs and a text' collated to produce a triptych 'in which the three scales are represented side by side'.[44] The production of narratives (in diverse media) was also the aim of many of the workshops organized by Writing Urban Places, including the production of co-constructed narratives that weave visual material, poetic practices and interviews into a 'visually expressive-form of scholarly communication' in Tampere; the construction of travelogues in Çanakkale; and production of ethnographic visual material in Tirana. See the chapters on these three cities in this publication.

Moreover, some contributions are aimed not only at producing narratives, but at using those narratives for the production of space. This is the case of 'Co-creating', in which the contributors organize a workshop with a community and invite them to tell 'stories of places and actions' as a way to learn about the sites of intervention. These stories are shared and further explored in a storytelling session where texts and images are produced. Subsequently, together these stories, texts and images are translated into 'inhabitable spaces'.[45]

These are just a few ways in which narratives shape our understanding of urban places and small samples of the methods we gathered to unearth them. While our task comes to an end, the Repository of Methods continues to evolve and has now taken a life of its own. This is evident in the second part of this book, in which a diverse range of methods were tested or further developed in different cities and contexts.

On Cities

The original plan of the COST Action, in 2018, established that the initial phases – focused on investigating the possibilities of cross-disciplinary tools and techniques and previewing key literature on methods and concepts relevant to narrative analysis – should be followed by an engagement of the group in the exploration and 'testing the possibilities of identified methodologies and tools through site-specific workshops' in a series of medium-sized European cities.[46] This took place on different occasions: working group meetings, workshops and training schools for PhD students and young researchers. Throughout these activities, the members discussed various methods, aiming to raise the awareness of city dwellers in their own urban environments and to build democratic places. These processes involved highlighting a series of narratives, identifying their origins and multiple sources, and producing new outputs that could generate knowledge and convey various interactions with those urban places. Although the activities that unfolded in those cities are discussed in detail in other chapters, grouping them according to their objectives and methods employed has turned out to be quite a productive exercise.

The first group, predominantly referring to the initial two years of the Action, corresponds to a series of meetings that provided the occasion for different looks at cities. Various activities made use of written or visual forms of communication – such as literary texts or graffiti – for the construction of meaningful itineraries. This was true of the WG3 and WG4 joint meeting in Almada, Portugal, in November 2019 and the WG2 and WG3 joint meeting in Limerick, Ireland, in December 2019, where the analysis of literary excerpts provided clues for the discovery of certain parts of the city. Confronting nineteenth- and twentieth-century literature with the present conditions of a specific urban area revealed significant changes in cities' flows, reading patterns of phenomena over extended periods of time and documenting those changes'. A similar experience was later provided during the mid-term conference that took place in Porto, Portugal, in October 2021. Thanks to the occasion offered by other projects affiliated with the Action, the walks through the easternmost area of Campanhã allowed for some activities of reading the city through the presence of graffiti and other physical elements. The perception of such traces offered opportunities to research social change and physical and cultural expressions as they develop, over time, in a particular material or cultural space.

A second group of activities, mostly corresponding to the PhD training schools and workshops, offered not only opportunities for reading the city but also to engage in the analysis and production of textual and visual material. This was the case of the training schools 'Local Stories and Visual

Narratives' that took place in Tallinn, Estonia, in September 2021 and 'Urban Chronicles in Empirical Context' in Osijek, Croatia, in April 2022, as well as in the workshop 'The City and the Myth' in Çanakkale, Turkey, in July 2022. In all these experiences, participants explored historical perspectives of the city, either through the cultural identities forged in ancient myths (Çanakkale), a past rescued from oblivion through literature (Osijek) or local urban stories (Tallinn), in their multiple perspectives, agendas and reappearances throughout time. Complementing the tasks of discussing historical, semantical and archetypal settings of these narratives, participants used different creative methods to explore and produce heterogeneous materials, including visual narratives and scholarly articles (Tallinn), creative workshops for writing, drawing, creating psychogeographical cartographies and constructing plaster objects (Osijek), and the recording of the personal experiences of each researcher during the fieldwork activities into an individual personal travelogue (Çanakkale).

Finally, a third group of activities focused primarily on the contemporary city, adopting an activist approach to the current problems of urban development and the inequalities thus generated. It was the case of the workshop 'Narrating Hiedanranta: Stories of Objects and Subjects of Urban Places' in Tampere, Finland, in June 2022, the workshop 'Skopje Brutalism Trail' in the capital of North Macedonia in September 2022 and the training school 'The Planned, the Unplanned and Everything in Between' in Tirana and Kamza, Albania, in March 2023. All of these activities brought new perspectives on the present and the exploration of multiple methods to generate different forms of activism. Either regarding the erasure of the Brutalist architecture of Kenzo Tange's reconstruction plan after the 1963 earthquake under the classicizing urban plan Skopje 2014 (Skopje), the developments foreseen for the former industrial area of Hiedanranta into a creative technological hub (Tampere) or the contrasting realities of the commercially-oriented planned city versus the informal and unplanned approaches of the local residents (Tirana). Those occasions allowed for the exploration of visual, performative and literary methods, revealing how approaches similar to the ones explored in other activities can also be incorporated into different political, urban and architectural discourses. These methods include the use of video and cinema (Tirana), dance and performance (Skopje), graffiti making (Skopje), different types of visual representation methods, including the construction of new narratives with 'visually expressive-form of scholarly communication' (Tampere), poetic practices and midnight readings (Tampere), narratives of personal experience through situated-interviewing methods (Tampere), and the construction of multiple visual and poetic descriptions.

(Un)Classified Methods

As may be noted from the above, we attempted to group the city events under categories that come close to those of *reading*, *writing* and *activating*, following the titles of the three sessions of the webinar (Fig. 3). This classification was based on similarities in the scopes and methods used to engage with the city. Those under *reading* apparently focused on reading textual and visual material; those classified as *writing* not only read but also produced textual or graphic material; and the third group, *activating*, are those that seemingly are political in nature. However, organizing and classifying methods revealed to be a critical aspect of our work on methods and the motive of much debate throughout the entire process of the COST Action. During the webinar, one of the participants invited us to reflect on the usefulness of metaphors like *reading*, *writing* and *activating* and to question if the use of categories limits the scope of methods as they travel from one context to another. Another participant asked whether a city is something waiting to be *activated* and if the acts of *reading* or *writing* are any less political than others.

Classifying or grouping cities based on the 'main' methods employed in the different activities obscured 'minor' methods – those that are present, but seem to take backstage. This is problematic because what is particularly interesting about the fieldwork events in the different cities is that they reveal different combinations of methods to reveal, interpret and create individual urban narratives – like the travelogues in Çanakkale, as well as collective ones – like the co-constructed narratives in Tampere. Similar discussions emerged while editing the *Repository*, in which we ultimately decided to organize the contribution lassify the collected methods released them from categorical constraints, provoking unexpected and creative applications while inviting exciting approaches that might weave different methods, configuring new *ways* to explore the multiple dimensions of urban places. Countless opportunities emerge: one might choose to wander aimlessly, find a bench to sit to eavesdrop on conversations and collage these moments to create a new urban narrative.

1 Carlos Machado e Moura et al. (eds.), *Repository: 49 Methods and Assignments for Writing Urban Places* (Rotterdam: nai010 publishers, 2023), 5.
2 Lorin Niculae et al. (eds.), 'Narrative Methods for Writing Urban Places', *Writingplace: Journal for Architecture and Literature* 5 (2021), 4.
3 The Repository of Methods: writingurbanplaces.eu/library/links/.
4 The webinar is available at: youtube.com/watch?v=mpqk6if-rcU&list=PLXlMnpOPXf1eBmNLZbsQmQXSSZLdzI_jf
5 Machado e Moura et al., *Repository*, op. cit. (note 1), 12.
6 Lorin Niculae et al., 'Reading, Writing and Activating Urban Places: Methods and Assignments', Writing Urban Places March 2022; writingurbanplaces.eu/reading-writing-and-activating-urban-places-methods-and-assignments/
7 See: writingurbanplaces.eu/about/#.
8 Jeong-Hee Kim, *Understanding Narrative Inquiry: The Crafting and Analysis of Stories as Research* (Thousand Oaks: Sage Publications, 2016), 6.
9 Lieven Ameel, *The Narrative Turn in Urban Planning: Plotting the Helsinki Waterfront* (Oxfordshire: Routledge, 2021), 2.
10 Lieven Ameel, Jens Martin Gurr and Barbara Buchenau, *Narrative in Urban*

Planning: A Practical Field Guide (Bielefeld: Transcript Independent Academic Publishing, 2023).

11 Catherine Kohler Riessman, *Narrative Methods for the Human Sciences* (Thousand Oaks: Sage Publications, 2008), 14.

12 Marie-Laure Ryan, Kenneth Foote and Maoz Azaryahu, *Narrating Space/ Spatializing Narrative: Where Narrative Theory and Geography Meet* (Columbus: Ohio State University Press, 2016), 1.

13 Jo Woodiwiss, Kate Smith and Kelly Lockwood (eds.), *Feminist Narrative Research* (London: Palgrave Macmillan, 2017).

14 Ibid.

15 Roland Barthes, 'The Death of the Author', *Aspen* 5/6 (1967); Michel Foucault, 'What Is an Author?' (lecture, 1969), in: Michel Foucault, *Modernity and its Discontents* (1969); Jacques Derrida, *De la grammatologie* (Paris: Les Éditions de Minuit, 1967).

16 Ameel, Gurr and Buchenau, *Narrative in Urban Planning*, op. cit. (note 10).

17 Ibid., 57.

18 Jeong-Hee Kim, *Understanding Narrative Inquiry*, op. cit. (note 8), 8.

19 Woodiwiss, Smith and Lockwood, *Feminist Narrative Research*, op. cit. (note 13), x.

20 Jeremy Allan Hawkins, 'Collaging Community Narratives', in: Machado e Moura et al., *Repository*, op. cit. (note 1), 50.

21 Mark Wigley, 'Story-Time', *Assemblage* 27 (1995), 83.

22 Saskia de Wit, 'Imagining Dialogues with the Voiceless', in: Machado e Moura et al., *Repository*, op. cit. (note 1), 94.

23 Ameel, Gurr and Buchenau, *Narrative in Urban Planning*, op. cit. (note 10), 63.

24 Ibid., 63.

25 Umberto Eco, *La Struttura Assente. La Ricerca Semiotica e il Metodo Strutturale* (Milan: Bompiani, 1972).

26 Eyal Weizman, *Forensic Architecture: Violence at the Threshold of Detectability* (Cambridge, MA: MIT Press, 2017).

27 Jeong-Hee Kim, *Understanding Narrative Inquiry*, op. cit. (note 8).

28 Ibid., 6.

29 Clifford Geertz, *The Interpretation of Cultures: Selected Essays by Clifford Geertz* (New York: Basic Books, 1973), 448.

30 Benedetto Croce, 'La storia ridotta sotto il concetto generale dell'arte', in: Benedetto Croce, *Primi saggi* (Bari: Laterza, 1951), 26.

31 Etymology of the word 'method' obtained from: etymonline.com/word/method.

32 Definition adopted from the Oxford Advanced Learner's Dictionary: oxfordlearnersdictionaries.com/us/definition/english/method#method, and the Macmillan Dictionary: macmillandictionary.com/british/method.
33 Machado e Moura et al., *Repository*, op. cit. (note 1), 8.
34 Jerome Bruner, a cognitive psychologist, recognized that there are two modes of thought: paradigmatic and narrative. The paradigmatic mode of thought is linked to positivism, which borrows methods, concepts and procedures from the natural sciences. The narrative mode of thought 'uses stories to understand the meaning of human actions and experiences'. See: Jeong-Hee Kim, *Understanding Narrative Inquiry*, op. cit. (note 8), 11 and Jerome Seymour Bruner, *Actual Minds, Possible Worlds* (Cambridge: Harvard University Press, 1986).
35 Niculae et al., 'Narrative Methods', op. cit. (note 2). See also the chapters on Tampere and Çanakkale in this publication.
36 Alasdair Jones, 'Tailoring Ethnography: (Co-)Present Cognition in Public Realm Research', in: Machado e Moura et al., *Repository*, op. cit. (note 1), 178-181.
37 Alina Cristea, 'Eavesdropping: Overlooked and (Over)Heard in the City', in: Machado e Moura et al., *Repository*, op. cit. (note 1), 70-73.
38 Esteban Restrepo Restrepo, 'Uncannying the Ordinary . . . with Cortázar', in: Machado e Moura et al., *Repository*, op. cit. (note 1), 190-193.
39 Clara Sarmento, 'Mapping Graffiti and Street Art: The Construction of Meaningful Itineraries', in: Machado e Moura et al., *Repository*, op. cit. (note 1), 106.
40 Ibid., 107.
41 Onorina Botezat, 'Reading the City: Literary Texts and Urban Writing', in: Machado e Moura et al., *Repository*, op. cit. (note 1), 142.
42 Luc Pauwels, 'Re-Acting with Images: Respondent-Generated Image Production and Photovoice', in: Machado e Moura et al., *Repository*, op. cit. (note 1), 134.
43 Klaske Havik, 'Scaling Stories: Social and Spatial Layers of Urban Exploration', in: Machado e Moura et al., *Repository*, op. cit. (note 1), 154-155.
44 Ibid., 155.
45 Yazmín M. Crespo, Omayra Rivera Crespo and Irmaris Santiago Rodríguex, 'Co-Creating: Workshop Arquitecturas Colectivas', in: Machado e Moura et al., *Repository*, op. cit. (note 1), 46-49.
46 Memorandum of Understanding for the implementation of the COST Action 'Writing Urban Places: New Narratives of the European City' (*Writingplace*) CA18126, 2018, available online at cost.eu/actions/CA18126/.

Fieldwork for Writing Urban Places

Luís Santiago Baptista and Slobodan Velevski
WORKING GROUP 4

Fieldwork is an expanding field that crosses several disciplines, including art, architecture, urban studies, and the human and social sciences. This crossroads condition reveals a practice that works in-between disciplines without becoming one, although a theoretical and methodological framework for fieldwork is being established as it is increasingly receiving attention from scholars. There is an emerging debate about how these two terms, 'field' and 'work', should relate to each other and be put together. Several authors have been discussing this challenge, trying to cope with the expansion of the use of the term in multiple contemporary practices. A set of prepositions have been proposed to link 'field' and 'work' with the use of different notations, opening up a series of possible relationships between the terms as well as its potential variation as a verb or noun. On the one hand, work 'in', 'on', 'of', 'from', 'to' or 'through' the field reveal diverse subject's positions in relation to a specific place, differentiating the status of both fieldworker and fieldwork. On the other hand, the fusion or separation of the two words by language marks such as '[space]', ':', '–' and '/' opens up ideas of indistinction, continuity, proximity and distance between the practices and the sites, allowing for the establishment of different modes of action. As Suzanne Ewing put it in her introduction to *Architecture and Field/Work*:

> *Fieldwork operates as both a noun and a verb, and this oscillation correlates with a potential oscillation of work and worker which may inflect questions about and understandings of* project, construction, design, work *in the field. . . . Fieldwork is a practice, not a discipline. It is practised in different ways by different disciplines towards diverging ends, and may contribute to the consolidation, deepening and extending of disciplinary knowledge.*[1]

The editors decision to use a 'slash between field and work' both expresses that the 'field' is increasingly extended and expanded, including human and non-human, material and immaterial, real and fictional dimensions, and that the 'work' is multiplied and disseminated through fieldworkers from different disciplines and geographies, openly in interdisciplinary and transdisciplinary arenas. It is from this increasingly complex, multiple, contaminated and fluid condition that we propose to approach fieldwork and fieldworkers in the context of the COST Action *Writing Urban Places*.[2]

Fieldwork Engaging Sites

The fieldwork in the COST Action *Writing Urban Places: New Narratives of the European City* considers urban spaces through the performative experiences of on-site investigations and explorations of the built environment. As such, fieldwork is a research experience that crosses a theoretical understanding of space with distinctive methods of approaching place, engaging a particular site and its territorial array with its social and cultural multiplicities. This combination of theoretical and practical engagement with sites blends people, places and actions to reveal numerous planned and unplanned encounters with existing communities. Therefore, fieldwork should be seen as a critical practice and an exploratory tool by which to understand, articulate and facilitate present complexities that are part of the ongoing process of constructing contemporary urban conditions. Culturally and historically speaking, fieldwork can be traced to the beginning of modernity, both with the figure of the traveller of the *Grand Tour*, with its rational and emotional investigation of the cultures of historical and exotic places, and the urban dweller of the emergent modern metropolis, confronting an increasingly changing economic, productive, social and psychological environment. In this sense, we could say that fieldwork conflates the investigation of the distant archaeologic sites with the research of the near environment of a transient present. On the one hand, the *Grand Tour*, as a journey of discovery of the cultural roots and experience of the architectural and artistic artefacts of the historical past, is materialized in a series of notes, reports, essays, maps, sketches, drawings and photographs produced by erudite travellers.[3] From Goethe to Le Corbusier, passing through John Soane, fieldwork is undertaken as a formative activity and learning practice that builds an authorial cultural background based on the direct experience of reality.

On the other hand, the transition from the nineteenth to the twentieth century brings the experience of the urban dweller, introducing a new field of investigation that is structurally in line with the emergence of the social and human sciences, such as anthropology, sociology and psychology, and authors like Georg Simmel, Siegfried Kracauer and Walter Benjamin. For instance, Benjamin's essays on the metropolitan condition, based on Charles Baudelaire's poetry, captured the energized and transient urban experience of the *flâneur* of nineteenth-century Paris.[4] The *flâneur* is then a 'kaleidoscope equipped with a consciousness', as he/she moves through the city involving 'the individual in a series of shocks and collisions', taking into consideration that 'at dangerous intersections, nervous impulses flow through him in rapid succession, like the energy from a battery'.[5] But the urban dweller faces a double reversible condition, the active perception of the environment by the metropolitan individuals reflects their adaptive transformation by the intensified life of the metropolis. In this context, fieldwork becomes driven by the fascination and shock of these 'wanderers', a fascination that is generated by the multitude of the modern city, and that nourishes further research and exploration.

If Benjamin already called for new technical devices for apprehension of the metropolitan environment, it was Dziga Vertov's *The Man with the Moving Camera* of 1929 that turned this reflection into a ground-breaking filmic work, documenting the ongoing process of the Soviet revolution after 1917.[6] As Vertov mentions in the beginning of the film, it 'is an experiment in cinematic communication of real events' aiming at 'creating a truly international language of cinema' that conflates the experience of a reality in mutation with the technical means used to depict it, from the moving operator in action in real space to the creative *montage* done in the studio. Despite the various interpretations of the relationship between people and places, fieldwork could no longer detach personal subjectivity from its practice as an output of actions and reactions, taken by individual or collective endeavours that transform and are transformed by physical environments, social relations, historical movements and technical apparatuses.

The truth is that fieldwork only became properly named fieldwork after the Second World War, assuming a more radically critical and speculative position, in the context of full-blown modernization and a new geopolitical world order. The issue is not just the understanding of the tangible reality, with its now authorized theories and established methods from the different fields of knowledge, but how to engage with reality from an expansive transdisciplinary position to investigate the margins and invisibilities of an increasingly complex urban and territorial landscape. Searching for 'other spaces' both inside the everyday life environment of the city and outside in the dilapidated peripheral areas becomes the focus of fieldwork practices, intentionally crossing the realms of the political with the aesthetic.

First, the critical focus appears in the investigations of everyday life through fieldwork. For instance, the 'unitary urbanism' proposed by the members of Situationist International (SI) entails a critical exploration of the complexity of the social and spatial context of the city. In this context, Debord's idea of *psychogeography* was brought forward as a way to study spontaneous and intuitive encounters and overlap of people and places and the influence of the built environment on human behaviour.[7] His concept of *dérive* 'as a technique of swift passage through varied environments' is a 'ludic-constructive comportment, which contrasts it on all points with classical ideas of the journey and the stroll'.[8] Neutralizing the utility and pragmatics of everyday life, '*dérive*'s spatial field is more or less precise or vague according as this activity is aimed sooner at studying a site or at bewildering affective results'. The aim of *dérive* is the dislocation of the usual and constrained perception and cognition of the city, creating 'itineraries' and 'situations' that open up other emotional and constructive interpretations of the urban environment. But Debord claims that '*dérive* difficulties are those of freedom', revealing his utopian tone that hopes that 'one day, cities will be built for *dérive*'.[9] Fieldwork journeys, based on the psychogeographic temporal experience of common spaces, may develop interrelations among people and places, freeing us from fixed and established everyday identities, thus perceiving social and physical space from unexpected and ever-changing personal perspectives.

Second, fieldwork also reorients its focus outside of the urban centres towards invisible and abandoned urban areas, from the dilapidated infrastructural sites to rundown commercial settings that increasingly fascinated artists, architects and social scientists from de 1960s onwards. Eventually, the individual and collective fieldwork excursions taken by Robert Smithson are a paradigmatic example, which could be extended to other artists like Gordon Matta-Clark, Richard Serra and Dan Graham. Robert Smithson's 1967 textual and photographic essay *The Monuments of Passaic*, in New Jersey, introduces the relation of this mundane and dilapidated wasteland with the childhood memories of his hometown, exposing the artefacts and leftovers of this generic and informal urbanity.[10] His 'entropic' approach to these anachronistic and ambiguous 'monuments' leads to the pervasive concepts of 'ruins in reverse', as de-historicized 'anti-romantic' monuments, and 'nonsite', as a metaphoric displacement of a 'site' in his earthworks.[11] The reversion of time, of the former, and the dislocation of space, of the latter, implicate these 'zero panorama' landscapes in a world out of joint, interrogating the traditional understanding of place as permanent and stable. Therefore, with this idiosyncratic and evocative account of site, fieldwork is destabilized and questioned by the temporal ambiguity and spatial discontinuity of the process of perception and comprehension of place, turning curiosity and gaze into the guides of the exhilarating encounter with these somehow empty and ambiguous *terrain vagues*. In this sense, fieldwork becomes an entangled and unmediated immersion in the real itself.

Fieldwork was initially developed by individuals or groups that share particular interests, but since the 1970s it has increasingly established new alliances with institutions and the academy. Usually conservative and hierarchical, these collective organizations have been challenged by fieldwork projects that adopt critical and even subversive intentions in the relation between places and people as a collective endeavour, advancing new learning tools and experimental pedagogies. The 1968 workshop in Las Vegas that students from Yale participated in with their professors Robert Venturi, Denise Scott Brown and Steven Izenour largely changed the perception of urban space and the influence that architecture has on the human understanding of the built environment.[12] Their intentions were not only to '[learn] from the existing landscape' of the commercial strip in Las Vegas as a intensively perceived and lived reality, but also to challenge the emerging discourses of the autonomy of the discipline of architecture. As they say, 'architects have preferred to change the existing environment rather than enhance what is there'. They proposed to short-circuit the dominant disciplinary positions by 'withholding judgment' on the reality as found as 'a way of learning from everything'.[13] The collection of innovative *in-situ* research practices, taken from their fieldtrip and workshop, resulted in a series of images, diagrams of activity patterns, various charts, collages and texts, photographs and films that confronted architectural form and cultural meaning, enhancing *the forgotten symbolism of architectural form*. Their focus on interdisciplinary collaboration showed their aim to overcome the boundaries of pragmatic and physical approaches of modernist perception of space, or put in their words, 'we are evolving new tools: analytic tools for understanding new space and form, and graphic tools for representing them', because the 'representation techniques learned from architecture and planning impede our understanding of Las Vegas'.[14] With *Learning from Las Vegas,* fieldwork becomes an experimental practice of research within an academic framework, increasingly contaminating the university environment, from Reyner Banham to Rem Koolhaas.

The integration of fieldwork into an academic environment acquired, in the early 1990s, a new political and social configuration with Samuel Mockbee's Rural Studio, based in the School of Architecture, Planning, and Landscape Architecture of Auburn University.[15] Their engaged intervention in the poor and dilapidated areas in provincial Alabama in the United States is an example of action taken to confront the social weaknesses of the built reality, assuming their agency in society. As Mockbee stated: 'Theory and practice are not only interwoven with one's culture but with the responsibility of shaping the environment, of breaking up social complacency, and challenging the power of the status quo.'[16] The close and practical knowledge of the territory in which they take action allows for a strongly engaged and participated involvement with the place and its communities, from the understanding and debate of the problematics to the collective construction and appropriation of the projects. In the case of Rural Studio, fieldwork not only changed the physical space but influenced social and political reality through the involvement and participation of local communities out of which not only knowledge turns into action, but action transforms reality. The legacy and ongoing involvement of Rural Studio as a community-based practice with its 'Citizen Architect'-approach to fieldwork activity contributes to the creation of strong social cohesion in the existing neglected and impoverished communities, enhancing their integration in society.

Although given here in a chronological sequence of historical relevance, these different interpretations of fieldwork as a critical and engaged practice are in diverse ways manifest in our contemporary society, and present in the fieldwork activities of *Writing Urban Places*. The curiosity of the traveller, the investigation of the researcher, the performativity of the dweller, the production of the artist, the polemic of the architect, the activism of the academic – all on some level contribute to the plurality of the network's fieldwork events that engaged with real places and situated communities. The shift in these characters affects the meaning of fieldwork itself, which has now become intertwined with the actions taken to understand, develop, preserve or simply sustain everyday life. What seems evident today is that fieldwork is an everlasting instrument that not only records reality, but also influences our self-perception and our relationship to our political, social and spatial built environment. Moreover, it is important to acknowledge that fieldwork is an evolving activity, now facing new challenges brought by technological advancements, from evidence-based design to artificial intelligence, that we must synchronize with subjective and intuitive decisions.

Fieldwork as Spatial Practice

The opening of the spectrum of fieldwork as an experimental, exploratory and engaged activity follows the theorizations of what was to be defined as 'spatial practice'. In 1974, in *La Production de l'Espace,* Henri Lefebvre introduced the concept of 'spatial practice' as a way to bridge the traditional opposition between design activity and cultural framework, criticizing the dominant passive and neutral idea of space and proposing a more active and engaged relation to space.[17] Crossing the phenomenological and semiological approaches with a political and social focus, Lefebvre tried to acknowledge the 'social space' of everyday life in our experience of the urban environment in the context of advanced capitalism. The 'abstract space', homogeneous and rationalized, that characterizes and dominates modernity, should be 'spatialized', brought to the 'concrete' of reality where space is permanently being socially enacted and re-enacted. This *spatializa-*

tion is proposed by Lefebvre's new triad of *spatial practice, representations of space* and *representational spaces*. The 'representations of space' of the 'conceived' manifest the ideas and procedures projected on reality by those with an active role in designing and building space, the 'representational spaces' of the 'lived' reveal the historicity of the symbolic and imaginary realms of a continuously productive society. In a way, the 'conceived' determines the continuous conceptualization of the 'lived', and the 'lived' implies the historical codification of the 'conceived'. But the originality of Lefebvre's theory on the production of space is mainly in the introduction of the third term of 'spatial practice'. The 'perceived' of the 'spatial practice' focus on the empirical relation with space, acquiring the characteristics of 'competence' and 'performance' within social space, that 'must have a certain cohesiveness, but this does not imply that it is coherent'.[18] The 'spatial practice' connects the conceptual and cultural domains proposing an idea of space as practiced in daily life, bringing together the 'physical', 'mental' and 'social' dimensions of space. With this new theoretical framework, Lefebvre redefined the relation between space, ideology and history, between projects both designed and used and their conditions of production and reproduction:

> *If this distinction were generally applied, we should have to look at history itself in a new light. We should have to study not only the history of space, but also the history of representations, along with that of their relationship – with each other, with practice, and with ideology. History would have to take in not only the genesis of these spaces, but also, and especially, their interconnections, distortions, displacements, mutual interactions, and their links with the spatial practice of the particular society or mode of production under consideration.*[19]

Lefebvre's theory of the production of space also gives methodological insights for the practices of fieldwork. From the theoretical basis of *The Production of Space* emerges what Lefebvre would call, in the conclusive chapter, 'spatio-analysis' or 'spatiology', as a way to critically cross knowledge and experience, mind and body, in the investigation of social space. But, Lefebvre is conscious that 'space is becoming the principal stake of goal-oriented actions and struggles'.[20] In this regard, *The Production of Space* is the follow-up of the 'experimental utopia' presented before in *The Right to the City*, significantly published in 1968.[21] Even if the philosopher reveals a romantic and somehow nostalgic fascination with the pre-capitalist city that emerged with the Renaissance until Industrialization, he envisions the possibility, not without contradictions or obstacles assumed by himself, of emerging 'counter-projects' and 'counter-plans' that could interact with productive reality and power relations. This activist, even utopian, position manifests a strong influence on contemporary cultural, artistic and architectural debates, in terms of expansive spatial research and increasingly of strategies of design. Indeed, the openness and indeterminacy of the ideas of Lefebvre on 'spatial practices' allow for a critical reworking of the idea of fieldwork, gathering interdisciplinary research of our urban environment and experimental cultural practices to act on it. Similarly experimental, in *Writing Urban Places* investigation and performativity were the basis and motivation for fieldwork.

A decade after Lefebvre's book, Michel de Certeau published *The Practice of Everyday Life*, radicalizing some aspects of the concept in its immersion in the practices of daily life.[22] Rarefying the utopian guise of Lefebvre, De Certeau moves beyond the ideological discourse of the social and human sciences, bringing to the fore the 'ordinary' instead, emphasising the subversive potential of the users in everyday life. In fact, he now focused more on practices of '*another* production, called consumption' by common people. He changes the perspective from 'production' to 'consumption', taking into consideration that 'users make innumerable and infinitesimal transformations of and within the dominant cultural economy in order to adapt it to their own interests and their own rules'.[23] These collective 'ways of operating' acknowledge, in reference to Foucault, power structures and disciplinary apparatuses, constituting 'the innumerable practices by means of which users reappropriate the space organized by techniques of sociocultural production'. Assuming that 'marginality' became widespread in contemporary societies, De Certeau wants to 'bring to light the clandestine forms taken by the dispersed, tactical, and makeshift creativity of groups or individuals' that subvert the organization and distribution of power in everyday life, allowing a relation with 'otherness'.[24] Opposing 'strategies', as emanating from political, economic and scientific 'space' of power, to 'tactics', as insinuating from minor, alternative and fragmentary opportunities in 'time', he tries to escape the negativity framing everyday life, stimulating creativity and activating memory. The 'tactics' manage to elude the polarity between power and spatial practices, exercised in everyday activities like 'reading, talking, dwelling, cooking, etc'.[25] From the perspective of interpreting and activating place, the identification of 'spatial practices' with the unfolding of narratives and stories that are engendered in the multiplicity of everyday life guided *Writing Urban Places* fieldwork events as collective and shared experiences in real urban places.

In the new millennium, in 2006, Jane Rendell introduced a new definition in her inquiry into the *place between* art and architecture, manifesting its attraction to one another.[26] 'Architecture's curiosity about contemporary art', displayed in the free and subversive activity of the artist in relation to the conditions of production of society, mirrors 'art's current interest in architectural sites and processes', which reveals the sense of social purpose and real engagement of the architect with real places.[27] Re-reading Lefebvre's and De Certeau's theories, Rendell's intuition leads to the addition of the term 'critical' to 'spatial practice'. With this move, she stressed the engagement with everyday life but confronted its instrumentality and commodification, affirming the 'contextual' and 'site-specific' nature of spatial interventions. In her words:

> *I suggest a new term, 'critical spatial practice', which allows us to describe work that transgresses the limits of art and architecture and*

> *engages both the social and the aesthetic, the public and the private. This term draws attention not only to the importance of the critical, but also the spatial, indicating the interest in exploring the specifically spatial aspects of interdisciplinary processes or practices that operate between art and architecture.*[28]

Introducing post-structuralist, gender and post-colonial discourses, Rendell proposes an interdisciplinary approach to spatial interventions in public space that assumes a critical role in destabilizing the instrumental relation between theory and practice. Affirming 'criticism' as a 'situated practice', she deconstructs the autonomy of the work and the dominance of the medium, allowing for multiple critical intersections and contaminations between artistic and architectural practices. This unavoidable confluence of art and architecture, of spatial research and aesthetic practice, of project design and performativity, of producing work and engaging context, announces the prevalence of the curatorial studies in contemporaneity, something that Rendell's following book, *Site-Writing*, would confirm.[29]

Also in 2006, a more political and activist interpretation of the 'spatial practices' was developed by Markus Miessen and Shumon Basar in their co-edited book *Did Someone Say Participate?*.[30] Rather than with establishing a programme, this approach is mainly concerned with the agency of the 'spatial practitioner', radicalizing the 'tactical' approach of De Certeau. So they attempt 'to dismantle the idea of 'the architect' being the one in charge with 'space' and a critique of the 'author-architect in the centre of spatial production', defending a 'participatory' and 'inclusive' approach to urban problematics.[31] With a transdisciplinary basis and a global scope, they intend to develop critical action in reality to counter the dominating 'culture of consensus' and the 'ethos of compromise', instigating tension and conflict as a way to move forward. This 'alternative model of participation within spatial practice' responds to 'today's need for actors operating from outside existing disciplinary networks, leaving behind conventional expertise whilst inventing new species of knowledge-space'. In this sense, it envisions the 'future spatial practitioner' as an 'outsider' and 'an enabler, a facilitator of interaction that stimulates alternative debates and speculations', in close proximity with the urban, political, social and cultural context in which he/she acts.[32]

Fieldwork for Writing Urban Places

The COST Action *Writing Urban Places* created the space to reflect on the disciplinary and methodological variety implied in the processes of 'sensing the place' and defining its social history through site-specific and contextual exploration. The series of fieldwork events explained below studied urban space in five different cities. The collection includes various narrative approaches to exploring the built environment in relation with historical, cultural and social specificities of the local context.

The first workshop in Osijek was based on the relationship between places and texts, and the conceptual approach of reading the city as text and the text as a city. The method combined understanding and discussing a selection of textual excerpts about the city and using them as a basis to relate with the physical reality by performing specific city walks. This portrayal encouraged participants to create a new narrative for the places in the city that re-examine their meaning. This process enables participants to shift the usual perception of the cultural identity of the city and give different meanings to existing places.

The next fieldwork event took place in Tampere and focused on the relationships between places and people in its former industrial area of Hiedanranta. The idea of the workshop was to overlap the material substance of this urban space with the internal dynamics produced by its inhabitants. The current activities on site are rapidly disappearing due to new initiatives for the urban redevelopment of this area. The stories of local cultural groups and their engagement with the site were essential operative tools out of which new co-constructed stories were developed, reflecting on the production of space. The series of interviews with local citizens, visual recordings and writings aimed to contribute to the understanding of local sociocultural dynamics overseen by current redevelopment initiatives and to open a debate about the necessity to support the insurgent spatial and planning practices that give valuable creative contribution to urban living.

The third fieldwork event in the series was conducted in the historical area of Çanakkale, Turkey, and the archaeological site of the ancient city of Troy. The workshop intended to juxtapose the rich history of the place by combining the material artefacts, historical facts and fictional stories with one's personal encounter with the physical space. The fieldwork aimed to construct the subjective perception of space, a sentimental journey individually created using the experiences derived from the abstract space of the myth, history and memories. Therefore, participants created their own travelogues, comprised of texts, images and drawings, in which the traveller's ideas of space were recorded as personal reflection on the visited space.

The workshop held in Skopje introduced a fieldwork method that is enrooted in the principles of socially engaged art and public performance. The research aimed to connect places with architecture, emphasizing the brutalist architecture of a small neighbourhood community centre in the forefront of the fieldwork process. Instead of departing from texts, the workshop started with the building as a main character in a story out of which a narrative for this specific place was developed. Various combinations of facts and fiction, interviews with the locals and synchronicities between people, and stories of other brutalist buildings from all around the world were used as a background for a staged performance. The workshop culminated in a performative event in which the fieldwork research was transformed into a public performance instigating awareness for the meaningful value of architecture.

The last event took place in selected neighbourhoods in Tirana and Kamza, in which the fieldwork was used to establish a relationship between two proliferations of politics of built space that coexist simultaneously: the space of the planned and the space of the unplanned. The workshop aimed to relate places with spatial character relying on the theoretical concepts of 'situatedness' and the mutual interdependences of individual (and group) within the (built) environment, the 'commoning', by redefining the actual urban existence based on shared assets that are beyond the influence of market and state, and the 'material unrest' as an activity imbedded in an effort to confront the prevailing societal power structures. The fieldwork actions taken during the workshop used the medium of short films to record the transformational complexity and richness of encounters produced in this parallel system of political practices.

The fieldwork in *Writing Urban Places* followed the merging of practices from art, architecture, urban studies and social and human sciences that intentionally blurs the traditional boundaries between these fields of knowledge, developing experimental and speculative approaches to different places. To do so it explodes the traditional distinctions between academic research in universities and experimental practice in the real world, allowing for a creative and collective sharing and producing among individuals, associations and institutions. This activist and participatory orientation traversed the fieldwork in *Writing Urban Places* with its challenge of bringing together interdisciplinary academic research and real places in European cities.

Fig. 1a-b: Combining historical facts, fictionalized stories and actual places was part of the journey that took place in the fieldwork of Çanakkale and the ancient city of Troy. After the explorations in the field, the travelogues registered personal perceptions and reflections from the archeologic artefacts to everyday events. As such, the travelogue becomes a phenomenological and critical tool through which participants experience and relate with the physical reality. Photos: Eylül Nur Dinç (July 2022) and Giuseppe Resta (July 2022).

Fig. 2a: The training school in Osijek was focused on learning how the city walks are an essential practice of urban living and relation to specific places. 'Strolling' and 'wandering' on the streets of Osijek, enriched with reading excerpts of site-related texts, transformed the haptic nature of the walking practice into a new perception of the city in which the imaginative condition is embedded in the physical experience of the city. Photos: Onorina Botezat (April 2022).

Fig. 2b: Photos: Onorina Botezat (April 2022).

Fig. 3a-b: The fieldwork as an *in-situ* research practice allows changes of the built environment thorough enhancing its existing qualities. The researchers filmed fragments of Tirana and Kamza, aiming to acknowledge the political dimension of the city by recording the processes of 'unplanned utilization of space' versus the 'planned space' as an outcome of the established societal power apparatus. Photos: Holly Dale and Dorina Pllumbi (March 2023).

Fig. 4a-b: The Skopje Brutalism Trail workshop explored the tools of performance as a means to re-evaluate the modern heritage in the context of recent urban transformations of the city. The public performance *City as a Stage*, an after-event of the workshop, gathered members of the local community together with artists and architects in a joint venture in which dining, reading and singing become a form of civic activism in order to preserve and reactivate a small community hall. Photos: Mila Gavriloska (September 2022) and Slobodan Velevski (November 2022).

Fig. 5a-b:
The juxtaposition of people, places and activities is an essential part of forming the identity of the local community in the Hiedanranta district in Tampere. The form of practicing 'unitary urbanism' understands the artistic expression of everyday life as a critique of the neoliberal and materialistic urban development that often disregards the value of existing communities, and thus allows the activity to be explored both as performative event and informal exhibition. Photos: by Blagoja Bajkovski (June 2022).

1 Suzanne Ewing, 'Introduction', in: Suzanne Ewing et al. (eds.), *Architecture and Filed/Work* (London/New York: Routledge, 2011), 4-5.

2 See: Slobodan Velevski et al., 'Taking Place: Reflections from the Fieldworker', *Writingplace Journal* #7 (2023), 5-15.

3 See: Gabrielle Brainard, Rustam Mehta and Thomas Moran (eds.), *Perspecta* 41, *Grand Tour* (2008).

4 Walter Benjamin, 'On Some Motifs in Baudelaire', in: Neil Leach (ed.), *Rethinking Architecture: A Reader in Cultural Theory* (London/New York: Routledge, 1997 [1939]).

5 Ibid., 31.

See: Dziga Vertov, *The Man with a Moving Camera*, 1929.

7 Guy Debord, 'Theory of the Dérive', in: Tom McDonough (ed.), *The Situationists and the City* (London/New York: Verso, 2009 [1956]).

8 Ibid., 78.

9 Ibid., 85.

10 See: Robert Smithson, 'The Monuments of Passaic', *Artforum* 6/4 (1967).

11 See: Robert Smithson, 'A Provisional Theory of Nonsites', in: Jack Flam (ed.), *Robert Smithson: The Collected Writings* (University of California Press, 1996 [1968]).

12 Robert Venturi, Denise Scott Brown and Steven Izenour, *Learning from Las Vegas: The Forgotten Symbolism of Architectural Form* (Cambridge, MA/London: MIT Press, 1977 [1972]).

13 Ibid., 3.

14 Ibid., 73.

15 See: Andrea Oppenheimer Dean and Timothy Hursley, *Rural Studio: Samuel Mockbee and the Architecture of Decency* (New York: Princeton Architectural Press, 2002).

16 See: samuelmockbee.net/work/writings/the-rural-studio/.

17 Henri Lefebvre, *The Production of Space* (Cambridge, MA: Blackwell, 1991 [1974]).

18 Ibid., 38.

19 Ibid., 42.

20 Ibid., 404-410.

21 See: Henri Lefebvre, 'The Right to the City', in: Henri Lefebvre, *Writings on Cities* (Oxford: Wiley-Blackwell, 1996 [1968]).

22 Michel de Certeau, *The Practice of Everyday Life* (Berkeley/Los Angeles/London: University of California Press, 1984).

23 Ibid., xii-xiv.

24 Ibid., xiv.

25 Ibid., xix-xx.

26 Jane Rendell, *Art and Architecture: A Place Between* (London/New York: I.B. Tauris, 2006).

27 Ibid., 3.

28 Ibid., 6.

29 See: Jane Rendell, *Site-writing: The Architecture of Art Criticism* (London/New York: I.B. Tauris, 2010).

30 Markus Miessen and Shumon Basar (eds.), *Did Someone Say Participate? An Atlas of Spatial Practice* (Cambridge, MA: MIT Press, 2006).

31 Ibid., 22-23.

32 Ibid., 24- 25.

Limerick Extra Muros Urbanity from the Outside

Michael G. Kelly and Anna Ryan Moloney

> *Urbs antiqua fuit, Tyrii tenuere coloni,*
> *Karthago, Italiam contra Tiberinaque longe*
> *ostia, dives opum studiisque asperrima belli;*
> *quam Iuno fertur terris magis omnibus unam*
> *posthabita coluisse Samo*
> *– Virgil, Aeneid, Book I, 12-16*

The opening lines on Carthage in Virgil's epic poem (circa 13 BCE) could be read as one of the original examples of an 'urban narrative' in a 'European' context. Carthage as an urban *other*, as the adversary of the later imperial metropolis Rome, and, as a dynamic force to enter the narrative, has had a long history since then, but stands here at the beginning of a foundational text of classical literature as the figure of a redoubtable and well-endowed city, resistant to externally imposed narratives.[1] The celebrated English translation of Dryden as part of his *Works of Virgil* (1697) – itself a major contribution to the canon of a later imperial culture – renders these lines as follows:

Fig. 1. Civic signage near Treaty Stone featuring city arms and motto, Limerick City, March 2023. Photo: Michael G. Kelly.

Against the Tiber's mouth, but far away,
An ancient town was seated on the sea;
A Tyrian colony; the people made
Stout for the war, and studious of their trade:
Carthage the name; belov'd by Juno more
Than her own Argos, or the Samian shore.

Earlier in that final decade of the seventeenth century, a truncated version of Virgil's characterization of Carthage is said to have been in circulation concerning the city of Limerick. That formula – *Urbs Antiqua Fuit Studiisque Asperrima Belli* – has survived as the motto of the city to the present day. Usually translated as 'an ancient city well versed in the arts of war', it well conveys the city's self-understanding as an urban place defined by conflict and resistance, the possession of which equated to a stake in the broader historical narrative of Ireland and its place in the world. The representation of the city as a citadel on its coat of arms, which accompanies the motto, further reinforces this imaginary: it is a city, more than many others, defined by its walls and their effects, not only to those who would take possession of the urban space, but to those already there.

The historical 'walls of Limerick' are thus unsurprisingly a recurrent motif in textual treatments of the city and its specificity in both Irish and international contexts. The reference functions as a synecdoche for the city as a besieged place at key moments in the history of the island, notably the siege of 1691 at the concluding stages of the Williamite War in Ireland,

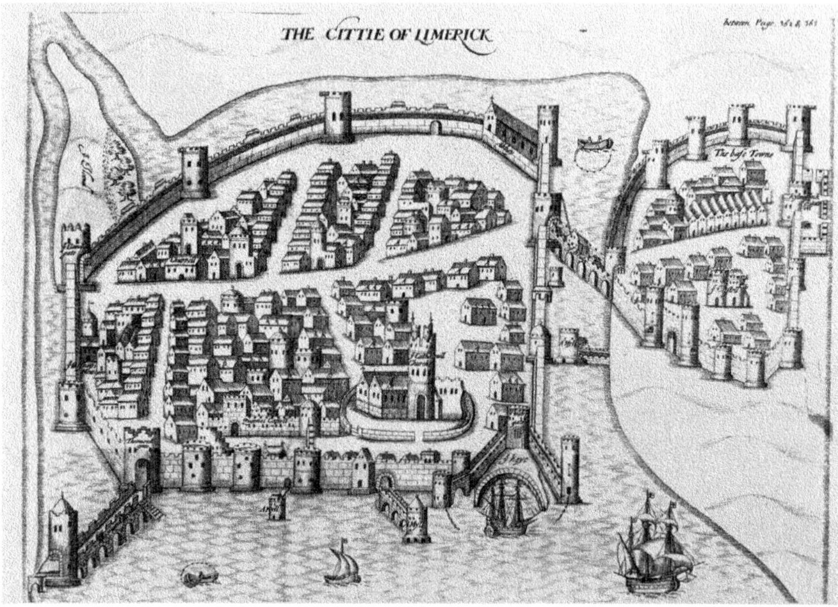

Fig. 2. Limerick, [1633]; size 30 x 37.5 cm (Pacata Hibernia 2) – showing the walls of Limerick and an early representation of the power structures within the city: the 'otherness' of Irishtown – extra muros – in relation to the garrison of Englishtown, connected by Baal's bridge across the Abbey River. Permission: University of Limerick Library, Special Collections, Norton Collection B/1989.

a major part of the Nine Years' War or War of the League of Augsburg (1688-1697), sometimes referenced as the first 'global' war. In this siege, the urban (walled) space of Limerick was the last bastion of resistance in Ireland against the Williamite order and the colonial regime it would subsequently (re-)enforce. The Virgilian motto is a key cultural trace of this event, while the (now ruined) walls today stand as a vestigial reminder, both of Limerick's position within a fully European history and of its status as a major urban site of colonial and post-colonial interactions, hybridizations and developments.

'The Walls of Limerick' is also, since the late nineteenth century, the name of the best-known Irish *Céilí* dance: an important participative, sociocultural practice in both Irish-based and diasporic Irish communities since then. The construction of a national narrative and cultural repertoire through the appropriation and configuration of elements of the past is a major feature of the 1800s in Ireland, with the traumatic caesura of the Great Famine in the 1840s marking both the nadir and a point of departure in modern Irish history. A decade prior to this event, in his *Topographical Dictionary of Ireland* (1837), Samuel Lewis offered a narrative of the successive waves of settlement and forms of cohabitation that characterized Limerick from its attested foundation early in the ninth century, as a result of the Danish incursion up the Shannon Estuary. This narrative mentions the Norman fortifications – including the castle still known as King John's Castle – built in the early thirteenth century, and is striking in its grounding of the city as an intercultural (and often conflictual) complex:

> *A succession of intestine wars among the native princes was carried on until the landing of Henry II., who soon after obtained possession of it and placed a garrison there; but after his departure, Donald O'Brien, King of Thomond, regained possession of it. In 1175, Raymond le Gros, with the assistance of the King of Ossory, invested it, and by fording the river in the face of the enemy, so daunted them that he entered it without opposition,*

obtained a great booty, and secured it by a garrison; but on the death of Earl Strongbow, it was again evacuated by the English and subsequently burned by order of Donald, who declared that it should no longer be a nest for foreigners. In 1179, Henry II. gave the kingdom of Limerick to Herebert Fitz-Herebert, who having resigned his claim to an inheritance so uncertain, it was granted to Philip de Braosa, and he, aided by Milo de Cogan and Robert Fitz-Stephen, advanced against the city, which the garrison set on fire. This so dispirited Braosa, that he immediately retreated, and so assured was Donald O'Brien afterwards of the security of his metropolis, that, in 1194, he founded the cathedral church of St. Mary, on the site of his palace. In 1195, the English appear to have regained possession of the city, for it was then governed by a provost; but Mac Arthy of Desmond forced them once more to abandon it.

King John afterwards renewed the grant to Philip de Braosa, with the exception of the city of Limerick, the cantred of the Ostmen, and the Holy Island, which he committed to the custody of William de Burgo, who formed a settlement there which from that period set at defiance all the efforts of the Irish. A strong castle and bridge were erected; and, encouraged by the privileges offered to them, English settlers flocked hither in great numbers, between whom and the inhabitants of the surrounding country amicable relations appear to to have been soon established, for, among the names of the chief magistrates for the ensuing century, besides those which appear to be English, Norman or Flemish, and Italian, there are several purely Irish. Money was coined here in the reign of John.[2]

The best-known literary offering from Limerick in the period of this historical account is Gerald Griffin's *The Collegians* (1829), a novel drawing on an infamous murder case from half a century earlier.[3] The dramatic fate of 'Colleen Bawn' (the fair-haired girl) at the centre of this narrative was reworked in a celebrated play by Dion Boucicault and also live on in

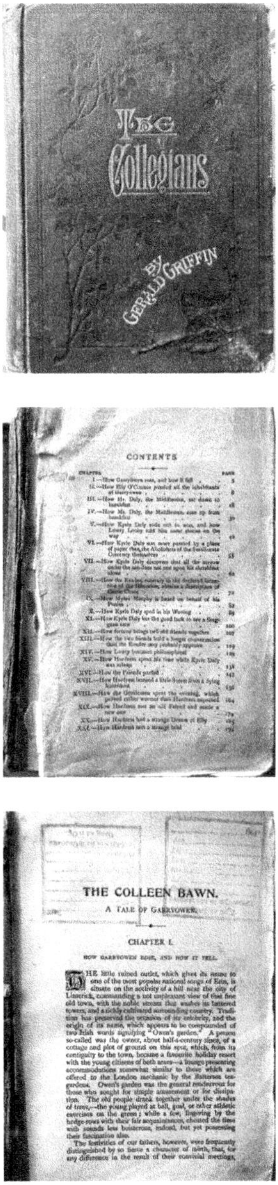

Fig. 3. Gerald Griffin.
The Collegians [1829].
Dublin: J. Duffy & Co, 1857[?].

the journalistic pen-name of novelist Flann O'Brien (Brian O'Nolan, 1911-1966), 'Myles na gCopaleen', indicating the work's entry into collective cultural memory in a manner transcending its strictly literary fortunes.[4] Griffin's novel opens with an evocation of life on the edge of the city at the time narrated – Garryowen (*Garraí Eoghan*, meaning 'Owen's Garden') is now a district within the city limits, forming part of what Cathal O'Connell describes as 'a "corridor of disadvantage" which runs from Moyross in the north west, through St Mary's Park in the city centre, to Garryowen, Prospect and Southill on the south-side'[5] – but Griffin presents it in opposition to the city as such: 'The name of Garryowen was as well-known as that of the Irish Numantium, Limerick itself, and Owen's little garden became almost a synonym for Ireland.'[6]

On the one hand, this assertion confirms and develops the *topos* of Limerick as a resistant fortress in the face of a bigger empire, Numantium being the Celtiberian antithesis of Rome, which reframes the Carthaginian origins of the city motto in a 'Celtic' context. It echoes the 'Hibernian' motif of liminality: Ireland (*Hibernia*) as beyond an imperial wall, before becoming an object of imperial interest. Limerick's walls are thus deeply ambivalent, readable both as evidence of conquest and its related violence, but also as 'outside the Pale' (to employ another Irish phrase), resistant to a more dominant power. Yet Garryowen – both part of and other to the city – is presented in terms of equality with the *urbs* and this equality has something to do with the not-fully-enclosed quality of the 'Irish' aspect in the construction, somehow at odds with the urban principle itself. Referring to his heroine as a 'suburban beauty' and 'this flower of the suburbs', Griffin's impersonal narrator assures us that 'her education in the outskirts of the city had not impaired the natural tenderness of her character'.[7]

Griffin's motif of peripherality is one that cuts deep as far as thinking about the specific meaning(s) of Limerick in an Irish and European context is concerned, but it is not a simple indicator of position. Peripherality here

Fig. 4. View of the Shannon at Limerick – including Thomond Bridge, King John's Castle, St Mary's Cathedral, and Potato Market (site of original Danish settlement) – from Arthur's Quay Ferris Wheel, March 2023. Photo: Michael G. Kelly.

could be argued to be embraced rather than endured, and thus seen as key to the emotional disposition and directionality of the subject. Developing from the earlier association with motifs of resilience and resistance, the civic 'psyche' emerges as Romantic in a sense quite different from the landscapes of the Irish West Coast (rebranded in recent years as the 'Wild Atlantic Way') that are not all that physically distant. It is an internally ambivalent civic romance, founded on motifs of conflict, separation, exclusion and a communal sublime to which the River Shannon can act as a living metaphor – too vast a presence to be simply picturesque, since, on occasion, it almost overwhelms the urban landscape that it moves through, structures or unmakes, connoting as much an inescapability of place, its dogged hold on the subjects who inhabit it, as a majestic persistence or resilience thereof.

While the figure of the wall thus summons up a considerable centrality of Limerick as a modest (mid-size) 'regional' European urban place, there is a parallel sense in which Limerick has, over many decades of modern Irish history, been cast in the role of an urban 'other' within the social and economic politics of the independent Irish state. The city of which the walls are a foregrounded signifier is indeed one that experiences itself consistently as occurring *extra muros*, which is a particular way of inhabiting peripherality in a modern and contemporary context. Associations of urban deprivation, impoverishment and dysfunctionality have frequently been mobilized in a national context to make of Limerick a kind of counterexample, a city, as it were, 'beyond the Pale' of improving governmental action (situated in Dublin, in this political imaginary), as far as national political agency and intentions are or were concerned.

Long before contemporary debates on the economic and structural regeneration of city centres, themselves preceded by national government-led regeneration initiatives in respect of the city's most disadvantaged, enclaved communities, the city (*urbs*) emerges in these reflections as de-centred, not in the sense of being without a centre, but of the 'centre' no longer being unquestionably located there where the walls appear to say it is. This imaginary of an urban reality being paradoxically *extra muros* entrenches Limerick in the role of the underdog, the outsider, disrupting the metropolitan order (latterly represented by Dublin as a prolongation of imperial figures such as Rome and London) and which is hence also a residually colonial one. Such imperial hierarchies do not validate the city's symbolic sense of itself, which has a resolutely diasporic or deterritorialized quality, while its representatives who make their own way into the wider world often present as mavericks, even as they enter an externally-validated cultural canon. Hence the resonance of figures such as Richard Harris (in cinema), Kate O'Brien and Frank McCourt (in literature), Dolores O'Riordan (in rock music), as well as an array of sports heroes, since engagement with sports is an especially prominent oral narrative form in the city and its surrounds.

This de-centring remains also a function of time as well as space, and this is at least in part a function of urban scale. While it is a frequent observation of economists and planners that Limerick's urban area (long divided between municipality and county governance) has the potential to host a population that is a multiple of the current one, Limerick is 'mid-size' as an urban reality in the persistence of at least a notion of complete impersonality. In his story 'Who's-Dead McCarthy' (2020), Kevin Barry offers what can be read as a partial rewriting of Poe's *Man of the Crowd* – that parable of the modern metropolis – in the context of the undead ghost of direct community. The question of scale is here inseparable not only from that of community, but from that of memory as well. The text presents a certain Con McCarthy, 'our connoisseur of death',[8] purveyor of the currency that is the news of recent deaths in a city not yet big enough for these to become a matter of pure indifference:

Fig. 5. Limerick actor Richard Harris facing Monica Vitti in Il Deserto rosso (dir. Michelangelo Antonioni, 1964) – an exterior filmed in Ravenna.

Fig. 6. Mural of singer Dolores O'Riordan, King's Island, March 2023. Photo: Michael G. Kelly.

I became morbidly fascinated by Con McCarthy. I asked around the town about him. I came to understand that in many ways he was a mysterious figure. Some said he came from Hyde Road, others from Ballynanty. The city was just about big enough to afford a measure of anonymity. You could be a great familiar of O'Connell Street but relatively unknown beyond the normal hours of the day and night. We might know broadly of your standing, your people and their afflictions, but the view would be fuzzy, the detail blurred . . . One night on William Street, I spotted him sitting late and alone in the Burgerland there over a paper cup of tea. That cup of tea was the saddest thing I ever saw. I sat in a few tables from him and watched carefully. As he sat alone his lips again moved and I have no doubt that it was a litany of names he was reciting, the names of the dead, just a whisper enough to hoist those names that they might float above the lamps of the city.[9]

The figure of McCarthy adrift around the streets of the contemporary centre suggests a place where memory is as much a matter of its inscriptions in the urban space as in the minds of those who refuse to let go. The cityscape becomes a partial 'chronotope', to use Bakhtin's term, where features both recall a transcendent civic fact and somehow suggest the elusiveness of that fact to the busy regime of contemporary individuality. As if the old walls themselves were both spectral invitations to pay attention to each other and reminders of the cruelty and indifference that also inhabit the social nexus.

The idea of urban space as chronotope can be extended to consider how the time and space of a city appear in its cartographic representations, in the dynamic visions for its future(s). These documents are texts in themselves. One such prospect for the city is palpable in the drawing made by engineer Christopher Colles in 1769. Commissioned by Edmund Sexton Pery as a design for a 'New Town' on Pery's lands in the south liberties of the city, this now iconic drawing sets out a strong ambition, a bold structure for a new urban form beyond the original walls, a grid-form alien to the dense weave of the streetscape of the earlier city.

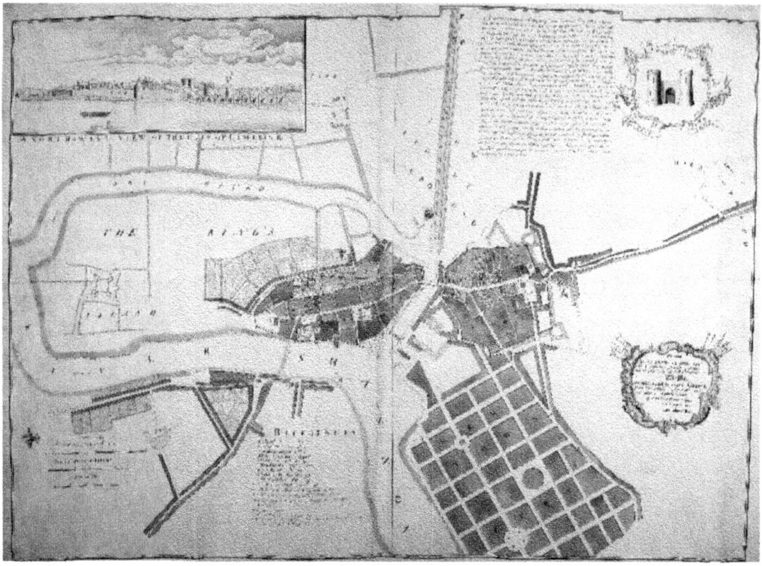

Fig. 7. Christopher Colles, Plan of the City and Suburbs of Limerick, 1769, 54 x 74 cm, © British Library Board.

With this grid, the concept – and experience – of walls in the city becomes inverted. The original stone walls formed the enclosure of the city, a physical boundary intended as both physical and metaphorical 'safety'. Following the direction of Colles' plan, Pery's New Town was developed during Limerick's highly prosperous nineteenth century. The grid was infilled, plot by plot, through speculative building, each individual landowner following a set of broad rules for its construction, including dimensions of approximate heights and widths, and material choices. This new streetscape, formed by the brick façades of the Georgian townhouses, turned the city inside-out. The walls of the city were no longer about enclosure and protection: these new, red-hued walls were a confident expression of its merchant expansion, where the city presented itself to itself, its life and activity framed by large windows on each *piano nobile* looking over the broad streets. In her novel of 1931, *Without My Cloak*, set in 1860s Mellick (a very lightly disguised Limerick, and an almost-anagram), Kate O'Brien captures this lived experience of her city through the eyes of her character Anthony:

> *Charles Street and his direction along it now went parallel with the seaward flow of the river. At the crossings, where short streets cut the New Town symmetrically from east to west, he could glimpse the great stream to the right of him down a short hill and observe the regular hurry of its course past the unhurrying docks; carts and ships and cargoes he noted, his own and other men's, and all he saw refreshed his knowledge of the town's business life and kept the surface of his mind in motion with trade affairs. When he looked eastward up the wide crossing streets, he snatched, one block away, a fragment of the life of King's Street, where the shops were gay at this hour, and where broughams and phaetons splashed arrogantly through the mud, bearing wives and daughters of the town to and fro between the tall brown houses at the southern end and all the fripperies and agitations of their social habit.*[10]

The scale and grandeur of the main thoroughfare of O'Connell Street stretched from the boundary of the original Irishtown and rose gently up the slope to the urban set-piece of The Crescent. Below this new brick city sat another network of newly constructed walls: the Georgian city was built one storey above the natural ground-level. A series of arches held up brick-vaulted cellars, basement 'areas' for coal and for servants, and culverts for waste – an arrangement of walls of the city concealed belowground, enabling the city above to function in both its public and private guises.[11] The upper-most street of the grid in Colles's plan was named William Street, an axis in the city that has, from its eighteenth-century origin, acted as a boundary between the two parts of the city, a metaphorical wall of sorts between a tangled network of mediaeval streetscape and the rational performance of grid city. In a transference from O'Connell Street – the street referred to as King's Street in O'Brien's Mellick – it is today, and since the mid-twentieth-century, William Street that instead occupies this place of trade and exchange. Many of its businesses are long-standing family affairs, shopfronts with names handed down over generations, giving it the presence of scale and familiarity of an Irish town as opposed to the anonymity of city. Kevin Barry (again) aptly captures this in his short story 'A Pirate, Dreaming', set in 1983. Barry gives an account of his home city through the eyes of the story's narrator, the presenter of an early-morning show on an illegal pirate radio station. Broadcast from the attic space of a Georgian building in the Newtown Pery brick core of the city, the 'pirate' simultaneously watches the city and talks to the city, the narrator acting as both the voice of the city fabric itself and of its people, communicating an accumulated lived knowledge of place:

> *The town below and beyond him was approaching its full throttle. The town had the lungs cleared on itself and a bit of colour slapped into its face. The old rooftops leaned into one and other, as though to confide. How-we-now, they enquired, but gently. He put the footstool directly under the velux and stood on it – the height would give the broader view – and he let his*

Fig. 8. The new brick walls of the city turn a corner, showing the inversion of the experience of wall in the newly expanded city. These new walls are punctured by large windows, revealing a generous proportional relationship between opening and solid.

> *busy, enquiring head emerge to the city, poked it this way and that and back again. Swallows darted back and forth and drew out their invisible threads and held the world together. He saw Billy Mac heading down towards William Street, was it Boyds he was working in, the hardware? Billy Mac stopped up in his stride, went to his haunches beside a puddle, took a comb out of his pocket, ran it through the puddled water, and then ran it through what was left of the hair on the top of his head. That was Billy for you. Smooth operator. Here and then gone again... Along by the Glentworth came a big, softly padding guard, beef to the heels, a countryish sort of lad he did not recognize – he knew most of the guards on a first-name basis. This fella looked as if he was straight in from the like of Askeaton or Knocklong. God help us.*[12]

Here again, Barry's narrative of the city – through the eyes of one of its inhabitants –exemplifies the scale of the mid-size city, where citizens become known intimately to one another through a weave of repeated patterns of behaviour. Furthermore, Barry's narrative emphasizes the complexity of the role and experience of the mid-size European city in Ireland specifically, where the relationship or tension between urban and rural is integral to any account of the Irish city, and to how one acts or performs the city and its meaning. Forty years on from that imagined scene, William Street today remains the commercial centre of Limerick's urban core, its character formed by its role as the main location of bus stops in the city, surrounded by a motley collection of shoe shops, pharmacies, clothing shops, chippers, bargain shops, charity shops, shops selling vaping equipment and wheelie suitcases, and a side-entrance to a branch of Ireland's most exclusive department store – an odd assortment of uses, vibrantly enjoyable in this eccentricity and centrality, and a reflection of the city's now multicultural population. It is a microcosm of the city within the length of one street, a street that gathers itself like a town.

This collage of street inhabitation was already captured very well by Limerick writer Michael Curtin in the early 1990s. In *A Plastic Tomato Cutter*, set in Limerick in the mid-twentieth century, the narrator, Mr Yendall, describes how a fellow character – Simpson, a shop boy who had climbed up to become a shop assistant – left the fictional Montague's tailors to establish his own drapery business in what was formerly the fictional Mayhew's Medical Hall. On making this announcement, his boss in Montague's, Mr Sloan, decries the location of his new shop:

> *'It's not a good street, Simpson.' Mr Sloan was emphatic. Simpson had no answer. How could he? A pawnbroker's offal and spare rib merchants, hucksters of balloons and holy pictures, an Italian chip shop, low pubs, betting shops, the promenade of the poor on their way to the dispensary for free cod liver oil, the wonder was that they had not bankrupt Mr Mayhew, a decent man but undoubtedly eccentric to prosper in such a community. It was not a street I would have strolled through after dark.*[13]

The urban river edge here offers another porously *mural* narrative of the city. The Shannon is the longest, widest river in Ireland, and Limerick is located at the most inland point of its tidal reach. Charles Mills's *View of Arthur's Quay* (circa 1860) offers a nineteenth-century prospect on how the city meets this material edge. The painting captures the energy and busyness of the river edge at a time where the river had a central role in the trade activities of the then-growing city. We see the hills of Clare offering their protective backdrop to the city, while the north shore of the river is populated by only a handful of large houses and their demesnes. Thomond Bridge reaches across to Englishtown and King John's Castle, where a red flag flies from one turret. Below it, the white water of the Curragower Falls rushes over the rocky riverbed at low tide. Smoke billows from the chimney of the distillery, while other industrial buildings jostle for space along the constructed urban edge, reclaimed from the river. The top of the

Fig. 9. View of Arthur's Quay c. 1860 by Charles Mills, oil on canvas (Dr Matthew Potter, Limerick Museum, Limerick), size 100 x 176 cm. Compare with the contemporary aerial view from the same position, in Figure 4 above.

stone tower of St Mary's Cathedral is presented as the city's high point, while the terrace of red-brick Georgian townhouses at Arthur's Quay closes the frame. In the foreground, the riverbed is a hive of activity, where mid-size merchant sailboats find mooring along a busy quayside filled with piles of materials, horses and carts, dogs, hens, while a mixture of well-dressed merchants and poorer workers carry out their business of conversation, exchange and labour.

As trade moved from water to rail to road, the river wall as a place of exchange and commerce lost its centrality in the life of the city. Ireland's towns and villages have a morphological tradition of turning their backs on their waters, whether river or sea. And through the twentieth century, Limerick was no exception: the narrative of the river in the city began to highlight it as a challenging presence, an untameable power. In *My Ireland*, a literary text that lies between autobiography and travel writing, Kate O'Brien describes the river of her city in a way that, over 100 years later, resonates with the description of Samuel Lewis, cited earlier:

> ***The Shannon is a formidable water; nothing parochial about it, nothing of prattle or girlish dream. It sweeps in and out of the ocean and the world according to the rules of far-out tides, and in association with dangerous distances. So its harbour has been long accustomed to news and trouble in and out, and in the general movement of time Limerick has been shaped as much by invasions and sieges as by acts of God and the usual weatherings. It is for Ireland therefore a representative city: whatever happened to Ireland happened also here – and some things happened to Ireland because of things that happened here.***[14]

Through the twentieth century, the river edge was, for many, a metaphorical wall, a neglected and cyclically shifting natural feature that became a symbol of the city's difficulties and poverty. Frank McCourt's globally successful memoir, *Angela's Ashes*, traces his childhood in the city from his birth in the 1930s, and the opening scene uses the river to set its narrative as the harbinger of ill-health:

> *Out in the Atlantic great sheets of rain gathered to drift slowly up the River Shannon and settle forever in Limerick. The rain dampened the city from the Feast of the Circumcision to New Year's Eve. It created a cacophony of hacking coughs, bronchial rattles, asthmatic wheezes, consumptive croaks. It turned noses into fountains, lungs into bacterial sponges.*[15]

One location along these walls stood as an exception to that predominantly oppressive narrative construction of the river: the place known as 'Poor Man's Kilkee'. Here, on the limestone quayside, its depth laid to lawn, city dwelling families who could not afford the train fare to the famous West Clare watering hole favoured by their wealthier fellow citizens would holiday and swim at low tide, enjoying the pleasures of the river.

An entire lifetime later, and since the mid-2010s in particular, the river has enjoyed a significant renaissance inside the city. With swimming, kayaking, rowing and stand-up paddleboarding, the stone-wall built edges between cityscape and waterway have been physically and metaphorically breached at every point. Moving across these boundaries and embracing the river has now become a symbol of health, vigour and prosperity, a narrative now recognized and promoted by the municipality. Walkers and runners circle the loop of the three city bridges (Thomond, Sarsfield, Condell). The presence of the river pulses through this stretch of the city, demanding attention. The city sees itself through new eyes, encircling its river, its people gathering to linger and socialize along the quaysides, looking west into a setting sun, as the quay walls stretch towards the softening edges of the river and its mudflats as it heads to the breadth of its estuary and the sea.

As with Virgil's narrative glimpse of Carthage, given at the outset of this essay – a city resistant to externally imposed narratives – Limerick, too, through the first century of Ireland's post-independence history, has resisted the narrative repeatedly assigned to it: its role as peripheral *other* in the network of Irish urban centres. This resistance relied on the generation and maintenance of a particular civic psyche, as mentioned earlier. This psyche of resistance can be seen much earlier, too, in the distancing, the *othering*, of the Irish native people from the garrison of Englishtown, as seen in contemporary cartographic representations, such as 'Pacata Hibernia' above. However, the city's darker history of these past hundred years lies in its own internal creation of a set of invisible walls around parts of the city – the walls of social segregation, of *othering*.

In the early to mid-twentieth-century, the generations of people living in dire conditions in the tenements of the Georgian red-brick houses (such as those depicted at Arthur's Quay in Mills's painting above) and in the network of laneways of the city (such as those recounted by McCourt in *Angela's Ashes*) were moved, wholesale, into newly constructed public housing estates at the far reaches of the city's boundaries. Each of the three new suburbs – Moyross, Southill and King's Island – were at a significant physical remove from the core of the city and, more importantly, were located in places of which the physical attributes rendered them even more invisible – a marsh, a hill, an island – and were further separated by poor public transport links and little services. This act effectively ghettoized a swathe of Limerick's people through the construction of these invisible but highly palpable walls, generating social divides. In the twenty-first century, various governmental efforts, national and local, have been made to regenerate and renew these areas, but it is the foundational act of physical segregation – placing city people wholeheartedly outside the walls – that has ensured this lived reality remains an immensely challenging one for Limerick's urban present, and central to the question of urban futures in its case. Drawing on the social research of Des McCafferty, Trutz Haase and Jonathan Pratschke, historian John Logan writes:

> *Using national census and other official data, they [McCafferty et al.] show how in the large public housing estates, a disproportionate number live lives of economic precariousness. These zones coexist with others where high levels of property ownership, secure, well-paid employment, educational success, and accumulated social capital is general. Though sometimes physically close, the zones are as culturally separate as if encircled by the impermeable walls of earlier times.*[16]

The clarity and commitment of vision in Colles's 1769 proposal for the expansion of the city – the creation of a formal cityscape of grand, inhabitable brick walls – is in sharp contrast to the creeping urban and suburban sprawl of twentieth- and twenty-first century Limerick, and the complex social, political and legal realities that have enabled this ongoing mutation. Recent and current powers of local governance have tended to favour policies of economic investment and physical development *extra muros*, driving processes of dispersal: motorway networks circling the city, new schools built on the edges, and intermediary tracts of land between centre and suburbs left to signify an urban potential both present and unrealized, as wasteland. Within the ruins of its earliest walls, the older centre of Limerick – this mid-size European city – continues to remind us of its value and its lessons, even as it calls for and awaits new narrative(s).

1 Flaubert's *Salammbô* (1862) comes to mind, for example.

2 Taken from the lemma on Limerick in Samuel Lewis' *A Topographical Dictionary of Ireland* (1837). See: Library Ireland, 'Limerick City', libraryireland.com/topog/L/Limerick-City.php, accessed 13 February 2023.

3 Gerald Griffin, *The Collegians: A Tale of Garryowen* (Dublin: J. Duffy & Co, 1857).

4 Dion Boucicault's *The Colleen Bawn, or The Brides of Garryowen* (1860) is a play written and first produced in New York, where the emigrant Irish playwright had discovered the Irish novel by chance. The incident exemplifies the interporosity of Irish and Irish-American cultural production and imaginaries – factors that play an important role in Irish cultural self-consciousness and production to this day. The most impactful literary 'memoir' of Limerick, for example, *Angela's Ashes* (1996), was authored in New York by Frank McCourt more than a century later.

5 Cathal O'Connell, 'City, Citizenship, Social Exclusion in Limerick', in: Niamh Hourigan (ed.), *Understanding Limerick: Social Exclusion and Change* (Cork: Cork University Press, 2011), 230–44: 233.

6 Griffin, *The Collegians*, op. cit. (note 3), 6.

7 Ibid., 9, 11, 9.

8 Kevin Barry, 'Who's-Dead McCarthy', in: Kevin Barry, *That Old Country Music* (Edinburgh: Canongate, 2020), 109-118: 109.

9 Ibid., 116-117.

10 Kate O'Brien, *Without My Cloak* (London: William Heinemann, 1931), 10.

11 For more on this, see: Peter Carroll, 'Fundamental Base: Thinking of the City from the Ground Up', in: *Architecture Ireland* 313 (2020), 13-17.

12 Kevin Barry, 'A Pirate, Dreaming', in: Tim Groenland et al. (eds.), *The Ogham Stone* (Limerick: The University of Limerick, 2022), 69-76: 73-74.

13 Michael Curtin, *The Plastic Tomato Cutter* (London: Thistle Publishing, 2015 [1991]), 114-115.

14 Kate O'Brien, *My Ireland* (London: Batsford, 1962), 22.

15 Frank McCourt, *Angela's Ashes* (New York: Scribner, 1996), 11-12.

16 John Logan, 'Settlement, Building, Segregation: A History of Limerick City', in: *Architecture Ireland* 313 (2020), 7-12: 11.

Porto — Campanhã Collage Stories from the City's Edge

Carlos Machado e Moura and Eliana Sousa Santos

Porto is the second-largest city in Portugal. With a population of only 292 thousand people in a municipality of around 41 km², it could be called a mid-sized city, although its metropolitan area, with approximately 2.4 million people (2021) and an area of 2.400 km², is the second-largest urban area in the country and one of the Iberian Peninsula's major urban areas. The city's eastern part corresponds to the parish of Campanhã, limited to the south by the river Douro and the east by the neighbouring municipality of Gondomar. The largest parish of the city, Campanhã, has an area of 8 km² and a population of 30 thousand people (2021) and results from the topography of the valley of the Tinto and Torto Rivers [Fig. 1].

Until the nineteenth century, Campanhã was primarily characterized by farms and small scattered settlements. A fertile land with many water lines, and agricultural activity as the basis of its economy, Campanhã

Fig. 1. F. Peixoto, view of Freixo from the Quinta da China estate, c. 1890.

Fig. 2. Postcard 'Porto: Boat race on the Douro River', c. 1905.

supplied the population of the city centre. Connected to these farms, the area became marked by the manor houses or mansions of the wealthiest families in Porto, with significant architectural and artistic value, dispersed across the landscape [Fig. 2]. Their present degradation mirrors the neglect and abandonment to which this part of the city was subjected as a consequence of the transformation of the territory.

From the second half of the nineteenth century, the transformations introduced by the railway and several industries rendered the valley of Campanhã the object of unbalanced growth. Among the industries installed is the mill next to the Freixo Palace by the river, now transformed into a hotel, and the Ceres mill next to the railway, which is still in operation. Establishing industries and housing to the east of the railway line was complex, due to the topography; to the west, the installation of factories and the need for a working population resulted in urban densification. This happened mainly through the adoption of the *ilha* housing typology – groups of tiny dwellings built in the backyards of middle-class houses and connected to the street via a narrow corridor – several of which still exist.

Throughout the last 150 years, several large-scale rail and road infrastructures crossed the territory of Campanhã but failed to provide quality urban conditions, which progressively isolated the area. Remaining free of dense construction, this eastern territory was later traversed and cut by new routes that aggravated the barriers created by the railroad in 1877 and followed by the Circunvalação road, built between 1889 and 1896. By the end of the twentieth century, the extension of the VCI ring road to the east intersected the territory of Campanhã again, followed by a new motorway, the Gondomar radial (A43), opened in 2011.

A number of recent projects and transformations, including the creation of metro lines (1999-2004) and the new intermodal terminal (2017-2022) next to the Campanhã railway station, along with a series of pedestrian paths and the new Oriental City Park (2010), have mitigated the discontinuities of this territory. Campanhã, however, remains a land with many problems of social and territorial cohesion. This led the municipality to launch the Campanhã Urbanization Plan (2023-2025), coordinated by Catalan architect Joan Busquets, to operate a profound transformation of the urban space, developing a new centrality in the eastern part of the city.

Our contribution provides a kaleidoscopic overview of Campanhã through the work on four different projects, for which completely distinct methods, agendas and aims were employed and that are focused on specific areas of the parish.

StreetArtCei, the first case, applies the method of digitally mapping street art routes to Campanhã, expressing specific cultural geographies, and serving as a barometer of the city's changing spaces. The Atlas of Literary Landscapes, the second case, proposes a collection of textual excerpts that allow the railroad and the Campanhã train station to be documented through Portuguese literature. The third case, The Worst Tours, is an initiative of walking tours that offer a critical perspective of the city, apart from the mainstream routes, envisioning possibilities of transformation. The study includes drawings, photos and a poetic text focusing specifically in the area of Freixo, in Campanhã. Finally, Adrift in Vacant Campanhã recounts the experience of the URBiNAT project, which aimed to design opportunities to co-create an inclusive public space in these underutilized areas, together with local citizens and stakeholders.[1]

The StreetArtCEI project in Campanhã

Clara Sarmento[2]

Campanhã is a neighbourhood of contrasts, a valley where council housing flourished in the 1940s, when a city born to the west expanded eastwards. Initially an agricultural area, then industrial, later of services, it experienced cycles of demographic growth followed by rapid desertification, it is a place of bourgeois estates, side by side with territories of drug trafficking. Campanhã is still torn between its past of rural tradition – which remains alive in the landscape and in many aspects of the community's everyday life – and the increasingly visible features of middle-class modernity with cosmopolitan aspirations. From a centenary railway branch to the modern Estádio do Dragão, from the Via de Cintura Interna to paths meandering among old farms, the history made of progress and setbacks of this neighbourhood can be read in the street art inscribed on its walls, where expensive commissioned works coexist with surprising illegal pieces.

Indifferent to the law or created for commercial consumption, the street art of Campanhã works as an unexpected sensory stimulus, as an aesthetic-intellectual challenge that goes along with the daily experience of the city. Here, we intend to apply to Campanhã a method for mapping digital routes of street art, routes that express specific cultural geographies, in the open and changing space of the city. By mapping these routes, significant itineraries emerge, and the act of walking becomes an immersive experience, rather than a mechanical dislocation of the body.

The method applied to Campanhã was developed by the Centre for Intercultural Studies (CEI) of the Polytechnic University of Porto, within the scope

Fig. 3. Approximate distribution of POI in Campanhã.
Credits: Google Maps and StreetArtCEI team.

Fig. 4-7. Factory in Rua de Justino Teixeira.

Fig. 8-11. Alfândega railway branch.
Photos: StreetArtCEI team

of the StreetArtCEI project.[3] The StreetArtCEI project contains an open archive of digital routes of street art in Porto and other cities in northern Portugal. StreetArtCEI considers legal and illegal pieces in absolute parity, whether they are located in high visibility streets or in the most remote alleys. Through a sequence of: a) observant movement, b) photography, c) location on a map and, d) design of connecting itineraries, the researchers-*flaneurs* of StreeArtCEI decode the spatial patterns of urban creativity, also in Campanhã.

In the fieldwork carried out so far in Campanhã, 383 images were collected, distributed by 26 POIs [Fig. 3], some of which in rather peculiar locations, such as the ruined building on Rua do Freixo, the electricity boxes on the Outer Ring Road (Estrada Exterior da Circunvalação) or the abandoned railway branch between Campanhã Train Station and Alfândega. The list of Points of Interest (POI) and the respective number of pieces is, in alphabetical order:

> Alameda das Antas, 7; Alameda Shop&Spot, 2 [Fig. 16]; Avenida 25 de Abril, 2; Avenida Fernão de Magalhães, 24 [Figs. 12-13]; Caminho do Ramal da Alfândega, 111 [Figs. 8-11]; Escola Básica de Ramalho Ortigão, 3; Estação de Campanhã, 15; Estádio do Dragão, 1; Estrada Exterior da Circunvalação, 16; Fábrica da Rua de Justino Teixeira, 34; Rua do Padre António Vieira, 2; Rua Vasques de Mesquita, 4; Rua da Vigorosa, 5; Rua de Justino Teixeira, 13 [Figs. 4-7]; Rua de Pinto Bessa, 12 [Fig. 17]; Rua de S. Rosendo, 3; Rua de São Roque da Lameira, 9; Rua do Bonfim, 3; Rua do Freixo, 60 [Fig. 15]; Rua do Monte da Estação, 18; Rua Esteiro de Campanhã, 9; Rua Igreja de Campanhã, 9; Rua José Monteiro da Costa, 1; Rua Pinheiro de Campanhã, 2; Rua Sociedade Protetora dos Animais, 6; Travessa de Bonjóia, 13 [Fig. 14].

Fig. 12-17. Avenida Fernão de Magalhães (12+13), Travessa da Bonjóia (14), Rua do Freixo (15), Alameda Shop&Spot (16), Rua Pinto Bessa (17). Photos: StreetArtCEI team.

A simple mapping of Campanhã's POIs critically positions the passer-by within the urban palimpsest, where street artists have built their own networks of communication, movement and meaning. The spatial concentration of POI around two axes of attraction becomes evident: Estádio do Dragão and the Intermodal Terminal of Campanhã, with their associated housing, commerce, transport and services. From here, the POIs extend radially through the surrounding streets and alleys, which are at the same time survivors of the once proletarian Campanhã and sentinels of the new urbanism and its technologies.

Commissioned, sophisticated, large-scale works are strategically located close to the gates of Estádio do Dragão and at the Alameda Shop&Spot shopping centre, thus paving the way of visitors, luring them into consumption, for the comfort of the city's ruling powers.

Some POIs stand out due to the number of pieces they host, such as the Freixo area and the Estrada Exterior da Circunvalação. Here, legal pieces adorn the electricity boxes, trying to bring to this peripheral and always jammed road a practice that is usual in the tourist centre of Porto. There, abandoned houses and factories retell the story of Campanhã's proletarian past, while offering their walls as canvas to the artists, duly hidden from the sight of those who visit the marina and palace of Freixo.

The path along the discontinued Campanhã-Alfândega railway branch as well as the wastelands of Travessa de Bonjóia reveal hidden galleries of street art, vibrant art studios on stone walls, tunnels and cement pillars. Until being domesticated and destroyed, they remain accessible only to initiates and adventurers.

In bourgeois housing areas, street art is almost absent, as the middle class isn't comfortable with illegal creativity. Avenida Fernão de Magalhães, for example, only hosts a considerable number of pieces at its southernmost end, at the edge of the neighbourhood, in the rubble of megalomaniac urban projects with their sad reminiscences. Here, time itself becomes a dimension of street art, as the social context that produces the image also supports its interpretation, when visualized. In this POI, we find pieces clearly alluding to Gisberta Salce Júnior's murder and pieces tacitly created as a transgression to the pandemic's lockdowns, all of them located in a space-time that works as a memory of the community.

When mapping the street art of Campanhã, places that are apparently threatening and unclassifiable become aesthetically welcoming, as they combine the turbulence of the city with the secrecy required by the creation of a mostly illegal art form.

The demographic dispersion and the open spaces that still characterize Campanhã make street art somehow rare in this neighbourhood, when compared with others in the urban and historical centre of Porto. Certainly, increasing urbanization will destroy many pieces and compromise existing POI, while bringing new spaces for artistic creation. The action of the StreetArtCEI project in Campanhã is still a work in progress, with much yet to be discovered.

LITESCAPE
The Atlas of Literary Landscapes and the Campanhã Train Station

Daniel Alves and Natália Constâncio[4]

The Atlas of Literary Landscapes of Mainland Portugal (Atlas), is an interdisciplinary project, with a markedly digital and academic methodology.[5] It also has pedagogical potential for teaching literature, history and geography, for instance, in addition to possible applications in the area of environmental education or tourist enjoyment. Its main objective is to bring to the fore the environment and landscape readings of Portugal's mainland territory as reflected in literary texts. Its methodology makes it possible to extract, categorize and map the representations that Portuguese and foreign writers of the last century and a half have produced about the territory and its natural, cultural and social heritage.

The Atlas is constantly being renewed and enlarged by means of incorporating literary texts from the nineteenth to the twenty-first centuries. The project investigates how this corpus can serve as an analytical resource for environmental, sociological and cultural changes, presenting itself as an indicator of the evolution of Portuguese landscapes in the popular imagination, in a diachronic perspective.

Based on the assumption that writers are also cartographers, one of the central purposes of the project is the mapping of literary texts. Each literary representation of landscapes from mainland Portugal is registered in a shared database as a single excerpt. These excerpts are distinct passages that can be read and understood independently and that, above all, convey a clear notion of the aesthetic aspects of the works from which they derive.

Fig. 18. A view of Freixo, Campanhã, from the railway (2022).

Fig. 19. Campanhã, excerpt of the topographic map of the city of Porto by Telles Ferreira, 1892.

In each excerpt, it should be possible to identify or imply the geographical references to which they relate. They are then classified into geographic, ecological, socioeconomic, cultural and/or historical categories. This cataloguing makes it possible to produce an interactive map that can serve as a basis for the development of various research of an interdisciplinary scope, but that can also be used for pedagogical or tourist purposes.

This is a hybrid methodology that combines traditional 'close reading' methods with a 'distant reading' perspective. It is a unique project in the field of Portuguese Literary Studies, as it includes not only works by contemporary and canonical authors, but also works belonging to less recognized writers. Nor is it confined to a region or a specific location, but encompasses the entire territory of mainland Portugal, with all its natural and cultural diversity. See, for example, the possibility of creating literary paths organized by themes, authors or works, available in the project's web application.[6] From the beginning, the project was conceived as a collaborative one, with the participation of academics and postgraduate students in Literary Studies, as well as teachers and researchers of Portuguese Language, Geography, History, Anthropology, Tourism, Biology, Architecture or Environmental Sciences, that help with the collection, introduction and classification of texts.[7]

Referring to the Campanhã train station, the literary excerpts that document older works show the evolution of the railways, the inauguration of routes that connect the Porto station to the Douro line or the North line, with the main focus on Lisbon. Many excerpts from canonical writers refer to the daily trade in the places surrounding Campanhã Station, as well as to the human landscape that inhabits and uses those places. The texts that we analysed for the purpose of this contribution – a selection of which follows below – show the existence of professions related to trains, such as the station manager or the ticket collector. They also allude to the hustle and bustle of street vendors, ordinary women, whose livelihood is based on purchases made by train passengers or by those who frequent the station. In contemporary texts, the intersection of villages by the railroad serves as a backdrop for the meditation of the narrators or the characters, the description of the landscape, its contemplation, or an association between the described landscape and the states of mind experienced by the characters.

Literary excerpts (selection):

> *He [Vilaça] added, in a postscript: 'It seems that the railway line to Oporto will be opening very shortly: with your permission, sir, I and my son will travel up and beg a few days' hospitality from you.' This letter was received on a Sunday in Santa Olávia, at suppertime. Afonso had read the postscript out loud. Everyone was pleased at the thought of seeing good old Vilaça back again so soon: there was even talk of arranging a picnic farther up the river.*[8]

> *The day had barely dawned and the street was already vaguely taking in, as if in a stretch, this cold and indecisive relief of the morning twilight, when there was a little woman passing by, elderly, livid, in a cloth mantle and black shawl, her shopping bag and lots of rings on her fingers. She was a legal pimp, who, as usual, went to Campanhã to see if the trains would dump . . . some collectible meat.*[9]

> *When the train rolled into the station, the train from Porto had not yet arrived, delayed in Pampilhosa by a breakdown in the machine. Manoel got off and, in front of Coimbra, which in the distance was a herd of lights scattered on a hill, a slight sadness invaded him again, thinking of his friend, happier, without a son to divert his lover's love, absorbing him. Streams of river gleamed between the bare trunks of poplars, and only a large stone pine rustled in the middle of the thick pool of darkness that soaked the land. He had to wait almost a quarter of an hour, the train due to arrive at eleven-thirty having left Sousellas at eleven-thirty. Alone in the almost deserted station, he took his time walking between the*

canteen and the unloading warehouses, until a blast from a horn sharply tore the silence of the frigid night. The train's headlights appeared from afar, scraping the earth in the distance like two faint embers, growing by the second amidst the murmur of a breathless monster that arrives at a gallop.[10]

Then came the solemn inauguration of the Douro railway line, which now finally ran from Caíde to Régua. It was the complement of this derisive gesture of assistance from the State, which belatedly came to help with the benefits of accelerated transport to a region struggling in poverty. It would, however, be a solemnity surrounded by the most praiseworthy features of official pomp, skilfully maneuvered by political calculating and noisily announced for a long time by the rulers. The Ministers of Public Works and Justice came to Régua expressly from Lisbon. And it even happened, for greater lustre and enhancement of the party, that the Minister of War could also accompany them, a tremulous and sweet old man who, in passing, was going to do his thermal treatment in Vidago. There would thus be, at the station, gathered on that rich day, the most distinguished representatives of the functionalism of the councils of Mesão-Frio, Vila Real and Lamego, all the officers and honour guard of the 9th Infantry, plus two regimental bands and five philharmonics. The station was decorated with flags, and on the side there was a large platform, with a blue and white cloth awning, for the ladies. At night, festival, fireworks, lighting and reception in the Town Hall.[11]

I was at Campanhã station when I heard: 'Transport of workers by rail, to France and beyond.'
Heavens! Treacherous words, which instead of sweat and tears carry the pollen of poetry! 'To France and beyond.'[12]

March 6th. Passing through Porto, on my way to Campanhã station, I saw these words painted on a wall: 'White National Power', adorned with a cross inside a circle. I wonder who this 'Gross National Power' will be against: against the Cape Verdean workers, or against the Japanese capitalists?[13]

To the east, my eyes reached as far as the heights of Campanhã, the Fontainhas and, peeking through the arch of the bridge, the entrances to the two tunnels of the railway. On the top line there was a constant passing of trains. In the other, many metres below, only occasionally did a locomotive appear, slowly pulling freight wagons that disappeared under the city, on their way to the Customs wharf.[14]

In the landscape stretched out to his left, once the river flows, only the bristling sea inspires affection, the only escape from that city stuck in granite. But even the sea evaded his understanding: the sun penetrated it and was lost in the depths, it was not like in the south, where it laid down in the waves and sometimes set them on fire. In the south, the sea was still a Hellenic sea; the one at Foz was barbaric, a sea of a southern island, restless, a foaming beast cornered.
Once the train was parked at the Campanhã Station, Pessoa said goodbye with a smile to the boy who had come in the compartment with his grandfather. He had lent him a pencil and paper so that he could draw to amuse himself instead of pacing restlessly between the seats. On his way out, the kid offered him the work: a human figure with huge glasses and a thick moustache, a semi-triangular head and a hat on top.
He jumped on the platform to clear his head. A smell of burnt oil came from the underside of the car. By the door, just behind the steps, a pipe drained a yellowish liquid that sloshed onto the gravel.[15]

THE WORST TOURS

Evenings of the Day When We Will Know What Freixo Is (Beyond the Name)

Pedro Figueiredo[16]

Freixo: Name.
Freixo: Bridge name, street name, palace, inn, power station.
Freixo: name of a lane (and a roundabout too).
In the beginning there was the name, it was the name of a tree *Fraxinus angustifolea* of the *Oleacea* family. More name than thing, more non-place than place, more memory and more scraps of life from a non-place, Freixo is a collage of things that I dare to try to describe.

Fig. 20. P. Figueiredo, Romanticization of the Freixo Power Plant, drawing, 2021.

Freixo is . . . two points:
Freixo is a non-place, an (im)possible intersection of Rua do Freixo and Rua do Noeda/Travessa do Freixo. Freixo is – they are – two realities, plus the context that frames and justifies them for one side and the other of Rua do Freixo and up to the edge of the Freixo Palace. Rua do Freixo has a brutal slope: it is an unfeasible road, uninhabitable pollution, it is ex-everything and ex-industrial; it has ruins with almost no people but with buses; street that crosses 'o Noeda' and its washing facilities; Noeda, a lane with islands in a rural context, a place with a hidden primary school. Freixo is a place, 'but' . . . but at the intersection there is the improbable 'Café Campanhã', plus its terrace at medium height (as a second balcony), shaded by a branch with a view and hearing the cars up and down on Rua do Freixo, surreal Freixo.

Freixo: If there is a crossing of straight lines, then there is a dot, there is a place, there is a train station, there is a Community (and everything makes sense again: 'eat chocolates little one, eat chocolates'[17]). 'Café Campanhã': a place overlooking a 'street impossible to all thoughts / real impossibly real'.[18]

Freixo: Street that connects ten medium-sized factory bulks, dispersed, stray and feverish. Some are anti-monuments to aspiring to a be monument, monuments waiting for speculation, monuments aspiring to cultural transformation or monuments aspiring to nothing, because beauty only exists in the eye of the beholder.[19]

Freixo is also a physical intersection and crossroads of urban layers. Not far from there nobody knows or nobody saw the past nor the future for the Ford garage.[20] But some knew or saw the self-organized creative intelligence of the musicians of the Stop Shopping Centre,[21] a possible guide of 'what to do' for buildings doomed to no solution. In the Stop Shopping

Fig. 21-24. Freixo Power Plant | The Freixo Power Station seen from Travessa do Rêgo Lameiro, and two drawings that propose a 'romanticization' of the main building, which dates from the 1920s. A company from the Edmond de Rothschild investment group has a real estate project for the site leading to its demolition.

Fig. 25+26. EIF / Freixo Industrial Company | The derelict Freixo Industrial Company (EIF – Epresa Industrial do Freixo) dates from the 1940s, and is part of the land of the Power Plant, corresponding to the facilities where chemical materials resulting from energy production were recycled.

Centre, they didn't 'break in case of emergency', they did it collectively; the property, although private, was not an obstacle.

And west of Freixo? Nothing new: The Maria Pia bridge and the freight railway line accumulate 30 years of simultaneous 'has been' and a missed opportunity, a future-of-the-past that seems mired in the limbo of the present, the limbo of postponed projects. Freixo, which is also the name of the bridge – the 'New Bridge of Freixo' – of which only the name is known ('in the beginning it was the name'): a hologram/lightsaber bridge, a real bridge, an impossibly real one.[22] Freixo – name of the Palace – also considered the easternmost limit of Porto, a baroque palace among industries ('to the east of the east . . . far to the east if it weren't for the west'[23])
The perspective changes, the will changes. Who knows if the far east of Porto could one day become the far west of Gondomar? And when is the eve of the day when we will know what Freixo is beyond its name?

Fig. 27-29. Viaducts 'between lines' | Between the elevation of the Campanhã–S. Bento/ Campanhã–S. João Bridge railway viaducts and the elevation of the former 'Railway branch of Alfândega' – deactivated and with provisional solutions under debate for its use – we find several massive railway viaducts, including one with slender reinforced concrete columns (which connects the Campanhã Station to the S. João Bridge) and one with large granite arches (providing pedestrian access to the Alfândega branch).

Fig. 30-33. Public Washrooms | In the 1940s, the peak period of the ilhas (a typology of low-cost housing that spread within the city in the nineteenth century), two washhouses were built: Lavadouro do Noêda (1941), with orange ceramic stripes, at the east of Rua do Freixo; and Lavadouro da Agra (1942), in Travessa do Rêgo Lameiro, to the west, the infamous 'Green Washhouse'.

URBINAT
Adrift in Vacant Campanhã

Gonçalo Canto Moniz
Vitório Leite[24]

During the last 60 years, Campanhã was transformed from a productive hinterland, characterized by ancient farms and industrial zones, into a living place. The fragmented agricultural and industrial patterns were given away to numerous new neighbourhoods, mostly of low-rent housing or social housing, and, at the same time, a network of motorways and subway lines added to the old train line and the ancient agriculture paths. These new layers created a fast connection between the towns around Porto and the city itself, but also led to increased mobility problems in the newer neighbourhoods.[25]

Invisible structures often fragment neighbourhoods, cities, or societies, shaped by sociospatial features and stories that limit people to certain areas. In this particular area, the structures are also physically visible, such as railways, roads, buildings and topography.

The modern and zoned neighbourhoods and the large-scale urban interventions have resulted in a fragmented morphology, filled with terrains vague and cul-de-sacs with very low connectivity and linked to illegal activities. However, these empty and informal spaces now often serve as paths for the local residents, used for commuting to work or visiting other parts of the city.

The European H2020 URBiNAT project is seizing the opportunity to co-create with local citizens and stakeholders an inclusive public space in these underutilized areas with low publicness, transforming them into 'healthy corridors'. These corridors will integrate nature-based solutions and harmonize material and immaterial dimensions.

Fig. 34-35. Livinglab with adults and children.

Fig. 36. URBiNAT Study area, Campanhã.

URBiNAT's aim is to co-develop an urban project for these healthy corridors that integrates nature-based solutions with a human-centred approach, enabling all citizens to engage in leisure, cultural, social and economic activities.[26] The healthy corridor is a public space that is being co-created with citizens and stakeholders in seven European cities – Porto, Nantes and Sofia, as frontrunners, and Hoje-Taastrup, Brussels, Siena and Nova Gorica, as followers.

In study areas in each city, the project attempts to continue rethinking modern values related to nature, mobility and functionality, while incorporating contemporary principles of inclusion and human rights, solidarity, circular economy, and health and wellbeing. In the case of Porto, the objective of co-creating a healthy corridor is being pursued by the local task force team in a specific group of unused plots between three neighbourhoods in Campanhã – Bairro do Falcão, Bairro do Cerco do Porto and Bairro do Lagarteiro.

Until the early twenty-first century, the urbanization of Porto's eastern parishes, where these neighbourhoods are located, was seen as less stimulating than the western part of the city.[27] However, this area is now undergoing one of the most interesting regeneration processes in the city.

The urban regeneration process of this territory and the contribution of the URBiNAT project to its sociospatial transformation was revealed during a COST Action 18126 *Writing Urban Places* visit, which guided participants through some of the urban elements and areas where the project is intervening. The aim of the visit was to show and describe the process and the place through the lens of the research team, which has been working in the field since 2019 and is still trying to understand the perceptions and wills of people who walk and live in these places.

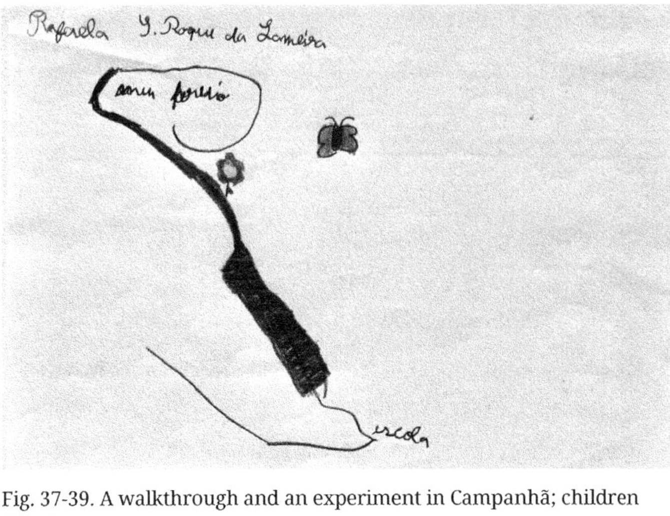

Fig. 37-39. A walkthrough and an experiment in Campanhã; children drawing.

Fig. 40+41. Campmarket and collage at Parque de São Roque da Lameira.

For the team, the project has offered a rich and creative experience of collective practice, enabling an understanding of deep critical proximity and the rethinking of our procedures and ways of doing, such as how to produce and communicate knowledge, how to plan from a micro-scale perspective, and how to use our standard disciplinary tools more accurately.[28]

During the walk, we attempted to explain these processes and give a glimpse into the everyday spatial experience of people who live in the area. Even if only briefly, we sought to integrate the visitors into the local daily life.

FINAL THOUGHTS

Carlos Machado e Moura and Eliana Sousa Santos

Despite the evident differences in the nature, objectives and outputs of these projects, the juxtaposition of these accounts provides alternative views of the fragmented territory of Campanhã. It also conveys a spatialized description of several of its multiple problems and possibilities. Although this collage falls short in offering a comprehensive reading of this part of the city, the methods and fieldwork experiences used testify to the rich potential of each medium and allow for the construction of new meaningful itineraries.

Whether through the exploration of a selection of textual excerpts and the discussion of their relationship with the physical reality of the city, via the recognition and reinterpretation of industrial remnants and public facilities and infrastructures at a time when they face processes of reappropriation and disappearance as a consequence of the urban redevelopment of the area, by means of the systematic documentation of urban traces like graffiti, or the actual engagement in participatory processes and collective practices with local residents, they all reveal lesser-known stories of the city's eastern fringes.

References

de Queirós, Eça. *The Maias*. Translated by Margaret Jull Costa. New York: New Directions, 2007 [1888].

Ferreira, I., & Moniz, G. C..'Healthy Corridors for Inclusive Urban Regeneration'. in: *How Many Roads* Rassegna di Architettura e Urbanistica, 2019 (158), pp. 51-59.

Latour, Bruno, *Critical Distance or Critical Proximity*. 2005, http://www.bruno-latour.fr/sites/default/files/P-113-HARAWAY.pdf

Pessoa, Fernando. 'Tabacaria', *Poesias de Álvaro de Campos*. Lisbon: Ática, 1944 [1915].

Pessoa, Fernando. 'Opiário', *Poesias de Álvaro de Campos*. Lisbon: Ática, 1944 [1933].

Tavares, D. 'A Centralidade - um conceito urbano em evolução'. In M. L. Real (Ed.), *A ponte e avenida: contradições urbanísitcas no centro histórico do Porto*. Porto: Câmara Municipal do Porto, 2001, pp. 13-19.

URBiNAT *Porto Local Diagnostic, Porto: Câmara Municipal do Porto*, DOMUS, CES, Universidade de Coimbra, GUDA, 2019.

1 These areas were visited by the members of *Writing Urban Places* during the Porto Mid-Term Conference in October 2021.

2 Clara Sarmento (CEI – Centre for Intercultural Studies, Polytechnic University of Porto).

3 See www.streetartcei.com. So far, StreetArtCEI has recorded and mapped more than 5,500 images, between 2017 and 2023, distributed along 15 geographic routes, organized into 420 Points of Interest (POI), in permanent update.

4 Daniel Alves and Natália Constâncio (LiteScape; Faculdade de Ciências Sociais e Humanas, Universidade Nova de Lisboa)

5 The Atlas started in 2010 under the coordination of Ana Isabel Queiroz and is currently coordinated by Daniel Alves and Natália Constâncio.

6 See: litescape.ielt.fcsh.unl.pt

7 The database is made available to all who collaborate on the project through a web platform that allows shared access to all content, enhancing networking and interdisciplinary work, with all the information entered by each person being immediately available to the group. From the collaborative work carried out since 2010, the database includes, by February 2023, a total of 8,206 literary excerpts, belonging to 422 works (essentially novels and short stories), by 205 authors (mainly Portuguese), comprising almost 2 million words.

8 Eça de Queirós, *The Maias*, translated by Margaret Jull Costa (New York: New Directions, 2007 [1888]), 70-71. Original in Portuguese: 'E depois num pós-escrito [Vilaça pai] acrescentava: "Parece certo abrir-se em breve o caminho de ferro até ao Porto: em tal caso, com permissão de Vossa Excelência, aí irei e o meu rapaz a pedirmos-lhe alguns dias de hospitalidade." Esta carta foi recebida em Santa Olávia um domingo, ao jantar. Afonso lera alto o P.S. Todos se alegraram-na esperança de ver o bom Vilaça em breve na quinta; e falou-se mesmo em arranjar um grande piquenique, rio acima.' Eça de Queirós, *Os Maias: episódios da vida romântica* (Lisbon: Livros do Brasil, 1993 [1888]), 84.

9 Abel Botelho, *O Livro de Alda* (Lisbon: Promoclube, 1984 [1898]), 145. Free translation; original in Portuguese: 'Mal apontava o dia e já vagamente a rua ia tomando, como que num espreguiçamento, este relevo frio e indeciso do crepúsculo matutino, quando aí deu com ela uma mulherzita que passava, idosa, lívida, de mantelete de pano e mantilha preta, sua malinha de compras e muitos anéis nos dedos. Era uma proxeneta legal, que, como de hábito,

ia a Campanhã ver se acaso os comboios despejariam . . . alguma carne colectável.'

10 Carlos Malheiro Dias, *Filho das Hervas* (Lisbon: Tavares Cardoso & Irmão, 1900), 19. Free translation; original in Portuguese: 'Quando o comboio rolou na estação, ainda o comboio do Porto não chegara, retardado na Pampilhosa por um desmancho na machina. Manoel desceu, e em frente de Coimbra, que era ao longe um rebanho de luzes tresmalhado n'um outeiro, de novo uma leve tristeza o invadiu, pensando no amigo, mais feliz, sem um filho que lhe desviasse o amor da amante, absorvendo-o. Cortes de rio lampejavam entre troncos nus de choupos e só um grande pinheiro manso rumorejava a meio do charco espesso de treva que ensopava as terras. Teve de esperar quasi um quarto de hora, o comboio que devia chegar ás onze e trese tendo partido de Sousellas ás onze e trinta. Sosinho na gare quasi deserta, levou o tempo a andar entre a cantina e os armazéns de descarga, até que um toque de busina rasgou asperamente o silencio da noite frigidissima. Os pharoes do comboio surgiram ao longe, raspando a terra á distancia como duas brazas desmaiadas, crescendo a cada segundo de entre um rumor de monstro esbaforido que chega de galope.'

11 Abel Botelho, *Próspero Fortuna*, 3rd edition (Porto: Livraria Chardron de Lello & Irmão, 1925 [1910]), 33. Free translation; original in Portuguese: 'Veio então a inauguração solene da linha férrea do Douro, que deitava agora, finalmente, de Caíde até à Régua. Era o complemento desse irrisório gesto de assistência do Estado, que tardiamente vinha acudir com os benefícios da viação acelerada a uma região debatendo-se na miséria. Seria, não obstante, uma solenidade rodeada dos mais louçãos primores da pompa oficial, manobrada habilmente pelo videirismo político e de há muito pelos governantes ruidosamente anunciada. Vinham de Lisboa à Régua, expressamente, os ministros das obras públicas e da justiça. E ainda aconteceu, para maior lustre e realce da festa, que pudesse acompanhá-los também o ministro da guerra, um trémulo e doce velhinho que, de passagem, ia fazer a Vidago o seu tratamento de águas. Haveria assim, na estação, reunidos naquele rico dia, os mais grados representantes do funcionalismo dos concelhos de Mesão-Frio, Vila Real e Lamego, toda a oficialidade e guarda de honra do 9 de infantaria, mais duas bandas regimentais e cinco filarmónicas. A estação embandeirada, e à ilharga um grande palanque, de toldo de paninho azul e branco, para as senhoras. À noite, arraial, foguetório, iluminações e recepção nos Paços do Concelho.'

12 Luísa Dacosta, *Na Água do Tempo* (Lisbon: Ed. Quimera, 1992), 116. Free translaton; original in Portuguese: 'Estava na estação de Campanhã, quando ouvi: "Transporte de trabalhadores pelo caminho-de-ferro, com destino a França e além."
Céus! Traidoras palavras, que em vez de suor e lágrimas carregam pólen de poesia! "Com destino a França e além."'

13 José Saramago, *Cadernos de Lanzarote* (Lisbon: Caminho, 1994), 67. Free translation; original in Portuguese: '6 de Março. Na passagem pelo Porto, caminho da estação de Campanhã, vi estas palavras pintadas numa parede: "Poder Nacional Branco", adornadas com uma cruz no interior de um círculo. Pergunto-me contra quem estará este "Poder Nacional Bruto": contra os operários cabo-verdianos, ou contra os capitalistas japoneses?'

14 J. Rentes de Carvalho, *Ernestina*, 2nd ed. (Lisbon: Quetzal, 2010 [1998]), 135. Free translation; original in Portuguese: 'Para oriente, os meus olhos alcançavam até ao longe dos altos de Campanhã, as Fontainhas e, espreitando por entre o arco da ponte, as entradas dos dois túneis do caminho de ferro. Na linha superior era um constante passar de comboios. Na outra, muitos metros abaixo, apenas de vez em quando aparecia uma locomotiva a puxar lentamente vagões de mercadorias que desapareciam sob a cidade, a caminho do cais da Alfândega.'

15 Rui Lage, *O Invisível* (Lisbon: Gradiva, 2019), 88. Free translation; original in Portuguese: 'Na paisagem estendida à sua esquerda, desaguado o rio, apenas o mar ouriçado lhe inspirava afecto, única escapatória daquela cidade emperrada em granitos. Mas mesmo o mar se furtava à sua compreensão: o sol penetrava-o e perdia-se nas profundezas, não era como no Sul, onde se acamava nas ondas e às vezes as punha a arder. No Sul, o mar era ainda um mar helénico; o da Foz era bárbaro, um mar de ilha meridional, indócil, fera a espumar encurralada. Estacionado o comboio na Gare de Campanhã, Pessoa despediu-se com um sorriso do menino que viera no compartimento com o avô. Emprestara-lhe um lápis e um papel para que se entretivesse a desenhar em vez de passarinhar irrequieto por entre os assentos. A saída, o petiz ofereceu-lhe a obra: uma figura humana com enormes óculos e bigode a traço carregado, cabeça meio triangular e chapéu no cimo. Saltou na plataforma para arejar as ideias. Um cheiro a óleo queimado vinha dos baixos do vagão. Junto à porta, logo atrás dos degraus, um cano escoava um líquido amarelado que chapinhava no saibro.'

16 Pedro Figueiredo (architect and author of *The Worst Tours* guide)

17 Fernando Pessoa, 'Tabacaria' (1915), *Poesias de Álvaro de Campos* (Lisbon: Ática, 1944).

18 Ibid.

19 Such 'monuments' include the monumental CUF (Companhia União Fabril), Freixo, Socipole, Mota-Engil, CACE Cultural, EIF (Empresa Industrial do Freixo), the Thermoelectric Power Station and the 'Noeda factory'.

20 Long abandoned, the former Ford Garage is the object of several projects to accommodate a hotel.

21 The musicians of the shopping mall Stop self-organized to create their own music festival. Online: expresso.pt/blitz/2023-03-07-Musicos-do-centro-comercial-STOP-no-Porto-vao-organizar-o-seu-proprio-festival-b3647994.

22 See online: rtp.pt/noticias/pais/nova-ponte-porto-gaia-pronta-em-2025-custa-369-milhoes-de-euros_n1319628.

23 Fernando Pessoa, 'Opiário' (1933), *Poesias de Álvaro de Campos* (Lisbon: Ática, 1944).

24 Gonçalo Canto Moniz (URBiNAT / CES, Centro de Estudos Sociais Universidade de Coimbra)
Vitório Leite (URBiNAT)

25 URBiNAT, *Porto Local Diagnostic, Porto: Câmara Municipal do Porto*, DOMUS, CES, Universidade de Coimbra, GUDA, 2019.

26 Isabel Ferreira and Gonçalo Canto Moniz, 'Healthy Corridors for Inclusive Urban Regeneration', *Rassegna di Architettura e Urbanistica* 158 (2019), 51-59.

27 Daniel Tavares, 'A Centralidade: um conceito urbano em evolução', in: Manuel Luís Real (ed.), *A ponte e avenida: contradições urbanísitcas no centro histórico do Porto* (Porto: Câmara Municipal do Porto, 2001), 13-19.

28 See also: Bruno Latour, *Critical Distance or Critical Proximity* (2005), bruno-latour.fr/sites/default/files/P-113-HARAWAY.pdf.

Tallinn Stories of Pictures and Pictures of Stories

Jüri Soolep

In September 2021, just when the world was slowly opening up again after the Covid-19 pandemic, the Department of Architecture of the Estonian Art Academy EKA hosted a PhD training school in Tallinn. A key topic of the training school was how local stories are connected to myths that, in other forms, also exist elsewhere.

On the Campidoglio Hill in Rome, we can find the sculpture of the river god Nile. The sculpture was made around 160 AD and comes from the vast stores of the Pope. Michelangelo set it atop the hill around 1536. It has several attributes, and interests us because the River Nile is all about the flood. Nile is reclining on the statue of the Sphinx, decrypting its essence and name. He has a clay tablet in one hand, looking after the geometry that is to be used to revive field markers after the Nile's annual floods. It also looks like a smartphone. In the other hand the river god holds the *Cornu Copiae* – the Horn of Plenty – so we see devastation and plenitude in one dialectical twist. The Horn of Plenty is one of those images that often migrate through the whole of European culture, in fine arts as much as in architecture. It exemplifies certain persistent meaning continuities, which migrate through different images. I have called them certain

Fig. 1. River God Nile. Photo: Jüri Soolep.

meaning continua, as certain visual, conceptual or even formal elements constitute a traceable historical shadow behind the images. Nowadays, particularly due to the development of digital networks, the amount of images around us has multiplied manifold.

In this contribution, such dynamic and varied meanings of poetic images will be discussed in relation to three particular local stories of the city of Tallinn. The stories discussed are chosen because they present meaning continuities that are quite persistent and stay with us for a long time. The first is about the Old Man from Lake Ülemiste. The second is about the Town Hall Square pharmacy and the pharmacist's able apprentice. It is a modern fairy tale of medieval Tallinn by the Estonian literary writer and scholar Jaan Kross. The third story is about a communist monument that was removed in 2007 and caused Russians to riot in Tallinn. For this contribution, we will disregard the political consequences of these events and focus on the meaning cores of these stories, that still can be distilled from the images concerned. While the Old Man from the lake and the Bronze Soldier are rather depressing stories, the fairytale of the pharmacy offers a brighter image of Tallinn, not in the least due to the beautiful illustrations by Estonian artist Edgar Valter, one of my favorite illustrators from my childhood.

Flood Stories

The image of Nile presented, as the title image already hinted at, the theme of the flood. The flood is a universal archetype that is currently gaining attention, as risks of flooding are becoming more common worldwide due to climate change. Ancient flood myths include that of the Egyptian mega-flood, with the revenge of the goddess Hathor who turned into a lioness and killed most of the people; the Sumerian flood and water epics; and of course the Biblical legend of Noah's Ark. In the myth of Sumer the fundamental element of starting the world and life is depicted as water. In the British Museum and in the Altes Museum we can see several gods with water flowing from their shoulders. The water is full of fish and the water gods deal with an eagle who stole the tablets of destiny. In the book of Genesis everything starts with the creation of empty space, which is somehow parallel to primordial waters: 'Darkness upon the abyss' and 'Spirit of God bore upon the water'. And then water is introduced into the world, 'parting between water and water'. It is worth mentioning that in this Greek text it is not water, but moisture that follows primordial water. In Berlin we can see a huge basin, with the main god depicted at the centre. Out of his shoulders the waters emerge and are on both sides enjoyed by priests, probably disguised as fish. The basin also reminds us of the baptizing basins in which one is submerged and rises reborn into Jesus. The original baptizing process demands full body submersion. This is symbolic creation, death and rebirth.

The Old Man from Lake Ülemiste

Lake Ülemiste is located quite close to Old Tallinn, high on the limestone cliff running along the northern Estonian coast. Several stories are connected to the lake, most of which are about a godly figure that lives in the lake and emerges from the water in unknown intervals. He comes down to the city and asks anyone he meets: 'Is Tallinn built already?' It also goes that everybody already knows what they should say: 'It is not ready yet!' Otherwise, if the city of Tallinn were complete, the Old Man from the lake would drown the city with a flood from Ülemiste.

The story of the Old Man from the lake was recorded first in 1866 by Fridrich Reinhold Kreutzwald. It seems to be an older myth, but Kreutzwald was the first to turn it into a modern fairy tale. Besides, there are other morbid stories of people who are stuck in the ice on the lake and have to make a deal with the Old Man, to not drown. So the lake has a sacred allusions connected to it. In the final version by Kreutzwald, the evil Old Man comes from the lake to find out if Tallinn is ready and everybody needs to answer that it is not. The story, at this stage, did not have any illustrations.

Like Vitruvius's book on the art of building, which didn't have any illustrations either, every generation has illustrated it anew, offering an intriguing range of depictions of the same story.

In 1946 Debora Vaarandi turned the legend of Ülemiste into a long poem about the Old Man from the lake and a young communist builder, illustrated by Asta Vender and Olev Soans, and published in 1952.[1] The next edition was published in the 1970s, and was illustrated by Viive Tolli with a totally different mood and graphic signature. Quite recently another novel was also based on this legend, and lavishly illustrated by Jaan Tammsaar.[2]

In Debora Vaarandi's communist poem, the Old Man from the lake is transformed into a comical figure, re-educated into the communist utopia of a future city. He has lost his mythical malicious character, and reminds us of a nice old man, talking to young people. He even forgets to ask the strategic question about the readiness of the city. Finally the Old Man even disappears, as if the communist propaganda had dissolved his evil myth. It should also be pointed out that recent studies have shown how Vaarndi actually took active part in communist deportations in 1949.

This version with the young city builder of the communist era is the perfect imagination of communist propaganda that started immediately in 1945, after the second Soviet occupation of Estonia. The young city builder wears a military uniform, depicted on the cover illustration (Fig. 2). Transforming into a communist society meant that all people, including school children, college students and pioneers, had to wear uniforms. When I entered first grade in 1970, I had to wear the uniform, but it had been tailored to look more civil than military. Only the red flag and neck scarf remained from the communist organization. It took about 20 years for the military iconography to gradually disappear from our clothes. The actual illustrations of the 1952 book probably depict the Tallinn Technical Railway School uniform. The school had been in Tallinn since 1880 and was taken over by the Soviets as

Fig. 2. The book by Debora Vaarandi, 1951. Photo: Jüri Soolep.

Fig.3. Viive Tolli, The Lake upon the City, 1967. Screen shot: https://www.osta.ee/v-tolli-jarv-linna-kohal-161192441.html

Fig. 4. CThe book by Arvo Valton, 2008.
Photo: Jüri Soolep.

Fig. 5. The book by Debora Vaarandi, illustrated by Viive Tolli, 1975. Photo: Jüri Soolep.

Fig. 6. The spread from the book by Jaan Kross, 1973. Photo: Jüri Soolep.

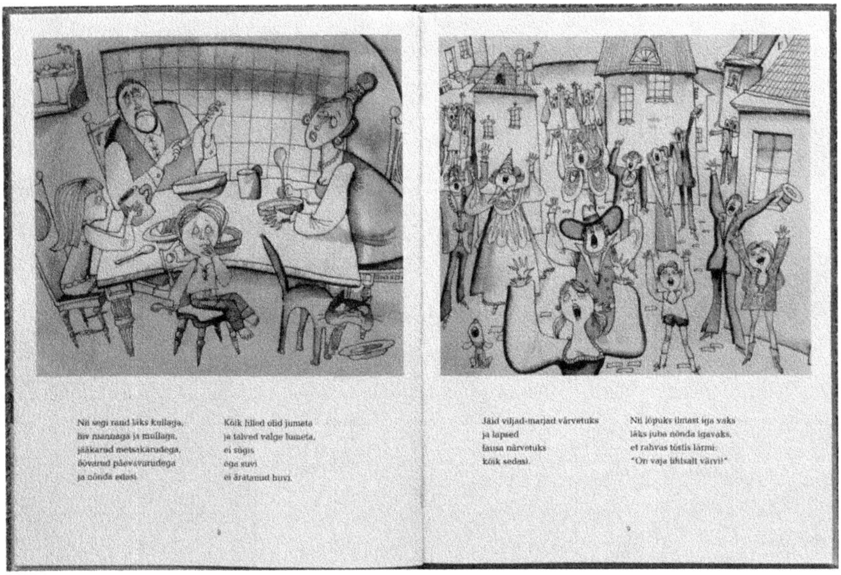

Fig. 7+8. The book cover and spread by Ellen Niit, 2020. Photos: Jüri Soolep.

the railway school. The railway remained the main military infrastructure until the end of the Soviet regime.

In the 1975 version, the imagery changed entirely, although the text remained the same and was used for the new publication, which also included the 1866 story.[3] It looks as if a whole new venture was started to publish new illustrations by a well-known graphic artist of that time. Viive Tolli had worked on the Ülemiste story for at least ten years before the opportunity came to use these illustrations in a book. Some of these preparatory sketches are extremely interesting as they depict the old city of Tallinn on the shore of the lake, or around and on both sides of the lake (Fig. 3). The drawing can be seen as the sublimation of the closed seashore of Tallinn in Soviet times, but we do not know exactly what ideas were behind all of these drawings. The illustrations in the book juxtapose the old and the new. In the first illustrations the old city has not yet been reconstructed, but by the end parts of the old city are all ready and festive looking. Debora Vaarandi's communist propaganda has disappeared and become just a background to the illustrations.

The most recent story about Lake Ülemiste comes from contemporary writer Arvo Valton. The protagonist Vambo is a fisherman who lives in a small shed at the lake. Like his father, who drowned, Vambo has an agreement with the Old Man from the lake, which ensures him good luck with fishing. In return he must also become the citizen of the lake. There is a love story with a young noble lady from the city, who is saved from drowning by Vambo. The story of obstacles between lovers is situated in the medieval Tallinn, and ends with a collective suicide (Fig. 4).

The Story of the Pharmacy on Town Hall Square

The second theme is a modern fairy tale of medieval Tallinn, first published in 1973,[4] written by Jaan Kross, who is also the author of several historical novels, such as *Between Three Plaques*. The story is richly illustrated by Edgar Valter, a celebrated Estonian artist and illustrator. The illustrations transform the story into a graphic novel about Mart, the pharmacist's apprentice. The pharmacy has been on Town Hall Square since 1422, and is still there today. The story also suggests that we walk on the same streets for hundreds of years and are therefore connected through a common space that has seen better and worse times. The story is about love between Mart and the mayor's daughter, who is sick. Mart has to help with the medicine because the pharmacist cannot do it himself. Instead of using awful drugs, Mart uses marzipan and everybody is happy in the end. Mart and marzipan are the recipe for love and health.

Here we could also look at another graphic story by Edgar Valter: a poem by Ellen Niit, published in 1971, is about a world without colours.[5] Suddenly, a hippy-like painter appears and starts to colour everything. Only now, far from my childhood, I see the political connotations implicit in the illustrations: the family sitting around the table with nothing to eat, the bleak look of the city in shades of grey as it was in Soviet times. Then of course, the great artist comes with colour and gayness and a happy new world is born.

The Story of the Bronze Soldier

Leading us into politics again, our third theme is more radical. In April 1945, at the end of the Second World War, 12 Soviet soldiers and officers were buried on Tõnismäe Hill in Tallinn. Their dead bodies were brought together from many different places. The circumstances and times of their deaths have remained obscure. It is quite likely that they did not perish in active combat.

In May 1945, a design competition was announced for a monument and its surrounding space on the burial site at Tõnismäe, which was to be called 'Liberators' Square'. Initial plans were to erect the monument on Victory Square, the present day Liberty Square, from which the sculpture of Peter I had been removed after Estonia won its independence. The new plan for

Fig. 9. The monument by architect Arnold Hoffard-Alas and Enn Roos in 1947. Now in the Military Cemetery. Photo: Jüri Soolep.

Fig. 10 + 11. Screen shot from the film: Bronze Night: the Russian Riot in Tallinn, Urmas E. Liiv, Tallinn 2007.

the monument was prepared according to drawings by architect Arnold Hoffard-Alas and the sculpture for the monument was made by Enn Roos in 1947. As Hoffard-Alas's student Tõnu Virve wrote, the conceptual basis of the monument is a portal to the realm of the dead.[6] Indeed, people familiar with the history of architecture may recognize the characteristic portal usually built in front of Egyptian temples, known as a pylon, in the proportions and pilasters of the limestone abutment of this monument.

The liberators' monument was a mandatory urban altar in all Soviet cities. Its supposed meaning, as stated in the conditions of the competition, was to represent the growth of patriotic feeling in the Estonian people and their battle against German fascists. The monument was also expected to represent friendship between different nations and the memory of the homeland's brave sons, who gave their lives in battle against the enemy.[7]

Regardless of the apparent atheism of Soviet power, the square was a highly charged sacred space. This became particularly apparent after the eternal flame was added in 1964. A short gas flame rose from a small angular pit at the centre of a bronze five-pointed star. The eternal flame is one of the oldest metaphors for the remembrance of war in Indo-European culture – inextinguishable honour – *kleos aftiton*.[8] Originally, a composition with five-pointed stars and the eternal flame was placed on the back of the pylon as a bronze relief. The place's ritual was connected to compulsory political liturgy on 9 May and on 22 September (the official date of the end of the Second World War in the USSR, and the official anniversary of the capture of Tallinn respectively).

The vegetation and the landscaping around the monument have changed several times throughout the course of its existence. Only the evergreen trees have retained their initial position. In the period 2003-2007, the forgotten monument was gradually energized again. It was seen as a forpost of Soviet propaganda of Victory Day, militarism and the occupation of Eastern

Europe. Meetings of war veterans at Tõnismäe began gathering steam again in 2003. This began to be referred to as the strengthening of Russian identity, part of which was actually hostility towards the Estonian state. These gatherings became quite large by 2006 and clearly opposed Estonian independence. The gatherings took place under Soviet red flags and imperial Russian flags.

Fearing the potential for a demonstration arising from the commemoration of Victory Day, the Estonian government dismantled the monument in April 2007 and reburied (or sent to Russia) the remains of the 12 dead soldiers and officers. The monument itself was taken to a military cemetery less than 2 kilometres away. The defenders of the monument led by the Night Watch organized a demonstration in Tallinn's Old Town and at Tõnismäe, which boiled over into mass unrest and violence that lasted for two nights. The group Night Watch – Nochnoi Dozor – was the organized activator of the iconic space of the Bronze Soldier.[9] It is quite probable that this name itself is taken from the Timur Bekmambetov *film НОЧНОЙ ДОЗОР – Night Watch*.[10] Let us consider what kind of iconography their self-identification is founded on.

Bekmambetov's film *НОЧНОЙ ДОЗОР* was completed in 2004 at the Pervõi Kanal film studio, which belonged to the Russian government. The film was based on the book of the same name by Sergei Lukyanenko. Both the film and the book proved to be very popular in Russia and abroad. The film's action takes place in contemporary Moscow, which is a battleground in the struggle between good and evil. The film is made in a 'magical realist' style, where everything seems ordinary, yet events themselves are totally unreal. To a certain extent, it resembles the language used in Andrei Tarkovsky's film *Stalker*, where everything is also ordinary and has acquired an unworldly meaning, or the atmosphere of Mikhail Bulgakov's book *Master and Margarita*. The film's plot is quite simple: it is the personal drama of Anton, the main character, in his struggle between good and evil. The Day

Fig. 12. The cover of the DVD of Night Watch, Timur Bekmambetov, 2004.

and Night Watch have agreed on a temporary truce, which is ruined when the Great Prophet is born – the Other, or Anton's unborn son Yegor, whom Anton is willing to sacrifice in order to win back his unfaithful wife. By the end of the film, things go wrong and his son joins the forces of evil. In the second part, the entire process returns to the beginning.

While the plot might not be very important from the point of view of this contribution, it is more interesting to study the representation of good and evil and the *imagosphere* that is depicted in the film. I suspect this is rather difficult to decipher for people who have not come across the Soviet sign system. Let us consider it more closely.

The dichotomy of good and evil is expressed in everything visible, starting with the location. The forces of evil reside and operate in the Kosmos Hotel, which was already a gathering place for high-class prostitutes in the Soviet era. Luxurious banquets and receptions take place in the hotel. The forces of evil's female hero performs there, at a huge rock concert. The forces of good's headquarters are in an office building with a granite sign on the door that reads: *ГОРСВЕТ (Gorsvet)*. Above the name is the Russian coat-of-arms with the two-headed eagle, which connects its image with the state. *Gorsvet* is an abbreviation of the Russian-language expression gorodskoi svet – light of the city. It is just one letter away from the former term *ГОРСОВЕТ*. This means *gorodskoi sovet* – city council. This is the Soviet-era municipal government, which carried out the city's administration in accordance with the general guidance of the city's communist party committee. Thus, the forces of good's headquarters have multiple meanings and is simultaneously the municipal government, a public bureau and a state structure. In addition, it is also a 'closed type of joint stock company'. The municipal administration office has its own 'information centre' that watches tomorrow's news (via website Regnum.ru – one of the most reactionary news agencies, later bought by the Russian state) and prevents accidents. The leader of the forces of good's office is recognizably similar to the office of a Soviet director. There is a set of telephones on a long T-shaped meeting table. Everything is a little bit worn but is prominently 'Soviet era chic'. At the same time, the chief of the forces of evil sits in the hotel playing video games and does business via a satellite telephone.

The forces of good's leader, Geser (evidently an allusion to the name Caesar, tsar), is dressed in a white shirt and a suit. His antipode Zavulon (with a biblical theme, the Jewish patriarch or ruler Zabulon, who operated in the vicinity of Nazareth) wears an undershirt and a woollen cap (like petty criminals from the Soviet era, working as dealers and illegal money changers – *fartshovshiki* or the opposite – a high class businessman's designer suit. In the end credits we also find out that Geser had been a deputy minister of the USSR *(zam-ministra pri CCCP)*.

The dichotomy continues in automobiles, women and clothing. Women from the forces of good are homely, dressed in simple clothing or work clothes. Olga, for instance, has been a bewitched owl for 100 years, and does not know how to dress in modern clothes. The women of evil, however, are unattainable sex idols in short skirts and high heels, *femme fatales* with satanic faces. The forces of good go about in wadded jackets and overalls with the name of their firm *ГОРСВЕТ* on their backs. They are clearly from the lower working class – *vatniki*. The evil guys wear designer clothes or expensive brands of sportswear.

The automobiles used by the forces of good are especially nostalgic and patriotic. They are Soviet lorries made (presumably) from converted GAZ-53 vehicles, with magical powers to jump and accelerate to the maximum. Lorries are painted yellow, like Soviet gas emergency vehicles. Even the number on the side of the lorry resembles the word GAZ, and connects them in spirit with the Russian government's media and economic *giant ГАЗПРОМ – Gasprom*. The forces of evil drive expensive Western European sports cars.

With the recent Ukraine invasion in mind, all of this looks like a mild mythopoetic experiment in which Estonia just got away with a slightly uncomfortable surprise, but actually this was a deliberate policy, a testing of countermeasures to see how far the global community will allow Russia to move. It was soon complemented by the invasion of Georgia in 2008, and that of Crimea and Donbas in 2014. After the Ukraine invasion everybody understood that the answer to Russian pictures and stories was nonexistent and led to real wars and loss of life.
These were the local stories of pictures and pictures of stories in Tallinn. The images carry different stories. Sometimes stories change with the images that are added to them. Sometimes it is stories that change the images that are used to illustrate them. Images, like stories, are never neutral – they carry complex value systems. The paradox enhanced by Digital Reality is that these value systems can only partly be orchestrated by the author or interpreter. Very often they go deeper into the archetypal levels of the human mind and tell the stories, both good and evil, of the places and people.

References

Vaarandi, Debora, *Ülemiste vanake ja noor linnaehitaja*. Tallinn: Eesti Riiklik Kirjastus, 1952.

Valton, Arvo, *Ülemiste Vanake*. Tallinn: PiktoGraaf (ordered by Ülemiste City AS) 2008.

Vaarandi, Debora; Kreutzwald, Friedrich Reinhold. *Miks Tallinn iial valmis ei tohi saada. Ülemiste Vanake ja noor linnaehitaja*. Tallinn: Tallinn: Eesti Raamat, 1975

Kross, Jaan, *Mardileib*. Tallinn: Eesti Raamat, 1973

Niit, Ellen, *Suur maalritöö*. Tallinn: Eesti Raamat, 1971

1 Debora Vaarandi, *Ülemiste vanake ja noor linnaehitaja* (Tallinn: Eesti Riiklik Kirjastus, 1952).

2 Arvo Valton, *Ülemiste Vanake* (Tallinn: PiktoGraaf (ordered by Ülemiste City AS), 2008).

3 Debora Vaarandi and Friedrich Reinhold Kreutzwald, *Miks Tallinn iial valmis ei tohi Saada: Ülemiste Vanake ja noor linnaehitaja* (Tallinn: Eesti Raamat, 1975).

4 Jaan Kross, *Mardileib* (Tallinn: Eesti Raamat, 1973).

5 Ellen Niit, *Suur maalritöö* (Tallinn: Eesti Raamat, 1971).

6 Tõnu Virve, *Pronkssõduri müür on värav surnute riiki* (Eesti Päevaleht, 12 May 2007).

7 Peeter Kaasik, *Tallinnas Tõnismäel asuv punaarmeelaste ühishaud ja mälestusmärk* (The Common Grave of Red Army Soldiers and Memorial Located at Tõnismäe in Tallinn), historical statement (Tallinn, 2006), 11. Online: valitsus.ee/brf/doc.php?34981.

8 Mihhail Lotman. *Märulisemiootika eesti pealinnas* (Riot Semiotics in the Estonian Capital) (Postimees, 2 May 2007). Online: valitsus.ee/brf/doc.php?34981.

9 Now editing the texts 15 years later, we can recognize the main organizers of the unrests in active imperial policy of Russia: Dimitri Linter visited Riga in 2014 as an official assistant of Vladimir Medinsky, the Russian minister of culture. A month before that he visited Crimea and participated in the conference with mental leaders of unrests in east of Ukraine: Sergei Glazev, Alexander Dugin and Igor Strelkov. Dimitri Linter was presented as a member of Novorossia. Online: rus.delfi.ee/archive/print.php?id=69994159.

10 Timur Bekmambetov, *НОЧНОЙ ДОЗОР* (Notshnoi Dozor) (OAO Pervõi Kanal, 2004).

Co-Constructed Narratives of the Grassroots in the City
Narrating Hiedanranta

Dalia Milián Bernal, Elina Alatalo, Jeremy Allan Hawkins and Panu Lehtovuori

With contributions by Sila Kartal, Mattias Malk, Mathilde Merolli, Hanna Musiol, Matej Nikšič, Dorina Pllumbi, and Elena Sitrakova in collaboration with different members of the grassroots of Hiedanranta: Henna Matanuska, Juha Sepponen, Matti Lankinen, Niko Lehtola, Taina Laaksonen and Ville Natunen

Introduction

In his seminal book *The City and the Grassroots*, sociologist Manuel Castells argues that 'major innovations in the city's role, meaning, and structure tend to be the outcome of grassroots mobilizations and demands'.[1] Like Castells, for years critical urban theorists have called for attention to the desires, stories, practices and spaces of the grassroots in the city, the ways they are shaping the territory, the material substrate of the city, and the meaning of the built environment, and how they are introducing 'into the city new identities and practices which disturb established histories'.[2] Nonetheless, these calls have received scant attention from mainstream urban planning and architectural research, education and discourse. In the words of Christian Schmid, 'their histories are yet to be written'.[3] In our view, as long as these stories remain invisible, not only is a theory of the city incomplete, but paths to alternative, diverse, possibly more democratic, just and sustainable urban futures are more difficult to imagine.[4] It is within this context that two initial questions emerge: How are the grassroots shaping the material and immaterial dimensions of urban places? And, how, in turn, are these spaces shaping the practices and identities of the grassroots in the city?

However, in order to be able to ask these questions, we are also faced with an epistemo-methodological conundrum. In the same way that Brazilian scholar Marcelo Lópes de Souza asserts that 'insurgent spatial practices cannot be exerted exactly in the same spatial environment created by old, status quo-confirming spatial practices', neither can grassroots spatial practices, narratives and stories be queried from the same status quo-confirming epistemological positions (like those linked to a positivist paradigm and objectivist epistemologies) or by employing the same status quo-confirming methodological repertoires (like those that aim for great generalizations, homogenizations and abstractions, such as the products of surveys or statistical analysis).[5] As Huq argues, these (insurgent, grassroots) practices 'shift the ground of knowledge from that of professional analysis to that of first-hand collective knowledge of social groups living under oppressive conditions'.[6] Here, two additional questions surface: How, then, can we unearth and understand the narratives of the grassroots? And how can their narratives be transcribed, translated and retold without being co-opted and instrumentalized?

To engage with these two sets of questions, we organized an intensive three-day workshop in the city of Tampere, Finland, held within the framework of the COST Action 'Writing Urban Places'. Titled 'Narrating Hiedanranta: Stories of Objects and Subjects of Urban Places' (hereafter refered to as 'Narrating Hiedanranta'), the workshop brought together an international and interdisciplinary group of participants, most of them researchers, in a former industrial area called Hiedanranta. Situated on the shores of lake Näsijärvi, Hiedanranta has been the site of vivid grassroots, which have been shaping the area for several years but whose future there is uncertain, as a large urban development project is underway. This project has already dramatically changed the material substrate of the area as well as the internal social dynamics of the site, as some cultural groups have been permanently displaced. Against this backdrop, the two objectives of the workshop were to, on the one hand, learn about and interact with the grassroots of Hiedanranta in a situated way and, on the other, explore *in-situ* different approaches to unearth, make sense of, visualize and retell the narratives of the grassroots of Hiedanranta, while these groups and individuals are still active and accessible.

The aim of this chapter is to present the three different methodological approaches introduced during the workshop, illustrate how these were woven together to produce co-constructed narratives of the grassroots in Hiedanranta, and discuss the usefulness of these approaches not only as a means to generate situated and subjective knowledge about the grassroots in the city and the value of their practices, but also as a method of representation that is difficult to codify and, thus, hard to instrumentalize.

This chapter will present six co-constructed narratives that build on the work produced during the workshop. For the purposes of this book, we asked different contributors to develop their initial narratives and arrange them to each fit in a two-page spread. Their contributions had to clearly link all methodological approaches to create a co-constructed visual narrative. Each contribution is accompanied by a short text that introduces the person they engaged with in Hiedanranta and explains the methods employed to represent their narratives.

In the following sections, we will first situate Hiedanranta within its context and provide an overview of the different grassroots groups active in the area. Then we will briefly describe the workshop and introduce the three different methodological approaches that were explored, which are visual methods, poetic practices and narrative (situated) interviewing. Subsequently, we will briefly describe the six co-constructed visual narratives, each presented in one spread, with some linked to video recordings. To conclude, we will discuss how these methods helped to engage with both sets of questions and argue for the potential of weaving these approaches together to produce creative and potentially subversive forms of scholarly communication as well as to generate co-constructed future narratives.

Hiedanranta as a Place to Invite the Grassroots
Tampere is the third largest city in Finland with a population of about 240,000 inhabitants.[7] Due to its long history of textile and pulp industry, the city was nicknamed the Manchester of Finland. As the city underwent major and rapid growth, many of its historical industrial buildings were transformed by or became replaced with new urban development projects. This is now also taking place in Hiedanranta, where a project is being developed to house around 25,000 inhabitants.[8]

When the Hiedanranta area was bought by the city of Tampere in 2014, it had been gated and some of its buildings had been unused for decades. The start was challenging, as the forgotten site is also somewhat far from the city centre and there was a limited budget. City officials responsible for the area took a leap of faith: instead of business as usual, they decided to rent out the premises cheaply to the kind of actors that would do something that could attract people to Hiedanranta. The area was given an experimental status to appeal to alternative cultures and start-up entrepreneurs. Hiedanranta is not the most typical former industrial site: in addition to the various factory buildings, there is also a manor with a garden towards the lake, and two wooden villas. This spatial and material diversity has attracted a variety of users and experiments, including social enterprises collaborating with a vocational school, big event spaces hosting alternative scenes, biochar production, circus performers, skateboarders, urban gardeners, artists and artisans. Many of the experiments have focused on new models of collaboration, trust and freedom. Without this, it would have proved extremely difficult to bring life to the area.

Bringing vacant spaces back into use has been a challenging learning process for all participants, with success stories as well as mistakes and unfortunate surprises. Many of the actors started as temporary users, without a certain future, yet some have settled at Hiedanranta and become more organized, following the pace of the place itself as it became more formal.[9] The experimental status created a window of opportunity for growth. For many, this has been a life-changing experience, as there has been room to test novel practices in a permissive setting.

Hiedanranta has become an excellent setting to explore grassroots' socio-spatial practices for several reasons. There is currently a vivid grassroots culture, in which local researchers are also participants. Regardless of certain losses, such as some of the active pioneering groups not finding a new space when the building they used was demolished, the attitude of the city has been mostly about supporting a variety of initiatives without prejudice.[10] Long-lasting relationships have built mutual trust. Over seven years, local people, researchers and city officials, supported by visiting groups, have built a community sauna together, avoided some unnecessary building repairs, designed a solar summer kitchen and a makerspace, created two new study programmes and developed a future space-sharing model, to name but a few.[11] For every successful project, there are at least three that were not realized. All of these shared adventures have made it possible to have local pioneers participate in an intensive workshop, offering direct and even intimate encounters for the guests from abroad, similar to the ones between the people of Hiedanranta itself. As such, the guests of the workshop had the opportunity to jump into the Hiedanranta bubble, feeling safe and welcome, prompted to try out something that might be outside their usual comfort zone.

Narrating Hiedanranta: The Workshop

Taking place from 8 to 10 June 2022, the 'Narrating Hiedanranta' workshop attempted to give participants the opportunity to engage directly with the question of how to work with grassroots narratives. Open to members of the COST Action 'Writing Urban Places', but also to local actors, the workshop assembled diverse backgrounds of research and practice. This created a need for shared spaces, including the physical spaces of the buildings and the landscape of Hiedanranta, as well as shared theoretical spaces, developed through lectures and activities relating to the workshop's theme. A particular focus on methods aimed to offer participants a non-exhaustive but substantial array of strategies for fieldwork sessions. These methodological approaches examined how visual methods for social research, poetic practices in spatial knowledge production and longform narrative interviewing can be used to engage with the grassroots.

To begin, sociologist Luc Pauwels presented a series of visual approaches to social research ranging from researcher-produced imagery, respondent-generated image production (RGIP), and 'visually expressive forms of scholarly communication'.[12] Whether looking at photographic methods such as Repeat Photography or visual elicitation techniques to generate respondent information, these methods were offered to workshop participants as means to query how the visual field can be drawn upon to develop new understandings of grassroots spatial practices. As a complement, poet and researcher Jeremy Allan Hawkins gave an introduction to poetic practices in spatial knowledge production, drawing on theories of poetic language and its relation to understanding, while also proposing strategies for *in-situ* writing that included the use of constraint, accident, play and collaboration.[13] These strategies were paired with practical experiments, including a prompt-driven site poem written during the lecture and a deambulating collective poetry reading as a site exploration. The presentations on visual methods and poetic practices worked together to question how text and image could be used creatively to produce data-rich and complex accounts of a site like Hiedanranta and the people currently shaping its character as space and place.

Finally, Elina Alatalo and Dalia Milián Bernal introduced narrative interviewing, a mode of interview through which longform recountings are produced.[14] Not fully structured and usually started by means of open-ended questions, this type of interview allows conversations to unfold in directions that are meaningful to the interviewee, often leading to unexpected anecdotes and stories. During the 'Narrating Hiedanranta' workshop, researchers in teams of two were each able to interview one individual part of the Hiedanranta grassroots. The interviews took place on the same sites where the grassroots work, have appropriated and transformed, and/or move within and around, thus adding a degree of situatedness to the process. The narrative and situated interviews had a duration of approximately two hours and were recorded. Before the interviews, interviewees were invited to bring visual material to the interview and both interviewee and interviewer were encouraged to produce visual material during the interviewing process. This led to multiform and varied results from the interviews conducted, which will become evident below.

Across the three methodological approaches – visual, poetic and narrative interviewing – the workshop organizers attempted to provide participants with tools for meaningful encounters and collaboration with Hiedanranta and its grassroots. On the one hand, this could mean soliciting narratives from the recent past or tracing extant marks of the activities that have shaped the site, but on the other it also implied a creative interaction with the people and the place, opening opportunities for the problematics of co-construction. It is a question of how, with these methodological tools, incoming researchers could participate in re-telling the stories of the grass-roots in Hiedanranta, whose voices would be preserved, what knowledge would emerge, and to what ends.

Six Co-constructed Narratives

The following six co-constructed stories, each presented on a spread, build on all these activities and weave together the three methodological approaches. The local people participating in these stories all have long-standing relationships with Hiedanranta. They have been among the first to arrive and have been central in materially and culturally making Hiedanranta what it is today. The first project, titled 'Quoetry: Hands, Words, Worlds', is the work of Mathilde Merolli and Dorina Pllumbi, who interviewed Ville Natunen, a skateboarder and professional skatepark builder, and member of Kaarikoirat association. During the workshop, Merolli and Pllumbi developed a method according to which they handpicked quotes from the interview and arranged them into a text with poetic qualities. This method, which they called 'quoetry', has been further adopted and adapted by other contributors to this chapter and is visible in subsequent stories. In addition, Merolli and Pllumbi made video recordings and took clips from the video to construct their project.[15]

The second project, 'Contouring with Universumi', is by Mattias Malk, who interviewed Niko Lehtola, a graffiti and urban artist and one of the founding members of SprayCanKontrol, a group mobilizing in Hiedanranta, that has been responsible for the organization of several international graffiti and urban art events in the area. Malk's work fuses his conversation with Niko during and after the interview with his own experience of the spaces of Hiedanranta, which he explored employing a method called 'bordering'.[16] It is through a form of bordering that, in turn, Malk presents the words of Niko from their conversation about 'what it means to live a good life and to be happy' as their co-constructed project.

This story is followed by 'Memory Strips', by Sila Kartal who interviewed Henna Matanuska, a circus artist and member of Sirkus Faktori. The group was active in Hiedanranta until they needed to move to make way for a new tramline. Inspired by Henna's work, which involves, above all, movements of the body, Sila uses a video of one of Henna's early performances and created image strips employing a method called 'slit scanning' to 'present varying layers of time' and movement as well as certain qualities of the space, though these remain abstract. The image strips are accompanied by powerful, short lines of quoetry, which clearly depict the way in which the places of Hiedanranta have inspired Henna's work.

In the project called 'Public Art in a Tight Spot', Hanna Musiol and Panu Lehtovuori reflect on their eye-opening conversations while touring around Hiedanranta with Matti Lankinen, another key artist of SprayCanKontrol, responsible for the impressive murals in the area. They bring forth a pair of features, a kind of tension between monumentality and fragility that exists simultaneously in a place. For example, murals are materially monumental and intended to bring art to everyday environments for anyone to enjoy. Yet, they are also very fragile, since the buildings can be torn down, the paintings can be painted over, or the people advocating for them may turn their interests elsewhere. Hanna and Panu invite us to think about this tension in a small, even claustrophobic, closet space.

Next, is the project titled 'Brooch' by Elena Sitrakova, who interviewed Taina Laaksonen, one of the key individuals behind the project for an edible garden that has been built by the community of Hiedanranta in collaboration with refugees from various countries. Here Sitrakova presents close-range images of the greenhouses accompanied by double-layered quoetry. The close-range images depict different abstract plants inspired by the flora in the homelands of the refugees, engraved in the glass of the greenhouses. Sitrakova's quoetry differs from the other uses of quoetry in that she highlights in bold certain lines that can be read as a poem on its own, hence, the name 'double-layered quoetry'.

The final project, titled 'Made of real...and not of some composites', is by Matej Nikšič, who invites us to see the importance of small entrepreneurs, such as artisans, in bringing life to areas like Hiedanranta. Our focus is often on the most visible and loud actors, who organize big events or deal with public space. Nevertheless, transformations also happen on more hidden and personal levels. People make use of cheap places as their work space, such as Juha Sepponen, to develop a more meaningful and sustainable livelihood. The photographs shot by Matej deliver us the sensory experience of Juha's new everyday life: the smell of wood, the sawdust, the hand-felt texture of wood. The story is not only about Juha, but also about how Matej was transformed himself. The discoveries he made in Hiedanranta now made him see similar places in his home country literally through a new lens.

Quoetry: Hands, Words, Worlds

Dorina Pllumbi, Mathilde Merolli, and Ville Natunen

Our encounter with Ville Natunen was one of the richest exploratory moments we had in Hiedanranta.

Ville has been part of the Tampere skateboarding scene all his life, both as a professional skateboarder and skatepark builder. He is an activist on different levels. Ville advocates and claims skating space in the city, but is also actively changing the skating culture from within by challenging and subverting existing problematic narratives through his designing and building of more inclusive slopes.

We arrived without predefined ideas about and methods for how to capture and represent the agency of his character. We followed Ville's lead while he guided us through buildings and skateparks, pausing at places that were meaningful to him to share his experiences with us.

Choosing video over audio recording was sparked by the desire to include a spatial dimension in the interview. We realized the potential of video recording as a less reductionist medium that would do more justice to not only the incredible spatial configurations we were emerging into but also to the conversation flow. Ville's confidence, openness and storytelling skills stimulated the dialogue between the interview questions, adding our own personal reactions and reflections to the recording.

Although time was limited to process the three-hour-long interview, we experimented with turning this encounter into a short documentary of selected pieces of the most meaningful moments, along with the QUOETRY compilation consisting of 110 quotes handpicked from the interview.

Ville's ability to narrate inspired the choice to pull quotes from the interview. By replaying the recording, we handpicked the quotes – focusing on message, keywords and humour. We used a text shuffler tool to randomize the order of the quotes. A handful of quotes were then repositioned to accentuate the poetic quality of the collected quotes. We named the poem 'Quoetry', a portmanteau of 'Quote' and 'Poetry'.

Interview: Ville's Story by Mathilde Merolli & Dorina Pllumbi www.youtube.com/watch?v=UDyh_b4553I

Quoetry

Something like ocean and jungle
It is big money / it is big stuff
Where they take the dogs from the street
There was no design for this
He will not understand them, he will not support them, he will not be, or maybe he will
It is just easier for him to say, yeah sure, instead of creating a conflict
This will be, like, our space
I go to my Instagram
But I think it is part of life
I am in a place of certain power
Three weeks, away three weeks back
This is tiny
Now I had to cut them out
Just two weeks ago
People do not want to have it
Their fathers never said any good thing to them
They are massive / they are beautiful
Nobody skates this ramp / there is no ramp to skate
I drew it on a piece of plywood
Probably he believes something / that all we do good
Whatever we do, you cannot drill anything through the floor
I want to drink whatever I want
Not on the sides meant for girls and kids
It would be, like, I do not know, fun for the kids to get to build ramps
Yeah, I do not know what is the truth
He said, everyone is happy
So, I have been thinking about her
I kind of started learning about feminism through her
Change is the only constant
Everything was big, and tall, and she is a small girl
We open the doors, we sell the tickets, we run the place
Kind of like, a private section of the city
My dad was a sailor
The name in Finnish, Muovitehdas
In the buildings
He would be, like, you are crazy
How long are you going to be in Tampere
We will make all this great for you
I know how it feels to skate there
It was nice to, nice that it was you, who came
Really young girls coming to talk to you
They were like, yeah, let us put you guys in that building
You are twenty years old
That is Temu, that is me
What is it?
It is right there, it is, I don't know
Against the concrete
If you have power, you do not want to argue with people that are not on your level
He manages big thing / we are little things
He is called Matti / he is my friend
What do you call that?
What the fuck are you talking about
It will get better
Now a friend
I want to eat to eat whatever I want
I hope my son will speak like you
She used to have short, blue hair
Or something
It looks good / it is not good
It seems like I have a lot of muscles
That is how he works
They will be skating in the Olympics, like, in the United States, like
One morning, everything was gone
It is kind of like a youth house in the end
What people speak
It has, like, a rough sound
White walls will create a lot of light in here
People working in swimming halls should pay rent
The Ukrainian situation had already started
Fit in this space
For a long time, it was in my taste, more beautiful
I have a plan
I am known
Somewhere
Maybe in ten years or stuff
Urban culture, rap culture
He was interviewing me in here
I would like to write stories
Yeah, it is good enough, it is good enough
This will be torn down, we will go somewhere else
This is not boring
Kids, and girls, and whoever skate
Different sound, different, maybe concrete
But it is also nice, we have, like, actual toilets
To actually have a space to go to work to
The buildings
When those kids, in ten years, they been skating this ten years
I do that all the time, I do that all the time
He teaches them
Then they leave, and you pick the next one
Some day, we all die
Why would you waste space inside for this
We are under them always
I do not care
How to skate this
This cannot be the space where we start, like, running this kind of thing
We do not know what is down there
You understood a lot
I wanted to, now, when I had the power
The roof is leaking
Please help us
It is already in the signs, in google maps
A glass ball spinning on it
I was expecting it to be boring people
You are now you
I have all the keys
Whatever we want, like, it is kind of good
Oh, okay
Let us put those kids in a chemical factory
I make changes and piss the architect off

Ville Natunen

Contouring with...

by Mattias Malk and Niko Lehtola

It is not easy to get to know a place only in a matter of days. The task becomes even more complicated if you are expected to relate this experience to others, to say something new or from a different perspective. In Hiedanranta we received many valuable insights from our hosts, but most importantly we were given the chance to speak to different local actors on our own terms. If there can be a story of a place, it is not a singular narrative. It is written and told in parallel by many.

This short project fuses my own walk on the periphery of Hiedanranta – my initial attempt to define the place by tracing its border – with insights from an interview with Niko Lehtola. Niko is also known by his street artist name Uni or Uni-versumi and has been active in the heart of Hiedanranta for years. Our conversation illuminated some of the changes taking place in the area and some of the anxieties that exist regarding its future. Still, we spent most of our breath beyond Hiedanrata, treading more universal topics of what it means to live a good life and to be happy. This continued long after the dictaphone was shut off, and in the steam of the evening sauna. These reflections fuse with the introspective documentation of the walk to create a portrait of Hiedanranta at a particular time and in a specific context. More of an ambience than a narrative, really.

Universumi

Follow the heart, not the profit.
It's not about not making profit, it's about making things for the right reasons.
Scale the reasons.
Make things for the right reasons.
Things that make a positive change.
This becomes difficult when there are businesses that need to make a profit, not really for the right reasons, but they still need to make a profit.
It is a difficult dynamic when there are corporations and agendas.
Each man or woman makes his or hers decisions or what they are willing to do.

If you follow what your heart wants to do, it's probably for the right reasons and it can bring you profit, also.
Because we see it happening a lot around that people and corporations are following the profit and we know already what it is doing to the environment and mankind and the animal kingdom.

Follow the heart, not the profit.
Niko Lehtola

Project: Hiedanranta ambient by Mattias Malk
www.youtube.com/watch?v=UPsbMOARzDE

Memory Strips

by Sila Kartal and Henna Matanuska

Inspiring to be here, everything was very open

There were lots of 'freedom' and 'opportunities'

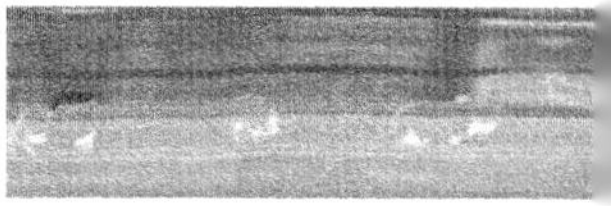

Henna Matanuska, a circus artist, discovered the idle spaces of Hiedanranta with her body and her art. Her tools were whatever she found in Hiedanranta with a scrap of her soul. She gets inspired by Hiedanranta. Henna feeds her creativity in this place while she is defining its spirit. The visuals were produced by slit scanning Henna's performance called 'Hiedanranta' as film strips. Film strips express the interaction between time, body and space. They present varying layers of time; past, present during the past, traces of now and they evolve into a memory. The strips are narrating inertia, precession and creation of Henna in Hiedanranta. One can observe the inertia of abandoned industry buildings, and alleys from consistent pinkish and greenish backgrounds. One can follow Henna's precession by looking at her black traces in the film strips. The hoop with fire was what she used to ensure her corporeal interaction with the space. She created that tool from what she found in Hiedanranta. What she told and shared during our narrative interview was clearly observed in her performance's strips. Her poetic expressions that attached to the strips elucidate the time-body-space interaction. Her movements were shaped by the space itself. She created many stories and narrated them with her art in Hiedanranta's abandoned places.

Alone, ghost -a good ghost-, 'I am here'

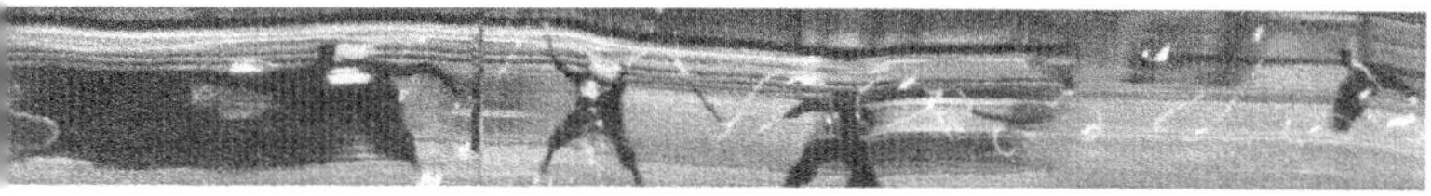

I worked with what I found.

The area behind the factories was inspiring

red bricks, alley, texture

Inspiring for creating the movement

You can go anywhere in abandoned factories...
...and create a story in your head.
Henna Matanuska

Public Art in a Tight Spot

by Hanna Musiol and Panu Lehtovuori, guided by Matti Lankinen

The Site Breathes, We Listen

Panu and I hail from architecture and literature, and work with different disciplinary fixations on words, histories, surfaces, scales, atmospheres. We bring, in other words, different ways of *disciplinary listening*. In Hiedanranta, we met Matti Lankinen, a visual urban artist and a member of SprayCanKontrol, one of the artivists who had imagined Hiedanranta, as a public art space, into existence.

Lankinen became our interlocutor and guide to this post-industrial neighbourhood of Tampere. We walked with him and listened. Touching concrete and brick surfaces. Recording sounds and images. Sneaking into vast industrial buildings, small crevices and indoor skating parks. Lankinen's guidance on our walk changed the cadence of our listening. Hiedanranta was alive and had much to say, we realized in the summer, and with his help we could hear some of its stories.

Monumentality and Fragility

Initially, we were just bewitched by the exuberance and magnitude of Hiedanranta's public art work. Yet, hours of walking, listening, and recording, however, made us also sense the site's paradox: its simultaneous monumentality, and its endangerment, fragility. Could we meet the storytelling need of this hurting space, which was literally being disassembled by bulldozers while we worked on our interview and recording?

Deeply moved by the dogged persistence of Lankinen and others to change, clandestinely, the public character of urban art for years, we also understood, felt, the physical and emotional heft of such monumental but ephemeral urban-scale visual work. Angered by the devaluing of grassroots public art in our socioeconomic profit system, we wanted to do justice to the expansive, tender, larger-than-life story of young graffitists who defied the odds and pried a public art space from a city that saw no need for it.

Experiencing Urban Scale in a Tight Spot

We wondered for a while how to best express the conflict over the right to public art and space, the ongoing demolition efforts, and to celebrate the aliveness of the site in an art exhibit. Ultimately, we decided to reverse-play with scale, in- and outside surfaces, media, and the atmospheres of

›› I have been collecting trash from the streams and rivers... I mean nature has always been there [but now] that I actively don't do [graffiti] anymore, I feel like working good for the nature feels more meaningful. It does not feel more meaningful if I just make a painting in my free time somewhere... I was talking about this with my [friends] what we would ask for more? ... "natural activism" feels meaningful now... hey... picking trash from the nature's feeling meaningful. ‹‹
Matti Lankinen

Hiedanranta. To this end, we designed a makeshift "Meditation Closet." This tiny, immersive, multimedia installation cabinet was created as a claustrophobic space in which to ponder the scales of public visual art and to feel the tenderness of and the threat to the site. Our inward gesture also mirrored the generosity of Lankinen, who guided us into his world, speaking intimately about his work, about Hiedanranta, and about its grassroots history. Our micro-cabinet of curiosities was ultimately an invitation to sense the different urban scales, their magnitudes and constrictions, dreams and disappointments, with our ears and eyes, on the skin, and in the body.

Brooch

by Elena Sitrakova and
Taina Laaksonen

The photo narrative story of the greenhouses was inspired by an interview with one of the coordinators of the floating garden and the Hiedanranta greenhouses. The idea for greenhouses originated from the organizer's grandmother's brooch, and it served as inspiration to create a square-like area where people could gather and feel a sense of community while farming. Designers worked in cooperation with immigrants to design greenhouses. They designed patterns using as an inspiration plants from different places so people can feel more at home.

Those images show how powerful collaboration and social interaction can be, and they tremendously motivated me. The way those greenhouses were built and the number of people who collaborated to make them a reality demonstrate their significance and success of that social project.

Double-layered quoetry

« **It was my grandmother's brooch.** I really liked the idea of a community around the greenhouses. So I thought that those greenhouses could be like jewels here in this region and that they could somehow **sparkle and glow**. So that was the first idea.»

« **I wanted to keep it as a non-formal activity**, like the refugees designed it by themselves and created it by themselves. just like with the floating garden. »

« We had that refugee crisis. I was working with other charity social projects and I thought that this would be a good opportunity to bring some kind of **healing aspect** to the refugees. »

« It was a design project, but it was also a social one. There were greenhouses here from the 30s, so we wanted to revive them too. We had a graphic designer who created that pattern, and we had a person who designed the light. All the time when we were designing those patterns, there were the refugees that were studying the Finnish language at the education centre. **They were like a peer group that evaluated the project.**»

« There are Nordic trees around, and in the greenhouse there are some **tropical trees in the form of a pattern**. Now I know how to combine design so it has more impact. »

« In some other places, it would be harder to persuade. I also like the aesthetics here; **everything is not finished or polished**. »

« **People come here and they leave their marks here, and I think I did it too.** »

« **It was nice here because it was so informal and quite creative. You can see the impact.** »
Taina Laaksonen

Made of Real . . . and Not

by Matej Nikšić and Juha Sepponen

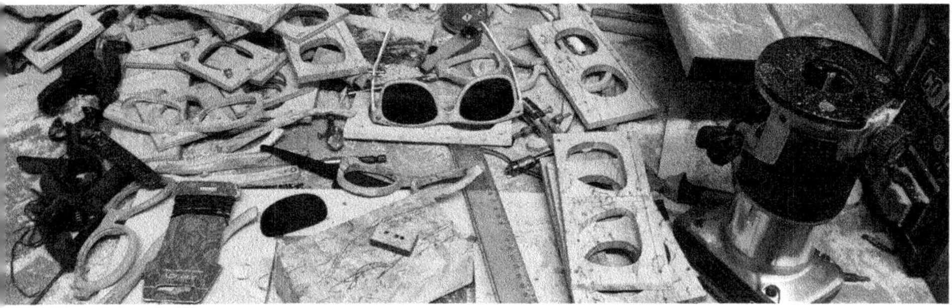

This is the story of Juha, a wooden-glasses maker from Hiedanranta. He did not enjoy his previous, eight-hour computer shift job and looked for a place where he could start his own production – he found it in Hiedanranta.

He has learnt how to produce glasses along the way. He mainly produces them for clients he knows. His glasses are made of real wood and not of composites. He likes to keep focused on the selected range of items and will keep producing glasses.

Juha occasionally joins the events organized in Hiedanranta and takes part in other activities in the area. After our interview he was going to heat up the sauna to be used in the evening.

# of Some Composites

'THE FUTURE

IS NOT OURS TO SEE,' Juha says.

He has some concerns about what will happen to Hiedanranta when the new development will be in full swing, but he is optimistic.

Juha Sepponen

Concluding Remarks

Since one of the principal characteristics of the grassroots in the city includes escaping and exceeding traditional measures, the knowledge production around their popular, spontaneous, emergent and often subversive spatial practices presents methodological challenges and requires engagement with epistemologies that take situated and subjective knowledge seriously. To inquire into these practices, status quo-confirming epistemological perspectives and methodological approaches would do nothing to account for the social value produced by, for example, a self-organizing urban gardening community or a self-built skateboarding park.

The co-constructed narratives presented here immediately offer an interesting 'visually expressive form of scholarly communication' worth exploring.[17] By weaving the different methods, the participants' situatedness and experience of place, and the stories of the grassroots of Hiedanranta all together, the different co-constructed stories introduce an interesting approach to tightly synthesizing knowledge. These methods of synthesis can be useful to represent interview material and stories of personal experience with spatial practices as well as the materiality of the built environment. Moreover, this approach to scholarly communication responds well to increasing calls for more creative, playful, and even 'rebellious' forms of representing research findings.[18] And while we are aware that these forms of representation might not be well suited for mainstream academic forums, they certainly have the potential to be powerful tools for academic communities willing to enact 'epistemic disobedience', seeking to decolonize research practices, engage with diverse audiences and/or emancipate the imagination.[19]

By following the visual, poetic and interviewing approaches introduced during the workshop, the participants were able to pursue and produce different types of material, discursive and relational knowledge. On one hand, this was about producing new and qualitative empirical documents about the present sociospatial context and relationships as well as the immediate history of the different actors living and working *in-situ*, available for further interpretation at later stages, including images, interview texts and recordings. On the other hand, the methods employed were also a means of breaking the boundaries of participation that might otherwise exclude outsider researchers from certain types of knowledge about a site.

To that end, whether in the photographing of an urban gardening project or the highlighting of quotes from an extended interview, the researchers were actively involved in the production of situated knowledge – engaged, embodied, entangled. As represented in the immediate outcomes of the workshop, which took the form of an impromptu exhibition, and in the continued developments partially represented in this chapter, the voices and perspectives of both insider grassroots actors were and are combined with those of outsider researchers in singular forms. In this way, we can see how the co-construction of narratives during the workshop, while mindful of the recent past, also created new stories from the collaborative encounters between researchers and local actors. This co-construction also ensures that distortive co-options of grassroots' narratives cannot happen so easily, even by researchers like us.

These strands of knowledge offer new accounts of the value and meaning of a site like Hiedanranta and the spatial practices that were able to flourish there. In practice, this ranged from the highlighting of an important feminist commitment in the local skateboarding association, materialized in the design itself of the on-site skate park. It also revealed the fragility of seemingly monumental works of art produced by the locally situated but globally recognized group of graffiti artists, suggesting a certain fragility of the site that is currently under pressure because of urban development. Or again, the poetic but tenuous occupation of space that can be seen in the ongoing history of a now-displaced circus association.

If these narratives bring forward knowledge of the Hiedanranta grassroots that was previously hidden or understated, they remain situated in the present tense of the site and its community, in part due to their co-constructed nature. Rather than performing purely archival work, the 'Narrating Hiedanranta' workshop participants engaged with the site and its actors using methodological approaches that called on forms of agency and creativity that, by design, entangle them in the now to produce situated knowledge in tune with the power relations at work.[20] In this way, we believe the workshop, while attempting to do justice to the recent past of grassroots activity in Hiedanranta, drew on the dynamics of co-construction to build new, future-oriented narratives of the site and its actors as they are in the present.

Acknowledgments

We would like to express our gratitude to all the interviewees for sharing their stories of Hiedanranta with us and to the workshop participants for their enthusiastic collaboration. In addition, we would like to thank Lorin Niculae for commenting on initial drafts of this chapter.

The co-constructed narratives which appear in this chapter were adapted from their original forms in order to fit the format of the *Writingplace journal.*

1 Manuel Castells, *The City and the Grassroots: A Cross-cultural Theory of Urban Social Movements* (London: Arnold, 1983), xvi.

2 James Holston, 'Spaces of Insurgent Citizenship', *Planning Theory* 13 (1995), 35-51; Leonie Sandercock, *Making the Invisible Visible: A Multicultural Planning History* (Berkeley: University of California Press, 1998); Niel Brenner, Peter Marcuse and Margit Mayer, *Cities for People Not for Profit: Critical Urban Theory and the Right to the City* (London: Routledge, 2012); Faranak Miraftab, 'Insurgent Planning: Situating Radical Planning in the Global South', *Planning Theory* 8 (2009), 32-50; Marcelo Lopes de Souza, 'Lessons from Praxis: Autonomy and Spatiality in Contemporary Latin American Social Movements', *Antipode* 48 (2016), 1292-1316.

3 Christian Schmid, 'Henri Lefebvre, The Right to the City, and the New Metropolitan Mainstream', in: Brenner et al., *Cities for People Not for Profit*, op. cit. (note 2), 42-62.

4 Castells, *The City and the Grassroots*, op. cit. (note 1).

5 Lopes de Souza, 'Lessons from Praxis', op. cit. (note 2), 1301; Efadul Huq, 'Seeing the Insurgent in Transformative Planning Practices', *Planning Theory* 19 (2020), 371-391; Dalia Milián Bernal, 'Challenging Methodologies: Deploying Liberatory Epistemologies to Unlock Creative Research Practices', *Qualitative Research* (forthcoming).

6 Huq, 'Seeing the Isurgent in Transformative Planning Practices', op. cit. (note 5), 381.

7 Tampere.fi, 'Information on Tampere', tampere.fi/en/information-on-tampere, accessed 29 June 2023.

8 Elina Alatalo et al., 'Co-designing Workshops of Hiedanranta: Vision of Dwellers', in: *University of Tampere* (Tampere, 2018).

9 Veera Turku, Ari Jokinen and Pekka Jokinen, 'How Do Time-Bound Practices Initiate Local Sustainability Pathways?', *Sustainable Cities and Society* 79 (2022); Veera Turku et al., 'Exploring the Catalytic Power of Temporary Urbanism through a Binary Approach', *Cities* 133 (2023).

10 Ibid.

11 Kirsi Pauliina Kalio et al., 'Skatescape in the Making: Developing Sustainable Urban Pedagogies through Transdisciplinary Education', *Sustainability* 13 (2021); Jonas Sjöblom et al., 'Crafting a Planning Issue with Citizens in the Context of Planning Competition: A Case of "Nordic Superblock"', *Journal of Urban Design* 26 (2021), 117-131; Klaske Havik and Alberto Arlandis, 'Choreography as a Tool to Understand Architectural Situatedness: A Mediating Intervention at Hiedanranta Industrial Heritage Ste, Finland', *Journal of Architecture* 27 (2022), 539-557. Elina Alatalo et al., 'Heating up the Sauna: Analogue Model Unravelling the Creativity of Public Participation', *Planning Theory* (March 2023).

12 Luc Pauwels, 'Conceptualizing the "Visual Essay" as a Way of Generating and Imparting Sociological Insight: Issues, Formats and Realisations', *Sociological Research Online* 17 (2012), 76-86; Luc Pauwels, *Reframing Visual Social Science: Towards a More Visual Sociology and Anthropology* (Cambridge: Cambridge University Press, 2015).

13 Jeremy Allan Hawkins, 'From Narrative Object to Poetic Practices: On Figurative Modes of Urbanism', *Urban Planning* 7 (2022), 430-439.

14 Jeong-hee Kim, *Understanding Narrative Inquiry: The Crafting and Analysis of Stories as Research* (Thousand Oaks, CA: SAGE, 2015).

15 The video is visible following this link: https://youtu.be/UDyh_b4553I and a video about the method can be found in the following link: https://youtu.be/roIW-0p-1SA

16 Mattias Malk, 'Bordering', in: Carlos Machado e Moura et al. (eds.), *REPOSITORY: 49 Methods and Assignments for Writing Urban Places* (Rotterdam: nai010, 2023), 30-33.

17 Pauwels, 'Conceptualizing the "Visual Essay"', op. cit. (note 12).

18 Cecile Badenhorst et al., *Re-imagining Doctoral Writing* (Colorado: University Press of Colorado, 2021); Pamela Burnard et al., *Doing Rebellious Research: In and Beyond the Academia* (Leiden: Brill, 2022).

19 Walter Mignolo, 'Epistemic Disobedience and the Decolonial Option: A Manifesto', *TRANSMODERNITY: Journal of Peripheral Cultural Production of the Luso-Hispanic World* 1 (2011), 3-23.

20 Donna Haraway, 'Situated Knowledges: The Science Question in Feminism and the Privilege of Partial Perspective', *Feminist Studies* 14 (1988), 575-599.

Travelogues of a Sentimental Journey through Çanakkale, Turkey

Giuseppe Resta and Sonja Novak

Mental maps are at the base of the construction of a sense of place, which is formed around social attributes, such as emotions and behaviour, and physical features that function as landmarks to represent that bonding sensation.[1] The workshop 'The City and the Myth', organized from 18 to 20 July 2022 in Çanakkale, Turkey, as part of the COST Action 'Writing Urban Places', intended to study the connection and separation between emotional topographies and tangible locations by proposing the use of a travelogue to navigate between these two dimensions. The mid-sized city of Çanakkale was chosen because it is charged with narratives: it is generally known as the World War One battleground of the Gallipoli Campaign, when the British Empire and France failed to capture Istanbul as the Ottomans used the surrounding geographical features to their advantage. Furthermore, Çanakkale lies in the region that is believed to be the same as ancient Troy, whose destruction is featured in Homer's *Iliad* and *Odyssey*. The Trojan War was considered to be a fictional event until the late nineteenth century, when pioneering archaeologist Heinrich Schliemann followed Homer's geographical descriptions and identified Hisarlık Hill as the site of the former city, together with the help of Frank Calvert. The site is now UNESCO World Heritage, but the boundary between myth and reality cannot be established with certainty. Additionally, Çanakkale is also the scene of the Greek myth of Hero and Leander, the lovers who swam across the strait every night, guided by the light of a tower. In 1810, Lord Byron re-enacted the myth by swimming in the Dardanelles and inspiring a race that has taken place every year since.

Arguably, Çanakkale plays a secondary role among Turkish centres: it is the 76th largest city in the country, though its relevance in immaterial fields such as history or literature exceeds its physical manifestation. The same thing is true in Europe of the Sintra Mountains in Portugal, the Rock of Cashel in Ireland, the Eisriesenwelt Ice Caves in Austria, the Acropolis of Athens or Stonehenge in England. There, as in Çanakkale, narratives function as a superstructure that enhances the significance of place beyond mere numeric data (population, economy, tourists). The many stories attached to the city and region of Çanakkale thus provide ground for the exploration of a topographical system of fictional events and memories.

From this perspective, while in Çanakkale, 30 researchers, professors and artists attending the workshop 'The City and the Myth' were exposed to various disciplinary fields such as architecture, archaeology, landscape, geography and literature. By means of outdoor itineraries, the participants collected personal, visual interpretations of the city using a travelogue, intended as a tool that could spatialize their sentimental journeys. Strolling through the city activated a combination of personal memories, biased interpretations of Troy and the situatedness of the travellers. In this article, we will analyse these three aspects, which together produce a sentimental map, with a focus on the methodology employed during the fieldwork.

Travel Literature and Travelogues

According to Christopher Brown's *Encyclopedia of Travel Literature*, 'travel literature designates those texts that recount the journey of a person from one place to a significantly different place and that have enduring qualities – be they formal or content based – that resonate with readers from different eras with different interests and backgrounds'.[2] The appeal of travel literature undoubtedly lies in the abundance of information about the different places it describes, the pleasure of imagining the mental images and maps, and the curiosity and desire for exploration and adventure it arouses in the reader. Travelogues, as a specific form of travel literature, are characterized by a truthful account of a voyage, written either in retrospect or during the endeavour of the journey, emphasizing the more memorable parts of the undertaking with detailed descriptions of the place, time, people, events and experiences of the traveller. Travelogues can be written in prose, poetry and dialogue, and can appear as diaries, letters, tour guides, scientific writings, commercial reports and other types of literary accounts. Due to its heterogeneous form and content, this subgenre of travel literature also distinguishes itself by the use of hybrid styles and a tension between truth and fiction that is at the heart of travel writing, as it mostly depicts solitary journeys to remote places that are witnessed solely by the author of the travelogue.[3]

As non-fictional pieces of writing, on the one hand, travelogues produce a chronotope that strongly resembles the real and actual place and time visited.[4] Through this act of simulation, they aim to achieve an effect of realism and truthfulness in the details and experience, and thus sometimes become an ethnographic account of the visited and experienced sites and geographic locations, but also of traditions, customs and culture (for example, of cuisine, art, myths and narratives). On the other hand, the stories that travelogues narrate are inevitably intertwined with and influenced by the author's personal experiences prior to the writing, including knowledge and education, attitudes and philosophy, memories, skills and a motivation for writing as well as any other factors that affect spatial and temporal descriptions, themes, style, perspective and other relevant narrative techniques and devices employed in the travelogue. Even though travel writing, like any

Fig. 1. Cover from the travelogue by Constance Hinfray, *The Fabric of Myths. Inter-species Entanglements and Perceptions*, 2022.

Fig. 2. Spread from the travelogue by Constance Hinfray, *The Fabric of Myths. Inter-species Entanglements and Perceptions*, 2022.

other type of writing, is a highly selective construct, the end result is often also permeated by an unconscious or involuntary mirroring of the author as a whole. For this reason, 'travel writing can serve as a complex and comprehensive repository of reflections' of the individual author and traveller, but also of their own cultural surroundings.[5] The following analysis from a readers' perspective – the recipients – will use a multifaceted and transdisciplinary approach to address some of the subjectivities of the authors' experiences of Çanakkale as well as the specificities of how they compete with or transform the place together with its existing material and immaterial culture, which the travellers – the authors – attempt to reconstruct in their travelogues.

Collective or Personal Memories

Personal memories are ordinarily based on the direct experience of individuals within a given society, while collective memory gathers 'the memories of the collectivity as a (necessarily fictitious) whole'.[6] In Çanakkale, it is the mythical nature of Troy that forms this fictitious whole. The notion of myth is pre-scientific by nature; it carries emotional connotations and is always shared within a group of people.[7] Even when epics are written by known authors, they usually translate existing popular stories or characters in a systematic narrative structure: 'History turns into myth as soon as it is remembered, narrated and used, that is, woven into the fabric of the present.'[8] Myths are always manifestations of a collective story, which is passed on from generation to generation and becomes contextualized according to the time and the place in which it is told. In the *Iliad*, for instance, Troy was the place of action where several travellers met their fate. The architecture and geography of Troy are an integral part of the *Iliad*, which seems to open up a space for the creation of other narratives after the destruction of the city. With the departure of the conquerors, the story of the city begins to travel on with the travellers. One can argue that in the *Odyssey*, where Troy is only the starting point, it is ultimately the story of two travellers: one is the celebrated Ulysses, who follows his journey far from home, thus embodying an archetype of the adventurer.[9] The second is Penelope, who also travels and controls the tempo of the narration while being confined to her chamber, with the act of weaving representing her journey. Ulysses' and Penelope's travels produce a topographical system that is made of events, unexpected in one case and iterative in the other, which characterize the space of their movements. They create a mental map. Geographers make a distinction between maps of tangible objects, those elements that have mechanical properties, and maps of the spatialized experience of the mind. The latter, like those of Ulysses and Penelope, starts from a blank map, a tabula rasa condition, and becomes increasingly populated every time a personal memory is recorded in this imaginary space.[10] Additionally, the geography of the mind prevails over that of the real because it is internally produced by the perceiving subject or, in this case, the traveller.

In 'The City and the Myth', we studied how individual emotional geographies, brought forward by the participants and further informed during the fieldwork, interacted with the myth of Troy. Travelogues helped the navigation between the two, accompanying their movement while fixing ideas, concepts and images of an exploration that lasted for two days. In half of the travelogues, authors make direct reference to their memories, for example to the state of destruction of their city, to the subjects they research on a daily basis, or to the preparation process for the very travels they narrate. These stories form a topographical system of fictional memories that can be charted, explored and attached to physical places.

The association of memory with geography has been explored extensively over time, starting from techniques for artificial memorization that supposedly were invented by the poet Simonides in the fifth century BC and soon formalized in the Latin textbook *Rhetorica ad Herennium* (86-82 BC), which became one of the cornerstones of classical education in the ancient world.[11] Quintilian and Cicero elaborated on these techniques, which teach one how to spatialize parts of a speech, known among the Romans as the 'method of loci': maps are organized systems, so the method consists of positioning each discrete memory in an imaginary place. Later, when the speaker needs to remember their speech, the narration unfolds while the subject travels through this mental topography, following an itinerary of successive loci.[12] Quintilian observed that when returning to a place, we also remember the emotions we felt there before. Legend has it that Simonides got this idea after he attended a dinner in the house of a nobleman in Thessaly, where at some point the roof over the hall collapsed; he survived and realized he could remember the names of all the victims by associating them with their seats around the table.[13] Hence, images and locations contextualized abstract notions visualizing imagined places populated with names. Joshua Foer points out that different cultures, such as Apache Indians, also associate memories with the landscape they inhabit as well as with the myths that took place there.[14] Geographical features interlock with mythical episodes in a way that a map coincides with the unfolding of epics. However, this becomes problematic when governments or companies transform such geographies, leading not only to material losses, but also to the disconnection of foundational myths from their geographical places. But the travellers of the workshop had never been to Çanakkale before, so their memories of Troy were inevitably formed by narrations such as movies, poetry and video games. Giuliana Bruno argues that emotional geographies are experiences at the juncture of art and science, and that custom tools are needed to capture the erotics of space, of which the impact goes beyond the seen.[15] In the case of the workshop, it was decided to keep a travel diary, where these newly created worlds could be rendered and collected. Additionally, geography and memory are bounded in terms of appropriation. Benedict Anderson observes how colonialist European countries produced historical maps to project political-biographical narratives that would justify their presence in other places.[16] Instead, participants in 'The City and the Myth' used their narratives to appropriate Çanakkale on a more personal and intimate level, injecting the mental map of their memories with the situatedness of their travels.

Fig. 3. Spread from the travelogue by Eduardo Côrte-Real, *To Troy or not to Troy, this is the Question*, 2022.

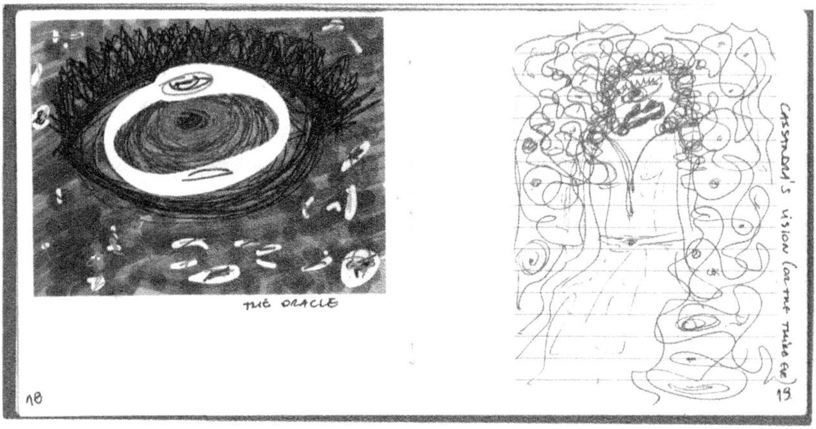

Fig. 4. Spread from the travelogue by Juliana Wexel, *A Letter to Cassandra*, 2022.

The Situatedness of the Traveller

Several scholars have compared the figures of the *flâneur* and the tourist as tropes of the traveller who visits places for recreation and enjoyment.[17] In Baudelaire's work, the *flâneur* is the subject of poetic life, prone to meet the unpredictable with a positive disposition in order to understand 'the world and the mysterious and lawful reasons for all its uses'.[18] There is a sense of mystery in the *flâneur*'s wanderings. After Baudelaire, the term *flâneur* was further developed by Benjamin, with a more spatial understanding. To the *flâneur*, the city 'opens up to him as a landscape, even as it closes around him as a room'.[19] Hence, one can travel from the infinite distance of Icarus's flight to the closest proximity of Georges Perec's domestic geographies. Their journeys take many forms (physical, metaphorical, fantastic or symbolic) and their motivations include work, pleasure, study and exploration. This practice was especially embraced by the Situationists, to be used as a technique to survey and analyse urban environments. Designed spaces were not only empty fields that responded to functional programmes, but very much charged with sociopolitical meanings to which a Situationist would resist through the construction of temporary situations.[20] This phenomenological stance added to *flânerie* a more critical and conscious behaviour that transformed wanderings into a precise methodology. As such, the means of transportation, communication and the recording of situations all became strategies to form a methodology for analysis.

'The City and the Myth' attempted a similar approach, facing the same problem the Situationists found in communicating these acts of *dérive* in aesthetic forms.[21] Henri Lefebvre, in an interview on Situationism, discussed how the essential element that creates situations is that of linking up different areas of the city, making them communicate. In this way, separate spaces would attain a certain simultaneity and take the form of a collective narrative.[22] The workshop, instead, was not aimed at connecting neighbourhoods, but mental maps with physical maps. Travelogues associate the individual with the collective, collapsing imagined places with tangible ones in a simultaneous cognitive stream that is recorded in a tangible medium.

Consequently, lived experiences and lived spaces were documented with words, drawings, collages, photos and diagrams, in the spur of the moment. Any postproduction or re-elaboration of the travelogues would have probably improved the quality of the outcome, but would at the same time have destroyed the synchronicity of the situation with the act of communication.

Clichés and Biased Interpretations of the Traveller

Considering the fact that visitors already carry interpretations of a place 'from home', before arriving at a certain destination, travelling implies an interesting paradox: it is an activity of enjoyment that, at the same time, requires preparation and organized work.[23] Travelling is a planned activity but seeks adventure, travellers wish to dive into the unknown, even though they already have an idea of what Çanakkale looks like. The experience of being a tourist triggers new or familiar, but forgotten, spatial, social and personal relations with the surroundings. It can happen, for instance, that a place we have never visited before may look familiar, while at the same time the street we walk through every day becomes an adventurous realm. In places like Çanakkale, the body of narratives surrounding its name and landscape echoes Homer's epics, Wolfgang Petersen's blockbuster movie *Troy* (2004), the art work *Fifty Days at Iliam* (1978) by Cy Twombly, the videogame *Total War Saga: Troy* (2020), as well as many contemporary literary texts.[24] Hence, the perception of visitors to Troy is grounded in these and other cultural productions before they even set foot in Çanakkale; their disposition towards what they perceive is not innocent. The critical thesis of the innocent eye, as posed by John Ruskin, which refers to the transition from an unbiased vision to one that is shaped by conventions, is indeed a relevant point of discussion for the travelogues: What is the relevance of memory, of cultural constructs, in charting a place that one visits for the first time? And especially regarding the example of Çanakkale as a highly branded cultural heritage site: How does information gathered before the visit influence the traveller's experience on the site?

Visiting Çanakkale with the task of keeping a diary questioned the mental imagery that everyone already had formed before their arrival. Strolling through the city, you can find the original prop horse used in the *Troy* movie, which is on show on the newly renovated seafront as a monument, as well as the profile of the Trojan horse on the packaging of bakeries, in music festival logos, at restaurants as well as in shops of medical equipment. Major cultural heritage sites have an image that is fed by stereotypes and city-branding initiatives.[25] Sabine Marshall called personal memory tourism the 'form of travel motivated by autobiographical memories, focused on the retracing of memorable previous journeys'.[26] In the case of Çanakkale, travellers are provided with an indirect personal memory of the site constructed by media, not by previous journeys. This confusing cognitive middle ground is caused by today's deterritorialization through mediated communication as well as through a hypermobility that renders the notion of home unstable. The faraway, Çanakkale, becomes intertwined with the very near, because it is first perceived elsewhere in its virtual forms.[27] This biased interpretation accompanies the visit and influences our real-time perception because, as we have previously discussed, its geography is produced by the mind of the traveller and tends to prevail over the physical one.

Clichés and stereotypes are the simplest way to represent a heritage site over a distance and thus also affected the participants. Gulnaz Garaeva maintains that the act of travelling does not necessarily engage with a deeper intercultural understanding of the destination.[28] On the contrary, stereotypes encourage a staged representation of the site that is in line with the visitors' expectation. Hence, the more virtual simulacra are distorted through mediated communication, the stronger Troy will resemble its

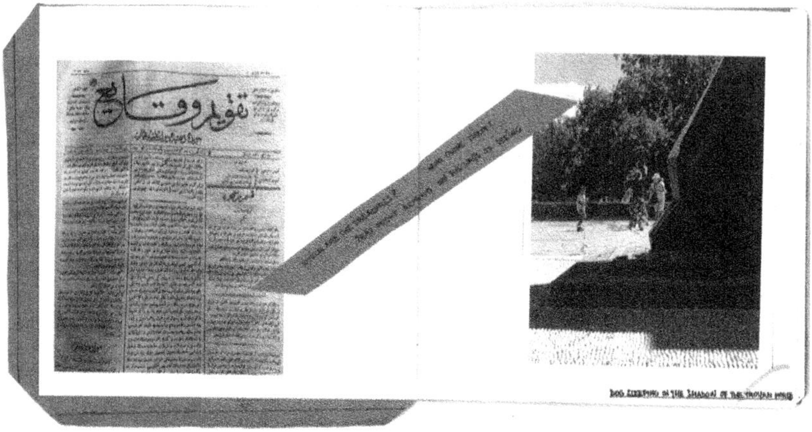

Fig. 5. Spread from the travelogue by Noemi Alfieri, *Red Lines in Çanakkale, this is the Question,* 2022.

Fig. 6. Spread from the travelogue by Saskia de Wit, *Sleeping dogs and the sea that disappeared,* 2022.

narrative twin. At the same time, getting to know the Turkish city in two days was a challenging task: it was observed that the travelogues, together with the perspective of having them exhibited and published, pushed participants through several stages of editing their first ideas. Initial ideas, carrying the traces of stereotypical references, were re-elaborated through more complex tools for expression, finally producing several thought-provoking contributions.

The Sentimental Journey through Çanakkale

The outcome of the fieldwork has recently been published in the book *The City and the Myth*, with the support of the COST Action 'Writing Urban Places'.[29] Presented as an archive of scanned travelogue spreads, the body of work became a collective system of knowledge pivoting around the fieldwork. In the first phase, it was important to reduce the excess of information of Troy's excessive media presence. On-site, participants first had to forget and leave behind their prior understanding of Troy. In Jorge Luis Borges' short story 'Funes the Memorious', Ireneo Funes is able to remember everything: not only does he remember every leaf of every tree of every forest, he even remembers every time he perceived the leaf.[30] Thus, he builds a useless catalogue containing all of the images in his memory, and in this way, however, finds himself in a sort of parallel world that perceptively disconnects him from reality. Funes is overwhelmed by information and is confronted by the same risk as those who acquire notions of a place through their media representations and are then satisfied with the level of detail they have attained. The fieldwork was crucial to instil doubt and uncertainty in the participants. This required different perspectives on the historical city of Troy as well as forgetting Schliemann's narrative, which was aimed at by visiting the exhibition at the Museum of Troy as well as the archaeological site of the city itself. Both are incomplete renderings of Troy, because the one only has small fragments, assembled within a contemporary building, while the other is a ruined place where the former reality is merely suggested by the remnants of walls. So, the museum is an intermediate point between the

Fig. 7. Resta Giuseppe (ed.), *The City and the Myth* (Melfi: Libria, 2022).

ruins and the contemporary city of Çanakkale, separated from each other by 20 kilometres, but also the platform that delivers an overarching narrative of the site. Indeed, it is the official and most scientifically accurate explanation of the historical evolution of Troy to date. The participants' visit to the exhibition space was an occasion to confront the body of narratives and develop a fragment of it with a more personal approach, which could be the wind, a certain statue or the landscape. As Borges writes, it is important to forget to be able to propose a synthesis. Instead of providing a synthesis, the juxtaposition of myth and fact that the travellers were exposed to provoked them into forming their own memory and perception of the site as well as the city of Çanakkale. Travelogues served as a tool to record an emotional journey, blending the realm of intimate experiences and that of grand mythological narratives together. Forgetfulness was trained and employed as an important skill to perceive the situatedness of the traveller, their body in space, and its impact on the surroundings. In this way, moods could emerge in the narration and change according to the different times of the day, based on light and weather conditions, which is something one cannot experience in or through media representations.

The reference to Laurence Sterne's *A Sentimental Journey* in the title of this text is an attempt to stress the importance for scientific disciplines to allow biased and subjective accounts of places to complement quantitative data. The sentimental traveller/researcher, as Sterne admits, is 'aware, at the same time, as both [his] travels and observations will be altogether of a different cast from any of [his] forerunners, that [he] might have insisted upon a whole niche entirely to [himself]'.[31] All observations of Çanakkale are partial by definition, because the branding of the city is highly connected to the narrative of Troy, which hovers between truth and fiction, myth and reality, similar to travel writing itself.

Travelogues are not disconnected from a sense of reality, but rather accept human limitations while facing Çanakkale's layered context. The museum as the place of truth, where evidence is stored and catalogued, also occupies a place within the media representations. Berna Göl, in the publication on the workshop, observes the recurrence of ramps in the travelogues, which is also the architectural element that characterizes the design of the building by architect Ömer Selçuk Baz. Here, 'the visitors' gaze going from one exhibition floor to another, is framed by vertical slits on facades which hold these ramps behind the perfect prism of the structure'. [32] The building itself is a device, a viewing machine, that visitors use to overlook the flat landscape and the archaeological site. On top is a terrace where the wind blows fully, making the traveller's experience really tangible.

This quixotic challenge produced, as an immediate result, 30 new narratives of the city in relation to the myth of Troy, but also an open-ended project that others can continue. The methodology of the travelogue allowed for very different types of output to coexist. First, the background of the travellers ranged from sociology and architecture to comparative literature and literary history. Some were very much focused on textual output, others worked predominantly with visual means. We wanted these travel journals to be instinctive, spontaneous and essentially empirical. As a result, among the produced travelogues, there is the story of a murder, a collection of QR codes linked to AI-generated visuals, drawings of a fictional species invading the archaeological site, and parallels between ancient Troy and today's Kharkiv that reflect on how a destruction of contemporary Troy(s) is possible. Twelve European countries were represented in the group of doctoral students, early-career researchers and professors. Analysing the output, we observed that architects tended to employ textual techniques, while participants with a background in literature experimented with drawings and photography. This confirms that the multidisciplinary dimension of the workshop implicitly encouraged individuals to go beyond their comfort zone. In six cases, the travellers merged the exploration with their personal research topic, creating interesting references to different places and subjects. It shaped a network of associations that starts in Çanakkale and reaches towards every corner of Europe, in the same way in which the destruction of Troy was the beginning of several foundational mythologies for other countries as a result of the diaspora of populations that fled west.[33] In these cases, stories and fragments followed the researchers back home, providing perspectives for further development. Research in architecture is often believed to be too far removed from the environment that it intends to study and assess, hence the importance of fieldwork, where methodologies are tested, revised and employed to generate new views on the contemporary world.[34] Architecture can learn from such travelogues by discovering new ways of narrating and making sense of the world. The travelogues are not meant to sustain or reconstruct a memory, but they should reorganize the old and propose new interpretations, where the dichotomy between truth and fiction is replaced by sentimental accounts.

References

Anderson, Benedict. *Imagined Communities: Reflections on the Origin and Spread of Nationalism.* London-New York: Verso, 1991.

Assmann, Jan. *Moses the Egyptian. The Memory of Egypt in Western Monotheism.* 1st Harvard Univ. Press pbk. ed. Cambridge, MA: Harvard University Press, 1998.

Bakhtin, Mikhail. "Forms of Time and of the Chronotope in the Novel." In *The Dialogic Imagination. Four Essays*, edited by Mikhail Bakhtin, 84–258. Austin: University Texas Press, 1981.

Baudelaire, Charles. *The Painter of Modern Life and Other Essays.* Translated by Jonathan Mayne. London: Phaidon Press, 1995.

Benjamin, Walter. *The Arcades Project.* Cambridge, MA: Harvard University Press, 1999.

Berger, Thomas. "The Power of Memory and Memories of Power: The Cultural Parameters of German Foreign Policy-Making since 1945." In *Memory and Power in Post-War Europe*, edited by Jan-Werner Müller, 76-99. Cambridge: Cambridge University Press, 2002.

Borges, Jorge Luis. *Labyrinths; Selected Stories & Other Writings*. New Directions. New York: New Directions, 1964.
Bruno, Giuliana. *Atlas of Emotion. Journeys in Art, Architecture, and Film.* London: Verso, 2018.

Chen, Chun-Chu, Yueh-Hsiu Lin, and James F. Petrick. "International Stereotype and the Collective Construction of Destination Image." *Tourism Analysis* 17, no. 1 (// 2012): 55-66. https://doi.org/10.3727/108354212X13330406124133. https://www.ingentaconnect.com/content/cog/ta/2012/00000017/00000001/art00005

Cicero, Marcus Tullius. *Cicero. De Oratore.* Translated by Edward William Sutton. The Loeb Classical Library from Old Catalog. 2 vols. Cambridge, MA: Harvard university press, 1942.

Çiğdem, Zeynep, and Uysal Ürey. "The Use of Orientalist Stereotypes and the Production of Kitsch: Tourism Architecture in Turkey in the Face of Social Change." *International Journal of Sport Culture and Science* 1, no. 4 (2013): 108-18. https://doi.org/https://doi.org/10.14486/IJSCS37.

Dundes, Alan. *Sacred Narrative, Readings in the Theory of Myth.* Berkeley: University of California Press, 1984.

Ewing, Suzanne, Jeremie Michael McGowan, Chris Speed, and Victoria Clare Bernie, eds. *Architecture and Field/Work*, Critiques: Critical Studies in Architectural Humanities. New York, NY: Routledge, 2011.

Farinelli, Franco. *Geografia. Un'introduzione Ai Modelli Del Mondo.* Torino: Einaudi, 2003.

Foer, Joshua. *Moonwalking with Einstein: The Art and Science of Remembering Everything.* New York: Penguin Press, 2011.

Forsdick, Charles, Zoë Kinsley, and Kathryn Walchester, eds. *Keywords for Travel Writing Studies: A Critical Glossary*, Anthem Studies in Travel. London-New York: Anthem Press, 2019.

Garaeva, Gulnaz. "„Interkultouralität?" Oder: Kritische **Überlegungen** Zu Interkulturellen Aspekten Des Tourismus." 4, no. 2 (2012): 209-20. https://doi.org/doi:10.1515/tw-2012-0207.

Gleber, Anke. *The Art of Taking a Walk : Flanerie, Literature, and Film in Weimar Culture*. Princeton, NJ: Princeton University Press, 1999.

Hazel Hahn, H. "The Flâneur, the Tourist, the Global Flâneur, and Magazine Reading as Flânerie." *Dix-Neuf* 16, no. 2 (2012/07/01 2012): 193-210. https://doi.org/10.1179/12Z.00000000017

Knabb, Ken. *Situationist International Anthology*. Berkeley, CA: Bureau of Public Secrets, 2006.

Mac Sweeney, Naoíse. *Troy: Myth, City, Icon*. Archaeological Histories. London-New York: Bloomsbury, 2018.

Marschall, Sabine. "Tourism and Remembrance: The Journey into the Self and Its Past." *Journal of Tourism and Cultural Change* 12, no. 4 (2014/10/02 2014): 335-48. https://doi.org/10.1080/14766825.2014.890208.

Morley, David. "Belongings: Place, Space and Identity in a Mediated World." *European Journal of Cultural Studies* 4, no. 4 (2001/11/01 2001): 425-48. https://doi.org/10.1177/136754940100400404

Resta, Giuseppe, ed. *The City and the Myth*. Melfi: Libria, 2022.

Ross, Kristin, and Henri Lefebvre. "Lefebvre on the Situationists: An Interview." *October* 79 (1997): 69-83. http://www.jstor.org/stable/778839.

Ruskin, John. *The Elements of Drawing*. London: Smith, Elder, & Co., 1857.

Sterne, Laurence. *A Sentimental Journey through France and Italy*. London: T. Becket and P. A. De Hondt, 1768.

Urry, John. *The Tourist Gaze: Leisure and Travel in Contemporary Society*. Thousand Oaks: Sage, 1990.

Vachon, Marc. "From Flâneur to Arpenteur." *Prairie Perspectives: Geographical Essays* 7 (2004): 44-56.

Virilio, Paul. *The Vision Machine*. London: British Film Institute, 1994.

Voet, Caroline, Eireen Schreurs, and Helen Thomas, eds. *The Hybrid Practitioner Building, Teaching, Researching Architecture*. Leuven: Leuven University Press, 2022.

Zilcosky, John. *Writing Travel. The Poetics and Politics of the Modern Journey*. University of Toronto Press, 2008.

1 Lindsay J. McCunn and Robert Gifford, 'Spatial Navigation and Place Imageability in Sense of Place', *Cities* 74 (2018), 208-218.

2 Christopher K. Brown, *Encyclopedia of Travel Literature* (Santa Barbara, CA: ABC-CLIO, 2000), viii.

3 John Zilcosky, Writing Travel (2008), p. 9

4 Mikhail Bakhtin, 'Forms of Time and of the Chronotope in the Novel', in: Mikhail Bakhtin, *The Dialogic Imagination: Four Essays* (Austin: University of Texas Press, 1981).

5 Charles Forsdick, Zoë Kinsley and Kathryn Walchester (eds.), *Keywords for Travel Writing Studies: A Critical Glossary* (London: Anthem Press, 2022), xxvi.

6 Thomas Berger, 'The Power of Memory and Memories of Power: The Cultural Parameters of German Foreign Policy-Making since 1945', in: Jan-Werner Müller (ed.), *Memory and Power in Post-War Europe* (Cambridge: Cambridge University Press, 2002), 80.

7 Alan Dundes, *Sacred Narrative: Readings in the Theory of Myth* (Berkeley, CA: University of California Press, 1984).

8 Jan Assmann, *Moses the Egyptian: The Memory of Egypt in Western Monotheism* (Cambridge, MA: Harvard University Press, 1998), 16.

9 Comparable to the *Odyssey Aeneid*. While, in the first, Odysseus (Ulysses) is driven by his own desire to reach home, in the latter, Aeneas is obeying the commands of the gods to go on a journey to Rome.

10 Franco Farinelli, *Geografia: Un'introduzione ai modelli del mondo* (Turin: Einaudi, 2003).

11 Joshua Foer, *Moonwalking with Einstein: The Art and Science of Remembering Everything* (New York: Penguin Press, 2011).

12 Paul Virilio, *The Vision Machine* (London: British Film Institute, 1994).

13 Marcus Tullius Cicero, *Cicero: De oratore*, translated by Edward William Sutton (Cambridge, MA: Harvard University Press, 1942).

14 Foer, *Moonwalking With Einstein*, op. cit. (note 11).

15 Giuliana Bruno, *Atlas of Emotion: Journeys in Art, Architecture, and Film* (London: Verso, 2018).

16 Benedict Anderson, *Imagined Communities: Reflections on the Origin and Spread of Nationalism* (London: Verso, 1991).

17 Anke Gleber, *The Art of Taking a Walk: Flanerie, Literature, and Film in Weimar Culture* (Princeton, NJ: Princeton University Press, 1999); Hazel H. Hahn, 'The Flâneur, the Tourist, the Global Flâneur, and Magazine Reading as Flânerie', *Dix-Neuf* 16/2 (2012).

18 Charles Baudelaire, *The Painter of Modern Life and Other Essays*, translated by Jonathan Mayne (London: Phaidon Press, 1995), 7.

19 Walter Benjamin, *The Arcades Project* (Cambridge, MA: Harvard University Press, 1999), 417.

20 Marc Vachon, 'From Flâneur to Arpenteur', *Prairie Perspectives: Geographical Essays* 7 (2004).

21 A *dérive*, from the French verb *deriver*, which means 'drifting', was defined by Guy Debord in 1958 as 'a technique of rapid passage through varied ambiences. *Dérives* involve playful-constructive behaviour and awareness of psychogeographical effects, and are thus quite different from the classic notions of journey or stroll.' See: Guy Debord, 'Theory of the Dérive', translated by Ken Knabb, in: Ken Knabb, *Situationist International Anthology* (Berkeley, CA: Bureau of Public Secrets, 2006), 50.

22 Kristin Ross and Henri Lefebvre, 'Lefebvre on the Situationists: An Interview', *October* 79 (1997), 69-83.

23 John Urry, *The Tourist Gaze: Leisure and Travel in Contemporary Society* (Thousand Oaks, CA: Sage, 1990).

24 For example, novels such as Peter Ackroyd's *The Fall of Troy* (2007), David and Stella Gemmell's *Troy* trilogy (2005-2007), Margaret George's *Helena, genannt die Schöne: Mein Leben zwischen Sparta und Troja* (2009), Gisbert Haefs' *Troja* (1997), Colleen McCullough's *The Song of Troy* (1998), Dan Simmons' *Ilium* (2003), Stephen Fry's *Troy: Our Greatest Story Retold* (2020), or Christoph Ransmayr's play *Odysseus, Verbrecher* (2010) and many more. Petersen's blockbuster starred many

Hollywood celebrities such as Brad Pitt, Angelina Jolie, Orlando Bloom and Eric Bana, ensuring the audience's enthusiasm and interest in the theme.

25 Chun-Chu Chen, Yueh-Hsiu Lin and James F. Petrick, 'International Stereotype and the Collective Construction of Destination Image', *Tourism Analysis* 17 (2012); Zeynep Çiğdem and Uysal Ürey, 'The Use of Orientalist Stereotypes and the Production of Kitsch: Tourism Architecture in Turkey in the Face of Social Change', *International Journal of Sport Culture and Science* 1/4 (2013).

26 Sabine Marschall, 'Tourism and Remembrance: The Journey into the Self and its Past', *Journal of Tourism and Cultural Change* 12/4 (2014).

27 David Morley, 'Belongings: Place, Space and Identity in a Mediated World', *European Journal of Cultural Studies* 4/4 (2001).

28 Gulnaz Garaeva, '"Interkultouralität?" oder: Kritische Überlegungen zu interkulturellen Aspekten des Toursimus', *Zeitschrift für Tourismuswissenschaft* 4/2 (2012).

29 Giuseppe Resta (ed.), *The City and the Myth* (Melfi: Libria, 2022).

30 Jorge Luis Borges, *Labyrinths: Selected Stories & Other Writings* (New York: New Directions, 1964).

31 Laurence Sterne, *A Sentimental Journey through France and Italy* (London: T. Becket and P.A. De Hondt, 1768), 16.

32 Berna Göl, 'How to Get out of the Route, or Finding the Staff Door', in: Giuseppe Resta (ed.), *The City and the Myth* (Melfi: Libria, 2022), 37.

33 Naoíse Mac Sweeney, *Troy: Myth, City, Icon* (London: Bloomsbury, 2018).

34 Caroline Voet, Eireen Schreurs and Helen Thomas (eds.), *The Hybrid Practitioner: Building, Teaching, Researching Architecture* (Leuven: Leuven University Press, 2022); Suzanne Ewing et al. (eds.), *Architecture and Field/Work* (New York: Routledge, 2011).

Skopje Brutalism Trail Rebuilding Social Fabric through Architecture and Performance

Marija Mano Velevska, Slobodan Velevski, Aleksandar Staničić and Blagoja Bajkovski, reflection by Holly Dale

Skopje: City of Solidarity

Skopje's urban history, dating from the turn of the first millennium, is marked by discontinuous periods of prosperity that were interrupted by a series of hazardous events, such as wars, fires, floods and earthquakes. The overlapping of different historical layers makes it a heterogeneous city, which embraces the traces and artefacts that its vibrant history has left behind. Each period in Skopje's modern history can be seen in the imported theoretical models and practices of city-building, adapted to its specific, local conditions. One exceptionally significant event that defined the course of the city's urban development is the devastating earthquake of 1963, when more than 80 per cent of the city was destroyed and over 75 per cent of the inhabitants were left homeless.[1] This condition created the opportunity for a new start and the construction of yet another sociospatial dimension of Skopje by means of a modern approach to planning and a series of exuberant (mostly brutalist) architectural designs. This massive redevelopment of the city is the result of a 'world solidarity', a term that refers to the help it received from 77 countries from all over the world, who responded both to the immediate as well as the long-term needs of the city and its citizens. Thus, the project for the reconstruction of Skopje was driven by a new perspective for redevelopment, one that was nuanced and entailed a profound and extraordinary sense of humanity and ethics.

This article is based on the experience of the 'Skopje Brutalist Trail' workshop, organized as part of the COST Action 'Writing Urban Places', in line with the activities led by Working Group 4, which focuses on the development of fieldwork. The fieldwork in Skopje focused on the general topics of brutalist architecture and solidarity, which are still present in the city, and offered a new perspective on social engagement through activism, where creative writing and artistic performance were used to develop urban narratives that link the city's architectural legacy with *in-situ* findings and the memories of people and places.

Solidarity and Community-Building

The powerful idea that underpinned the theoretical and disciplinary framing of the 'Skopje Brutalist Trail' workshop was that solidarity and community-building can be achieved through acts of collective thinking, co-creation and meaningful interventions in an urban setting. The origins of this line of thought can be traced back to the 'contact theory' developed by Louis Wirth, who argued that an exposure to diversity in dense urban settings increases the chances for tolerance to emerge.[2] Since then, a whole discipline of urban and social tolerance developed, which can roughly be defined as the 'capacity of the citizenry to negotiate harmonious encounters with difference and to engage with difference to secure improvements to social wellbeing'.[3] Today we understand that mere contact with diversity in itself is not enough; what is necessary for social cohesion to develop is meaningful interaction between different social groups, which can only be achieved through a set of interconnected conditions: a) a strong governmental apparatus that rests on or presupposes the legal equality of different social groups; b) the striving towards the common interests of the members of those groups; and c) a focus on spatial practices, meanings and forms that might promote positive contact.[4] On the other hand, the co-creation of space (but also meaning) rests on an in-depth dialogue between all parties involved, as a respectful exchange of opinions and ideas, until a deep collective understanding and a balance between creators and users are achieved. It respectfully takes into account multiple cultural backgrounds in an effort to reconcile them and create the basis for mutual cohabitation.[5]

Rebuilding communities and fostering social cohesion after large-scale urban destructions has already been recognized as a key component of disaster resilience and disaster risk science, of which Socialist Yugoslavia – and Skopje in particular – is an excellent example.[6] The global effort put into the reconstruction of the city following the 1963 earthquake is still cited as a precedent where a divided, Cold War-era world overcame its differences in an undivided act of solidarity with the Macedonian people. This enormous endeavour came out of (and perhaps occurred thanks to) the spirit of the Youth Work Actions in Socialist Yugoslavia, in which the country was rebuilt and modernized following the Second World War destructions.[7] These voluntary, community-based works acknowledged the plurality of the local contexts, while physically, politically and culturally (re)building the nation through a collective effort. The younger population and government bodies were bound by a shared, common vision of the future and a belief in collective power to improve society as a whole. What community-building and co-creation (of space) have in common is, first, the understanding of social tolerance as a dynamic category; then, the focus on citizen participation as well as on inclusive and transparent planning processes; and, finally, a framework for meaningful interaction with difference, organized through strong governance and with an equal status for all groups involved, to not only build a shared environment but also a shared future – together. Long-lasting relationships that survived even the Yugoslav civil wars of the 1990s are a testament to this model's success.

Skopje's Brutalist Architecture: Utilization of Solidarity

The post-earthquake reconstruction of Skopje is most visible in the presence of brutalist architecture that emerged in the process of its reconstruction. The immense redevelopment in the aftermath of the tragic event of 1963 was guided by the United Nations in cooperation with local authorities. One of the most valuable aspects of Skopje's reconstruction is its enormous emancipatory impact on society in general. The reconstruction of the city (then, the capital of the Socialist Republic of Macedonia within the Yugoslav Federation) employed not only the technical and material support from the country itself and from abroad, but also the latest knowledge and skills in the programming and governance of various institutions, which guided the cultural development over the following decades. Besides reforming everyday life, the architectural masterpieces that were built for public functions and official institutions not only shaped the physical space but also the character of society. Modern architecture in the 1960s had appropriated the already established, global brutalism movement in architecture and as such made a great impact on the city of Skopje and Macedonia in general, resulting in what has recently become the generally accepted, international position of considering Skopje as the capital of brutalist architecture.

Beyond the architectural merits of brutalism and its stylistic qualities of formal, structural, and material legibility, promoted by figures like the architects Alison and Peter Smithson as well as the architecture critic Reyner Banham, Skopje's brutalist legacy affords an exceptional sociocultural production in the city and in society. Indeed, Skopje's brutalist episode offers the chance to reassess the essential question of brutalist architecture: whether its virtue is a question of ethics or aesthetics.[8] While the general perception of brutalist architecture focuses merely on its tactile and visual qualities, it becomes more important to perceive this movement beyond mere aesthetics and to see these structures for their social and urban innovations rather than for its purely superficial appearance.[9]

In the case of Skopje, brutalist architecture propagates its true ethical value because the sociocultural utilization of architecture was institutionally embedded and became a societal goal. The series of remarkable buildings that were realized following the earthquake's devastation is both bold and progressive. They vary in programmatic category, size and typology, and they are aesthetically abundant and socially generous in their own specific ways.

New Narratives for 'Domche':
Perhaps the Smallest Brutalist Building in Skopje

Over the last decade, almost 60 years after the heroic and collective, international effort to rebuild the city, and after 30 years of endless sociopolitical and economic turmoil in the modern Macedonian state, various initiatives have been taken to understand and valorise the specificities of the architectural (brutalist) legacy, which has been endangered either by the processes of decay or by intentional negligence. While most of these activities are inspired by the alluring formal appearance of the brutalist buildings and limit themselves to the visual domain, some initiatives are trying to examine and re-establish the social and cultural values of these buildings within everyday life. In that way, the fieldwork in Skopje fosters the intersection of the social values of collective spaces with neglected and outdated public buildings.

The 'Skopje Brutalist Trail' workshop focused on a particular building from 1973, which served as a community centre for 30 years and is colloquially referred to as 'Domche' (a diminutive form of the noun 'home'). Occupying an area of less than 500 m^2, this building is perhaps the smallest brutalist project in Skopje. Although the building has been out of use for more than a decade, it is still vividly present in the memory of the people – both the inhabitants of the neighbourhood and of the city. In an attempt to re-enact the social role of architecture, the workshop on the case of Domche expands the notion of architecture and its formal language in the way Kica Kolbe described a building as a 'stone book where the walls and rooms are the "letters"'.[10] As such, during the workshop, the sculptural, concrete building was turned into a collection of narratives.

The significance of narratives as used in the process of understanding places and activities lies in their capacity to bring together personal experience and material reality. While the first is related to perception as a rather subjective element, the second refers to the spatial notion of place as a physical and thus objective element. The participants of the workshop conducted their subjective, interdisciplinary research to create distinctive narratives about the building. The new narratives for Domche were created through a specific combination of facts and fiction, based on the synchronicity of places, personas and events, thus bringing together various people and buildings in unexpected encounters. This approach expands the meanings of a building beyond the physical aspects of the place, representing a dynamic relationship between the subjective and the objective, between perception and cognition.

Furthermore, the 'Skopje Brutalism Trail' workshop followed a method of theatre-making protocols and used narratives to develop artistic interventions in the actual urban context.[11] At the beginning of the three-day workshop, participants from 12 different counties were first introduced to the local context – the city and its brutalist architecture, including the specific site of Domche. More importantly, they were introduced to each other through a performative presentation titled 'I Am Building', in which each participant performed a short monologue by taking on the role of one building located in the place they came from. That brought together 18 different buildings from 16 different cities that share key features: they belong to the modernist/brutalist legacy, have a certain architectural and/or historical relevance to the city, and house some form of public function. Although in a very limited time span, and analogue to the rehearsal readings during a theatre-making process, a common ground was established so that each participant of the workshop could reflect on their individual perspective. It culminated in a form of public rehearsal, where the workshop findings were presented publicly. The outcome of the 'Skopje Brutalism Trail' workshop was a theatrical performance in three acts (performed by the participants of the workshop) and showed three general approaches in telling Domche's stories: the first act told stories of far-away buildings, as distant relatives of Domche; the second act told stories inspired by Domche in different languages, spoken by the participants of this working group (narrations in the form of poems, short stories or scripts); and the third act told Domche's stories through artefacts found on the site by staging an auction through which the audience could directly participate in the play.

As the workshop demonstrated, the interdisciplinary assembly of participants allowed for the exploration of the meaningfulness of architecture to go beyond discursive or visual observations of spatial attributes, while the combination of architectural elements with visual and performing arts made it possible to communicate the variety of findings directly within the group and to the public. The combination of narration with acting and performing created an emotional chronicle of the building's past and present, but also produced synchronicities that open up towards its possible future.

The modus operandi of the 'Skopje Brutalist Trail' workshop took the key points for community-building, as applied in the processes of Skopje's post-earthquake reconstruction. It focused on empathy in thinking, designing and knowledge exchange, which was symbolized in the slogan 'I Am Building' (the building as the main character). Methodologically, reading rehearsals as used in theatre-making were undertaken for the co-development of characters and narratives. Finally, the text was transformed for a performance on stage where a degree of situatedness was achieved through the co-creation of space through movement. Writing (urban) stories and places thus became a tool for narrating shared futures.

Conclusion

As a form of a socially engaged art, public performances aim to mobilize communities towards a common goal.[12] This transforms the artistic approach of acting into a tool for advocating, making the artistic act political in the sense that they do not only represent an objective reality, but create particular situations.[13] The performative event as the final outcome communicates a narrative plot and its characters to a wider audience, thus transforming the writing (a rather intimate act) into an open (public) interpretation. Although the performance happens instantly and has a fleeting presence, the immediateness of the performance makes the act an effective mode for communicating the meaningfulness of architecture in relation to the cultural production of urban space. Its repetition over time is never a facsimile reproduction, but an evolving process where narratives are adapted to the momentum of the performance. In that manner, the public performance of the 'Skopje Brutalist Trail' workshop in the park of the Faculty of Architecture in Skopje in late September 2022 follows the similar activities already conducted, and was further developed in a performance that took place in December 2022 at the site of Domche, as part of the MOT international theatre festival.[14] This suggests that new releases of Domche-stories are to be expected, each time reaching a wider audience and producing new interpretations. Every rendition of the building as a main character provides new layers in its meaningfulness and creates new possibilities for its integration in the context, through various appropriations. Therefore, the series of performative events on Domche serve as a platform in which the deteriorated condition of a once highly appreciated neighbourhood space can find its way back to the community.

Reflection on the Theme and the Workshop Experience

Holly Dale

In September 2022, the COST Action 'Writing Urban Places' conducted fieldwork in Skopje to investigate the brutalist heritage of the city and used literary tools to generate an image of an inclusive, shared future.[15] This review will elaborate further on the two literary methods used in the fieldwork: descriptive writing and transcription.[16] In doing so, the review aims to explore how literature can help residents make sense of the brutalist heritage in their communities, using past, present and future narratives. Today, a growing number of heritage conservation projects make efforts to reflect on past inconsistencies, integrate contemporary values and develop approaches to ensure more inclusive futures.[17] This research draws from the concept of 'urban literacy', introduced by Charles Landry and developed further by Klaske Havik, to understand how literature can be used to explore brutalist heritage.[18] Havik proposes to connect architectural research to literature by addressing three interrelated concepts: description, transcription and prescription.

The first literary method used in the fieldwork was a performance titled 'I Am Building'; the method used descriptive writing to rediscover the meaningfulness of the brutalist community centre, 'Domche', by exploring twelve stories of 'Domche'. The 12 stories had been written as part of the project The City as a Stage by Filip Jovanovski. Each story has been created through a close collaboration with the community, recounting memories of the past community centre. Literature provided insight into lived spaces, communicated through the descriptive memories of the characters in the stories. Pallasmaa's work on phenomenology highlights how literary descriptions can explore a broader range of scenes than traditional image-based architecture, allowing for a greater understanding of past events.[19] During a theatrical table reading (rehearsal reading), participants from across Europe appropriated the lived spaces represented in the 12 stories of Domche, with discussions including their personal associations with brutalist heritage in an engaging cross-cultural exchange. Through participation, the boundaries between subject and object were blurred. The role of fiction encouraged the dualism of subject and object to be seamlessly exchanged as the participants' perspectives on complex social and historical narratives generated new meanings. Bachelard already stressed that the phenomenological approach to architecture actively encourages the reversible relationship between subject and object, affording meaningful relationships between people and places.[20]

The second research method transcribed the current use and appropriation of the City Gate and the City Wall, two of Skopje's most significant pieces of brutalist infrastructure. Transcription is the act of writing another version; the literary group Oulipo explored experimental methods of transcription to find new potentialities in their work, a generator of unforeseen possibilities. In the second method, the two brutalist sites were documented in the style of George Perec's work, as 'an attempt to exhaust a place'.[21] The technique records the everyday objects that pass through one's field of vision, highlighting urban and social rhythms. The technique of documenting the everyday use of a space through creative writing provided the characters and perceived settings for the reader to appropriate, giving them principal control over the production of space. The outcome of the method was a series of speculative narratives developed through the transcription of the documentation. Characters unseen in Skopje's current brutalist legacy became the protagonists.

Both research methods used literary tools to address Skopje's brutalist heritage through past, present and future narratives. The bottom-up rather than the top-down approach allowed participants to engage in the production of space. The literary tools applied in these two methods afforded a multitude of new narratives, as the roles of subject/object and author/reader were intertwined through describing, transcribing and prescribing the city. The outcomes highlight contradictions and omissions in Skopje's current brutalist legacy.[22] While the first method used description to offer critical interpretations of the past brutalist legacy, the second used transcription to offer speculative scenarios by actively engaging the reader. This review highlights how these literary methods can help drive the development of heritage conservation to reflect past inconsistencies, integrate contemporary values, and develop approaches to ensure more inclusive futures.

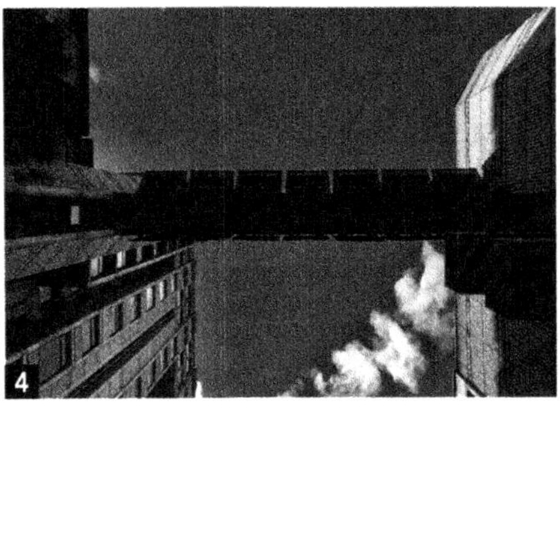

Photos previous page:
Fig. 1. Krsto Todorovski (architect), Hydrometeological Center, Skopje, 1975.

Fig. 2. Mimoza Tomikj and Kiril Muratovski (architects), Museum of Macedonia, Skopje, 1971.

Fig. 3. Janko Konstantinov (architect), Post Office Hall, Skopje, 1981.

Fig. 4. Gjorgji Kostantinovski (architect), Student Dormitory 'Goce Delchev.

Fig. 5. Janko Konstantinov (architect), Telecommunication Center, Skopje, 1981.

All photos: Blagoja Bajkovski with technical support of Boshko Stolikj.

Fig. 6. Performative Reading 'I Am Building' at the Museum of Contemporary Art, Skopje. Skopje Brutalism Trail workshop (September 2023). Photo: Mila Gavrilovska.

Fig. 7. Site visit to the community center 'Domche' and the Taftalidge neighbourhood, Skopje. Skopje Brutalism Trail workshop (September 2023). Photo: Mila Gavrilovska.

Fig. 8–9. Rehearsal Readings. Working in groups with tutors Filip Jovanovski (FR/U, AKTO Skopje), Miodrag Kuc (Z/KU, Berlin), and Boris Bakal (ShadowCasters, Zagreb). Skopje Brutalism Trail workshop (September 2023). Photos: Mila Gavrilovska.

Fig. 10–13. Public performance in the park of the Faculty of Architecture, Skopje. Skopje Brutalism Trail workshop (September 2023). Photos: Mila Gavrilovska.

1 United Nations, *SKOPJE RESURGENT: The Story of a United Nations Special Fund Town Planning Project* (New York: United Nations, 1970), 312-315.

2 Louis Wirth, 'Urbanism as a Way of Life', *The American Journal of Sociology* 44 (1938), 1-24.

3 Jon Bannister and Ade Kearns, 'The Function and Foundations of Urban Tolerance: Encountering and Engaging with Difference in the City', *Urban Studies* 50 (2013), 2700-2717.

4 Pnina Werbner, 'The Dialectics of Urban Cosmopolitanism: Between Tolerance and Intolerance in Cities of Strangers', *Identities: Global Studies in Culture and Power* 22 (2015), 569-587; Gordon W. Allport, *The Nature of Prejudice* (Boston: Addison-Wesley, 1954); John Dixon, 'Contact and Boundaries: "Locating" the Social Psychology of Intergroup Relations', *Theory & Psychology* 11 (2001), 587-608.

5 Corelia Baibarac and Doina Petrescu, 'Co-design and Urban Resilience: Visioning Tools for Commoning Resilience Practices', *CoDesign* 15 (2019), 91-109.

6 Lorenzo Chelleri, 'From the "Resilient City" to Urban Resilience: A Review Essay on Understanding and Integrating the Resilience Perspective for Urban Systems', *Documents d'Analisi Geografica* 58 (2012), 287-306.

7 Reana Senjković, *Svaki dan pobjeda: Kultura Omladinskih Radnih Akcija* [Every Day a Victory: The Culture of the Youth Work Actions] (Zagreb: Institut za etnologiju i folkloristiku, 2018); Rudi Supek, *Omladina na putu do bratstva: Psihosociologija radne akcije* [Youth on the Way towards Brotherhood: Psychosociology of the Work Action] (Belgrade: Mladost, 1963).

8 Reyner Banham, *The New Brutalism: Ethic or Aesthetic?* (London: Architectural Press, 1966).

9 Antony Vidler, 'Brutalism: Aesthetic or Ethic?', *CLOG* 'BRUTALISM' 6 (2013).

10 OKNO, Kica Kolbe, 'Бетовенхале во Бон и Универзална во Скопје – паралели и идеи' [Bethovenhalle in Bonn and Universal Hall in Skopje – Parallels and Ideas], https://okno.mk/node/85717, accessed 19 July 2023.

11 Filip Jovanovski et al., 'Performing (on) Architecture through Theatre Protocols', in: Carlos Machada e Moura et al. (eds.), *REPOSOTORY: 49 Methods and Assignments for Writing Urban Places* (Rotterdam: nai010, 2023), 118-121.

12 The notion of 'engaged art' refers not only to the interactive performance where actors, space and audience actively co-participate, but also to the process of its creation, which, in the case of the Domche narratives, is largely based on participative collaboration with local communities.

13 Dérives, Jean-Luc Godard, 'Que faire?' (1970), http://www.derives.tv/Que-faire, accessed 19 July 2023.

14 The public performance in December 2021 was the result of a four-day interdisciplinary workshop titled 'Lost Modernist Utopias' with students from the Faculty of Architecture, the Faculty of Dramatic Arts (Theatre) and the Faculty of Fine Arts (Painting), tutored by Miodrag Kuč from ZKU (Berlin) in collaboration with FR~U/AKTO, Skopje; MOT, '47. MOT 2022: City as a Stage (Lost Modernist Utopias)', https://mot.mk/en/event/city-as-a-stage-en, accessed 19 July 2023.

15 Writing Urban Places, 'Workshop Report: Skopje Brutalism Trail', https://writingurbanplaces.eu/workshop-report-skopje-brutalisam-trail%EF%BF%BC, accessed 19 July 2023.

16 This review is the outcome of a Short-Term Scientific Grant (STSM) 'Props and Appropriation: Exploring the Everyday Narratives in the City', awarded in 2022 to Holly Dale.

17 Juan A. García-Esparza, 'Narrating the Urban Fabric of Our Historical Towns', *Writing Places* 6 (2022), 120-135.

18 Charles Landry, *The Creative City: A Toolkit for Urban Innovators* (London: Comedia/Earthscan, 2000); Klaske Havik, *Urban Literacy* (Rotterdam: nai010, 2014).

19 Juhani Pallasmaa, *The Eyes of the Skin* (Chichester: Wiley, 1996).

20 Gaston Bachelard, *The Poetics of Space* (New York: Penguin Books, 1958).

21 Georges Perec, *An Attempt at Exhausting a Place in Paris*, translated by Marc Lowenthal (Cambridge, MA: Wakefield Press, 2010 [1982]).

22 Ophélie Véron, 'Contesting the Divided City: Arts of Resistance in Skopje: Contesting the Divided City', *Antipode* 48 (2016).

Almada The Other Margin

Luís Santiago Baptista and Susana Oliveira

Almada is both a city and a municipality on the south bank of the Tagus River, which faces historical Lisbon to the north and the Tagus River mouth and the Atlantic to the west. While it is part of the metropolitan area of Portugal's capital, it has an identity of its own, marked simultaneously by its proximity to and its distance from Lisbon. As part of its singular geographical condition, Almada also extends towards the southern Portuguese plains, where the city of Setúbal and the Sado River's estuary are located. Almada's topography is characterized by natural cliffs in the west and the north, respectively looking towards the ocean and the city of Lisbon, and a very slight slope towards the south with excellent climatic and geographical conditions. The proximity to the Portuguese capital naturally defined the settling and development of the different activities in the region as well as the foundation of the town of Almada itself. The region has a long history of all kinds of production, but mainly as the agricultural extension of the capital, due to its rural environment including fisheries, wine and olive oil production, and cork farms and warehouses. This so-called 'other margin' historically played a fundamental role in the defence system of Lisbon until the second half of the twentieth century, with the presence of a series of military forts and batteries, as well as quarantine and prison facilities, close to but separated from the capital. Interestingly, the proximity to Lisbon was also appealing to the royal family, whose summer palaces have been located there since the eighteenth century, in the coastal and forest areas to the east. Later, in the 1930s, these ludic and touristic activities would spread towards the opposite Atlantic waterfront, which became a popular beach and vacation destination in contrast to the aristocratic and elitist Estoril, which lies to the west of Lisbon, towards the Atlantic coast.

With Lisbon dominating the area north of the Tagus, the other margin, also often called the 'Margem Sul' (south bank), increasingly became dependent on Lisbon, as a result of the relatively late industrialization of the country, and as such became a suburb. The capital's agricultural supply, mainly organized by water transport, resulted in the presence of quays and the development of coastal fishing villages like Cacilhas, Porto Brandão and Trafaria. But the industrialization also brought new activities to the riverfront, especially those related to naval industry. Some of these activities were relocated from the port of Lisbon, others were new, with an increased scale and spectrum of action. The Alfeite arsenal, a huge military port facility, opened at the end of the 1930s, but above all the Lisnave shipyard, inaugurated in 1967, became a very relevant international enterprise within the naval industry. This massive naval and industrial presence along Almada's riverfront gave the city its social and cultural identity, defined by the working-class context with its strong left-wing politics. While the shipyards occupied land on the coast, appropriating huge areas for industrial activities, the city of Almada developed a strong working-class character through a myriad collection of new places and buildings intended for cooperatives, unions, associations and other communal gathering spaces. New public housing estates like the Almada Economic Neighbourhood, from 1952, and the huge Integrated Plan of Almada, from 1972, on the expansion area of the city to the west, responded to the increasing demographics of the municipality. But the population growth was mainly driven by the more generic suburban housing estates, promoted by private initiatives and located around the city and towards the south, in Laranjeiro and Feijó.

This acceleration of suburban growth in the municipality since the 1960s was further enhanced by the construction of a bridge over the Tagus, establishing a connection that had long been desired, but that until then had only been possible via fluvial transport. The connection had been promised for a long time, with several failed attempts since the end of the nineteenth century, including a bridge, a tunnel and a funicular system. The new bridge, inaugurated in 1966, first facilitated crossings by car and bus, and later, in the beginning of the 1990s, also by train, on a lower platform inside of the steel structure of the bridge. Unsurprisingly, Almada officially became a city in 1973, which gave it a new status that balanced between reinforcing its strong working-class character, while increasing its dependency on the capital, since it became embedded within the Greater Lisbon Metropolitan Area.

Almada's suburban condition must be understood within the singular context of its development. It is quite surprising that the dominant, generic suburban environment of the Almada municipality looks like the result of an absence of territorial and urban planning, while it probably has one of the richest planning histories in Portugal, albeit one marked by continuous inefficiencies and failures. The Urbanization Plan of Almada of 1946 by Étienne de Groer and Guilherme Faria da Costa and the establishment of the Urbanization Office of the municipality in 1955 as well as the more localized urban plans that followed, like the Integrated Plan of Almada of 1972, the several Margueira plans in development since 1999, and the recent Ginjal quay plan, reveal that there was and is no lack of planning ideas for this metropolitan area. However, only a few of these planning efforts saw real or consistent concretization.

Almada has a strong social and cultural identity and an incredible memory of its own singular history. The urban life of Almada persists in resisting the suburbanization, even with the continuing disappearance of its agricultural and industrial production and its increasing dependency on Lisbon.

The evolving identity of Almada should consider and integrate its urban and historical narratives as a way to preserve and reinvent the bonds between its inhabitants and communities to the place.

We present Almada here not only because it was one of the locations for one of our first meetings, in November 2019, at the Casa da Cerca, a beautiful cultural centre in the old town of Almada. From multiple perspectives, in different spreads, we also want to reflect (on) the place's character, the tensions between suburbanization and the larger metropolitan area of which it is a part, and the identity of Almada. To do so, we used different means of representation, times, histories and stories, presented by using literary, artistic or documentary sources, such as novels, illustrations, models, photographs and film.

The first narrative focuses on a fisherman's life on the beach of the Costa da Caparica, as presented in the silent movie *The Lighthouse Keepers*, showing the harsh living conditions of these communities.[1] Next, there is the 'Atlas das Paisagens Literárias de Portugal Continental' (The Atlas of Literary Places of Mainland Portgual, a collaborative project connecting literature with the territory, of which we present a few literary excerpts (which were part of the literary trail to explore how Almada's memory and identity were experienced *in situ* during our Cost meeting in 2019), which focus on the Cacilhas quay, a place that goes back to Almada's industrial and agricultural past in the twentieth century.[2]

The emergence and decay of the naval industry's huge presence on the eastern riverfront is the focus of the following two urban narratives about Almada. First, there are Nuno Barros Roque da Silveira's contrasted photographs of the Lisnave shipyard in full operation, from around 1970, which simultaneously capture the scale of the industrial enterprise's ambition as well as the working conditions in the naval repair infrastructure.[3] Second, there is the unbuilt urban plan for the Margueira shipyard by architects

Manuel Graça Dias and Egas José Vieira (the so-called 'Cacilhas' Manhattan'), which announced the closing of the naval shipyard and its transformation into a new urban centre in 1999, but remains unrealized.[4]

The exhibition 'Almada: Um Território em Seis Ecologias' (Almada: A Territory in Six Ecologies),[5] curated by Luís Santiago Baptista and Paula Melâneo and shown at the Museum of Almada in 2020, provided the following two contributions that engage with Almada's present condition: on the one hand, the artist Nuno Cera investigated through film the current situation, not only of the abandoned and ruined *terrain vague* of the Lisnave shipyard but also the almost deserted and decaying Alfeite military arsenal that extends towards the south. On the other hand, artist Paulo Catrica explored through photography the different urban environments of the contemporary city of Almada, from the old town to the expansion plans for its modernization and suburban development in the context of the larger, metropolitan area of Lisbon.

Finally, the recent appropriation of Cassiano Branco's urban plan of 1930 by comic book authors António Jorge Gonçalves and Nuno Artur Silva brings us back to the Costa da Caparica and the first announcement of its transformation into a popular and informal tourist destination.[6]

With minimal explanations, the texts and images displayed in the spreads that follow, focused on these specific places, will give the reader the experience of jumping between past and present, between memory and reality, between the literary and the visual, constructing the urban narratives of Almada.

Fig. 1-10. Maurice Mariaud (dir.), *Os Faroleiros*, film stills, 1922.

MAURICE MARIAUD (DIR.), *OS FAROLEIROS* (1922)

Os Faroleiros (The Lighthouse Keepers) is a film by French director and actor Maurice Mariaud, produced and shot in Portugal in 1922. The film 'was lost for decades', reads the explanatory note of the movie theatre Batalha, and is considered a 'rarity of Portuguese silent cinema'.[7] It is a drama about a fatal love triangle between a woman, who lives in a lighthouse after her father's death at sea, and two lighthouse keepers. The film was partially shot outdoors, on Lisbon's and Almada's coasts, and at sea, showing the original landscapes and living conditions of that time, while also inaugurating a 'Portuguese verist' tradition, both in cinema and in fictional literature, which remain very relevant trends to this day.[8] In contemporary Portuguese cinema – for instance, in Pedro Costa or João Canijo's movies – these trends are not only expressed, but exacerbated. Fatalism and naval narratives are intertwined with local traditions, oral history, and Fado lyrics, especially in the *canalha* subgenre, which often deals with treason and jealousy.[9] Evidently, the 1922 movie distilled a number of Portuguese cultural clichés and tainted nationalist self-representations, which were part of the fascist regime's propaganda for decades, in ways that remain tangible in the other images of Almada that are also presented here.

ROMEU CORREIA (DIR.), *OS TANOEIROS* (1976) *O TRITÃO* (1982), *CAIS DO GINJAL* (1989)

by Ana Isabel Queiroz, Natália Constâncio and Daniel Alves

The descriptors inserted in the database of the 'Atlas das Paisagens Literárias de Portugal Continental' make it possible to carry out literary studies at different levels of the Portuguese landscapes, starting with those that relate to the past and show historical transformations at the political, social, economic and environmental levels.[10] Excerpts from the works of Romeu Correia show the evolution of the biophysical and human landscapes of the riverside area of Almada, referred to as Cais do Ginjal – a stonewall along the riverbank. Through an analysis of the content of these texts, the spacetime of intense industrial activity can be defined and situated in the period from the second half of the nineteenth century and onwards, including the manufacturing of cork products, wooden barrels, canned fish, cookies and biscuits, and the routines of men, women and children in this narrow strip of land where they lived and worked.

The literary excerpts focus on spaces that were once the setting for these narratives and describe the inhuman conditions of the families who worked there to earn a living. Through a comparative approach, which starts with the reading of literary excerpts and takes readers to the territory they represent, readers are simultaneously transported to past, present and future realities ('looking back, looking forward'), cultivating the perception of a dynamics that defined that place along with a sense of the depth of time. At the same time, a surprising confrontation between the material and the immaterial develops, which completes the aesthetic and emotional immersion that is developed along this literary path.

In fact, the places visited on the route between Boca do Vento and the Cacilhas pier nowadays reflect a new economic, social, and cultural configuration: some buildings are inactive or abandoned, in ruins; others have been transformed into bars or restaurants, departing from the image of precarious work that emerges from these texts. Connecting literature and the territory, the Ginjal literary trail was developed within the framework of the 'Atlas das Paisagens Literárias de Portugal Continental' at the 'Writing Urban Places' WG3 and WG4 meeting in November 2019. Alongside it, there are three novels by Romeu Correia (1917–1996): *Os Tanoeiros* (The Coopers), O Tritão (The Merman), and *Cais do Ginjal*. These narratives bring the reader back to the 1920s and 1930s.

> *And just knowing that he would not return to Boca do Vento any time soon, made him so unhappy . . . What a gorgeous place! There was the women's washhouse, the steps to the pier of Ginjal, and the river and the boats . . . Mostly the river and the boats! It was both delightful and confusing to admire that body of water – because, at times, it seemed to be in its rightful place, but at others, it looked like a long, blue cloth bound to the sky itself!*
> *Os Tanoeiros*, p. 12.

> *That boulder was about thirty metres from the vertical line of the rock. Seen from above, it resembled a giant toadfish, and when the tide rose, and the waters covered most of the stone, the portion that remained above the water resembled a lupin. That is why the stone was called 'Tramoceiro', a distortion of the Portuguese word for lupin [*tremoço*]. I once asked the good grandfather, José Correia, why this rock was on the beach of Fonte da Pipa. – That stone, he explained, was attached to the rock of the village many centuries ago. But it was thrown onto the beach by one of the many earthquakes that affected our planet. . . . There, before me, was the city of Lisbon, the vast blue sky and the Tagus River, flowing towards its mouth. . . . The workers from Olho-de-Boi, who were returning from their daily chores, with lunchboxes in their hands, cigarettes in their mouths, talking about football or women, passed nearby the rock. Some knew me and greeted me. Others pretended not to notice me. Time went by, fish took the bait, and some came to fill the baskets.*
> *Cais do Ginjal*, p. 131.

The workers swarmed to the warehouses and factories to start their work at 8:00 a.m., which would last until 5:00 p.m. Hours of intense work. Wine and olive oil warehouses, cooperages, fish canning factories, tinplate canned food, large and small casks in brine. There were Portuguese and Spanish employers, but also a Greek, a German, and for a wider variety, even a Russian employer . . .

Cais do Ginjal, pp. 39–40.

He learned the harshness of cooperage: the heavy sledgehammer blows, the fire that tamed the staves, dreadful clouds of smoke which created solid catarrh. His hands acquired calluses and nodules; muscular dilatations, blood clots, coarsened his juvenile arms. At the time, wood was plentiful, as was American oak, a delight to harvest – casks, with no lack of paraffin. It was a different time . . . The wine exporters had private cooperages guaranteeing the consumption of the casks in the warehouses.

Os Tanoeiros, p. 28.

That pier where we lived, that wall with a long series of buildings, had given rise to a curious riddle that was asked in the evening:

– Why does the pier of Ginjal look like a waistcoat?

And the answer always caused laughter:

– Because it only has houses on one side.

It was true: it only had houses on one side . . . In addition to some residences, there were cooperages, canning factories, wine and grain warehouses. Between the back of those buildings and the rock, there were vegetable gardens, fruit trees and trellis of good grapevines. There were also henhouses and dovecotes, as well as other hovels, which the walls of the beach-side hid from the hasty observation of the simple wayfarer on the pier.

O Tritão, p. 11.

At the time, Cacilhas was like a snake changing its skin. The beach and the ramp, where boats of small draught found shelter, gave way to a small portion of the wall, the first landfill. The trains and wagons were replaced by trucks and taxis, relegating the draught beasts to other tasks. The donkey rides were already rare, a business of the owners of the coach houses and the innkeepers, who were always ready to welcome the gentleman riding the beast to offer him a glass of wine. Almada, Cova da Piedade, Mata do Alfeite were the places visited by the donkeys. The dandies who came to Cacilhas to get a shave for a pataco [coin], paid for the boat and still had some money left for a glass of wine. The lighthouse and the fountain would still be there for many good years, illuminating the seafarers in the pitch-dark nights and offering water to canisters and barrels. Fish stews, boiled or grilled shellfish, the fresh sardines of Caparica or Sesimbra, those were the most appreciated snacks. Workers from the Parry & Son dock and the Symington dock, unloaders of British mineral coal, received at Black's warehouse, set the most prominent industrial tone, as well as the coopers of Ginjal, the cork workers and the fish canning staff. Cacilhas – a place of embarkation for Lisbon and a very old port, frequented by boatmen, unloaders, sailors, and caulkers. The youngest employed their energies and dexterity in playful fights, duels of strength, rope pulling, long dives in the river, which caused apprehension for the swimmer's life . . . They also sailed in the Tagus River, in constant competition, both during working hours and on their own time.

Cais do Ginjal, pp. 59-60.

NUNO BARROS ROQUE DA SILVEIRA, PHOTOGRAPH SERIES OF LISNAVE (1970)

Nuno Barros Roque da Silveira was one of the photographers from the municipality of Lisbon who documented the city's transformation. In the second half of the twentieth century, during the modernization of Lisbon and the country in general, the city council started to systematically register the changes in its urban context through a series of films and photographs, which have become crucial historical documents. Working with specific commissions from the municipality near the end of the 1960s and during the beginning of the 1970s, Nuno Silveira captured, for instance, the transformation of the Alcântara valley, after the construction of the Ceuta Avenue, or the opening of the Marginal Road that connected the city to Cascais along the coastline. At the same time, he repeatedly photographed buildings destined for demolition. Modernization confronts the disappearance of the old.

The photographs he took in 1970, of the early life of the Lisnave shipyard on the south bank of the Tagus River, acquire, in this context, a special relevance. It is difficult to see them just as documents due to their immense aesthetic and social qualities. Lisnave was one of the most challenging industrial developments in Portugal, a naval shipyard launched as an international partnership on the global market of naval repair. What was supposed to become the biggest dock in the world was built in Lisnave over the following years, a sign of ambition and international success. Portugal was governed by a dictatorship until 1974 and the Almada margin of the river was a historically grown working-class area, so political and ideological tensions were certainly present. Nuno Silveira's photos show the incredible scale of Lisnave, focusing on the naval workers' skilled labour. But the intense light casting the men working with the technical machinery could only be revealed by the deep darkness of its shadows.

Fig. 11-12. Nuno Barros Roque da Silveira, Lisnave Shipyard, photographs, 1970.
Source: Arquivo Municipal de Lisboa (PT/AMLSB/CMLSBAH/PCSP/004/NBS).

Fig. 13-14. Nuno Barros Roque da Silveira, Lisnave Shipyard, photographs, 1970. Photos: Nuno Barros Roque da Silveira Source: Arquivo Municipal de Lisboa (PT/AMLSB/CMLSBAH/PCSP/004/NBS).

MANUEL GRAÇA DIAS AND EGAS JOSÉ VIEIRA, *CACILHAS' MANHATTAN*, MARGUEIRA (1999)

The closing of Lisnave's Margueira shipyard in 2000 was already announced by its troubled history after the revolution of 25 April 1974. The shocks of successive oil crises and the changes in the geostrategic routes of the international naval infrastructure became intensified by political and labour-related turmoil, initiated by the workers against the administration, with significant strikes that had begun even before the so-called Carnation Revolution. The instability of the international markets was reflected in these social tensions, announcing the slow, productive decay and human desertification of the shipyard. From then on, Margueira became an enormous *terrain vague*.[11]

In 1999, a new and futuristic vision of Margueira hit the news: architects Manuel Graça Dias and Egas José Vieira, frontmen of Lisbon's ludic and bohemian, postmodern era, presented a huge urban project for the shipyard's unproductive land. It would become popularly known as 'Cacilhas' Manhattan', because of its metropolitan landscape of circulation viaducts, technical skyscrapers, and urban parks, marked by the monumental portico of Lisnave's dock.[11] The delirious metropolitan project's force and energy gave a visionary image to the speculative economic operation from which it originated. The plan would not be realized, though, and was replaced by a more domesticated and conventional urban plan, which still awaits its realization today. Cacilhas' Manhattan remains a plan on paper but its image persists in our memory. As the architects described it:

Fig. 15. Manuel Graça Dias and Egas José Vieira, *Cacilhas' Manhattan*, Margueira, photomontage, 1999. Source: Contemporânea / Caixa d'Imagens.

> *Now, here, on this side, the volumes are contrasted in glass and iron, being high, pointed, enormous, piercing the sky, seeking to compensate Lisbon's not having any space nearby and Almada's seeing so little of the river. Enormous towers in the morning sun, towers shining in the afternoon sun, structures with graceful profiles, directed over that vague chessboard that supported the warehouses and docks, violent towers like the violent and enormous ships that filled Margueira, superb volumes that would enter and depart, inhabiting this landscape of Lisbon, getting used to the landscape of Lisbon.*[12]

Fig. 16a. Manuel Graça Dias and Egas José Vieira, Plan *Cacilhas' Manhattan*, Margueira, sketch, 1999. Source: Contemporânea.

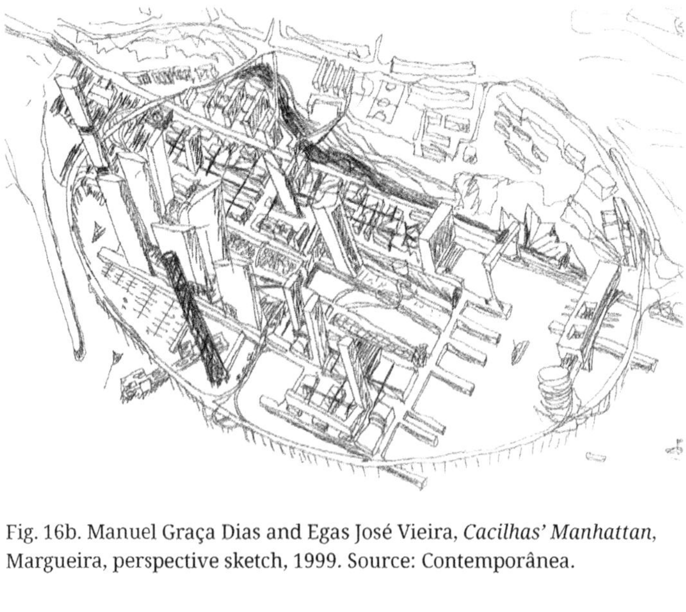

Fig. 16b. Manuel Graça Dias and Egas José Vieira, *Cacilhas' Manhattan*, Margueira, perspective sketch, 1999. Source: Contemporânea.

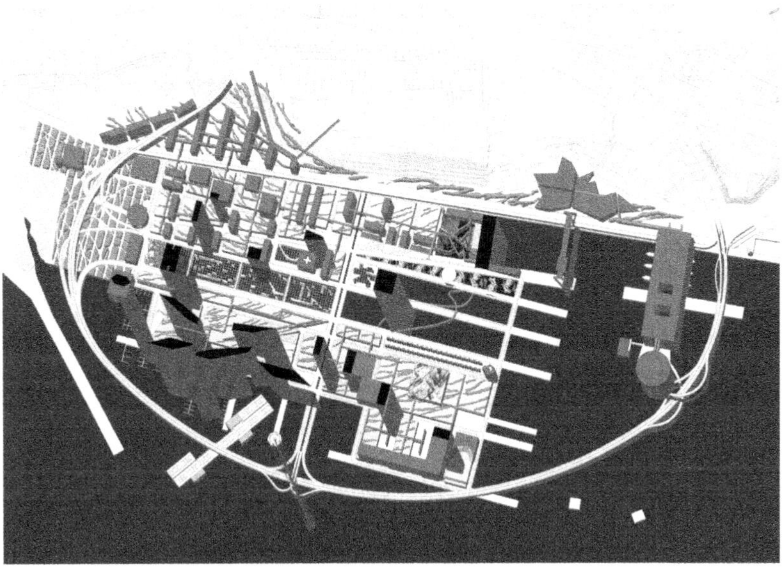

Fig. 17. Manuel Graça Dias and Egas José Vieira, *Cacilhas' Manhattan*, Margueira, axonometric drawing, 1999. Source: Contemporânea.

Fig. 18. Manuel Graça Dias and Egas José Vieira, *Cacilhas' Manhattan*, Margueira, model, 1999. Source: Contemporânea.

NUNO CERA, *ALFEITE ARSENAL* (2019) *LISNAVE NAVAL SHIPYARD* (2019)

Nuno Cera is a Portuguese photographer and video artist whose work – such as his well-known collaborations with architect and theorist Diogo Seixas Lopes – closely relates to architecture. Cera has a manifest interest in modern spaces, which appear to be haunted by presences and memories. For example, he worked on the ruins of violent pasts and disturbing presents in the abandoned national-socialist resort of Prora, Le Corbusier's Unité d'Habitation in Berlin, Ricardo Bofill's Abraxas urban complex, Aldo Rossi's San Cataldo Cemetery, and Carlo Scarpa's Tomba Brion. Likewise, Cera's work has also touched upon the desolate landscapes in the peripheries of Lisbon's metropolitan area. In all these works, photography or film capture or incorporate the anguish and anxieties of modernity as manifested in space.

Fig. 19-24: Nuno Cera, *Alfeite*, film stills, 2019. Courtesy of the artist.

Working with the presence of the naval industry, Cera focused on the two big shipyards built in the northeast area of the municipality. On the one hand, the Alfeite Arsenal was inaugurated in 1939, which housed military naval functions, including the Navy School that open the previous year in a modernist building and the Navy Command that was installed in the eighteenth-century Royal Palace. Still open, the Arsenal has now become a rare activity in a decaying industrial environment. On the other hand, Lisnave used to be a naval repair shipyard with an unusual ambition, involving one of Portugal's biggest private corporations combined with governmental supervision, which was in operation from 1967 to 2000 but became an enormous terrain vague afterwards. In the vertical still frame films about Alfeite and Lisnave, Cera sublimates the industrial, naval infrastructure into processes of decay, with fixed images subjected to the temporality of natural elements, going back and forth from landscape to detail. The decaying beauty of these huge technical buildings, structures, and spaces of our recent past mirrors the phenomenon of deindustrialization. Cera's work testifies to the last, disappearing presences of a territory that once promised a tabula rasa for urban development.

Fig. 25-30. Nuno Cera, *Lisnave*, films stills, 2019. Courtesy of the artist.

PAULO CATRICA, *'ALMADA: A TERRITORY IN SIX ECOLOGIES* (2019)

Artist and photographer Paulo Catrica offers us a perspective on the urban environment of Almada through a series of photographs. As a visual researcher, Catrica developed a deep interest in contemporary urban conditions, capturing reality 'as found' without prior moral and historical judgment, even if, in the case of Almada, some childhood memories could not be avoided. Catrica is interested in the life of the places he captures with his camera, but the images are devoid of any presence of the inhabitants of the city. Material reality is a desert, yet, their presence may be felt *in absentia* nonetheless. In this sense, architecture is never a pure, formal condition abstracted from the context of place, but the result of a continuous public appropriation that leaves material marks in space. There is always a strangeness in still, familiar urban places, captured at eye level; not only because people are absent, but also because of the the diffuse contrast between light and shadow in the photos shot in the early morning or evening.

Catrica shows the different urban contexts that constitute a possible identity for Almada. First, the old town is marked by the presence of a building that housed the most important collective association, the Incrível Almadense, founded in 1936 and which has become a shared symbol of the working class presence in the city. Second, the Nossa Senhora da Conceição plan of 1952. This typical, autonomous neighbourhood built under the dictatorship, with its ruralized basis that resisted metropolitan development, was originally located outside of the town, but is now part of the city. Third, the modern urban expansion to the west as a result of the Integrated Plan of Almada of 1972, which uncannily balances the violence of social housing with the idyllic, rural landscape. Fourth, the generic suburbanization of an increasingly densified and infrastructured metropolitan area that has conquered the whole territory, from the city centre to the peripheral suburban areas in the south.

Fig. 31-32. Paulo Catrica, photographs for *Almada: A Territory in Six Ecologies*, 2019. Courtesy of the artist.

Fig. 33-34. Paulo Catrica, photographs for *Almada: A Territory in Six Ecologies*, 2019. Courtesy of the artist.

NUNO ARTUR SILVA AND ANTÓNIO JORGE GONÇALVES, *AS AVENTURAS DE FILIPE SEEMS: ANA* (1993)

Cassiano Branco, one of Portugal's most important architects from the first half of the twentieth century, presented his most ambitious project in 1930. It was widely publicized in the general press at the time. However, the plan for the urbanization of the Costa da Caparica was never built. It was an exuberant and extraordinarily modern vision, echoing Le Corbusier's plans for Paris or the proposals for the Cittá Nuova by Antonio Sant'Elia, revealing Branco's interest in urban scale and the problems of urbanization; but it can also be considered as one of the great utopian projects of Portuguese architecture of the 1930s.

Presented as a single image of a tourist resort without permanent urban life, Branco's design for the Costa da Caparica also evokes António Ferro's Californian ideal. Ferro was responsible for the dictatorship's propaganda and envisioned this extensive beach as the Los Angeles that Europe lacked. Unlike the aristocratic Estoril and Cascais, the proposal to transform the Costa da Caparica was aimed at the masses – not a truly viable proposal from an economic point of view in Portugal during the early years of the Estado Novo. The plan was never built, but its image persisted in the collective memory of Lisbon's inhabitants.[13]

The only known drawing for this project was later appropriated, almost exactly from its *voile d'oiseau* point of view, in *Ana*, the first volume of the comic book series *As Aventuras de Filipe Seems*.[14]

In it, Ana Lógica, a photographer, goes looking for Filipe Seems, a private detective, who needs to find a girl just like her – the twin she saw in a photograph. This is a book with a dreamlike quality, especially in its portrayal of

Fig. 35. *Cassiano Branco, Costa da Caparica*: Praia Atlântica, aerial perspective, 1930. Source: Arquivo Municipal de Lisboa.

architecture, and specifically in the way in which it transfigures the Lisbon metropolitan area. Ana Lógica meets Cassiano on the beach.

As scriptwriter Nuno Artur Silva said in an interview, offering us coincidentally a beautiful way to end this brief series of Almada's representations:

> *'Lisbon (the bigger Lisbon, including the 'other margin') was a scenography ready to receive stories. A city with extraordinary potential. And there were stories to tell and images to draw . . . From this moment on, I wanted to do pop art. Collage, mixed media, crossings and overlappings. Everything comics allow, simple and immediate. To combine Borges' universe with Philip K. Dick. Combine the mythical past with futuristic visions. The Costa da Caparica presented here is the one of (modernist) Cassiano Branco (a project that was never built). All in a single moment of time.'*[15]

Fig. 36-37. Gonçalves, António Jorge, (drawings) and Nuno Artur Silva (script), *As Aventuras de Filipe Seems: Ana*, (Lisbon: Edições ASA, 1993), full-pages. Courtesy of the authors.

1 Maurice Mariaud (dir.), *Os Faroleiros*, 1922 [Film], 72'.

2 Daniel Alves (IHC) and Natália Constâncio (IELT), 'Atlas das Paisagens Literárias de Portugal Continental', https://litescape.ielt.fcsh.unl.pt, accessed 16 June 2023.

3 Arquivo Municipal de Lisboa, 'Nuno Barros da Silveira', https://arquivomunicipal3.cm-lisboa.pt/X-arqWEB/, accessed 16 June 2023.

4 Manuel Graça Dias and Egas José Vieira, *11 Cities: Projects 1995-2005* (Porto: Civilização, 2006).

5 Luís Santiago Baptista and Paula Melâneo (eds.), *Almada: Um Território em Seis Ecologias* (Almada: Câmara Municipal de Almada, 2020).

6 Nuno Artur Silva and António Jorge Gonçalves, *As Aventuras de Filipe Seems: Ana* (Lisbon: Edições ASA, 1993).

7 Batalha Centro de Cinema, 'The Arditti Quartet e Daniel Moreira: Os Faroleiros', https://www.batalhacentrodecinema.pt/program/the-arditti-quartet-e-daniel-moreira-os-faroleiros/, accessed 16 June 2023.

8 Teresa Barreto Borges (ed.), *Escritos sobre Cinema de João Bénard da Costa, Tomo I, Volume 4* (Lisbon: Cinemateca Portuguesa, 2021), 410-411.

9 Similar to the French term *canaille*.

10 IELT, 'Atlas of Literary Landscapes of Mainland Portugal', https://ielt.fcsh.unl.pt/en/portfolio/atlas-of-literary-landscapes-of-mainland-portugal/, accessed 16 June 2023.

11 Ignasi de Solá-Morales Rubió, 'Terrain Vague', in: Ignasi de Solá-Morales Rubió, *Anyplace* (Cambridge, MA: MIT Press, 1995), 118-125.

12 Graça Dias, *11 Cities*, op. cit. Manuel Graça Dias, op. cit., p. 148.

13 Notícias da Gandaia, 'Cassiano Branco 1930', https://gandaia.info/cassiano-branco-1930/, accessed 16 June 2023; Mar da Caparica, 'Sobre o projecto de Cassiano Branco', https://mar-da-costa.blogspot.com/2016/06/sobre-o-projecto-de-cassiano-branco.html, accessed 16 June 2023.

14 Nuno Artur Silva and António Jorge Gonçalves, op. cit.

15 Interview with Nuno Artur Silva by Anabela Mota Ribeiro, in: Publico, 'Filipe Seems, um rapaz de Lisboa', https://www.publico.pt/2009/11/11/culturaipsilon/noticia/filipe-seems-um-rapaz-de-lisboa-244928, accessed 16 June 2023.

Mapping the Fictional and the Physical City
The Spatiotemporal and Cultural Identity of Osijek, Croatia

Sonja Novak and Angeliki Sioli

Introduction

Osijek is the fourth largest city in Croatia with a population of about 100,000, including the surrounding suburbs. It is the largest city as well as the economic and cultural centre of eastern Croatia. It is located mostly on the right bank of the River Drava and has a rich, multicultural history, which is reflected in its contemporary cultural and urban identity. It is famous for the historical Fort Tvrđa as well as the European Avenue, the most representative street of Austro-Hungarian Secession architecture. The city's urban development has historically emerged from three locations: the fort or citadel Tvrđa, the Upper Town (Gornji Grad), and the Lower Town (Donji Grad), which were united in 1911 as a result of a regulation plan establishing one line along the Drava. This plan promoted the longitudinal development of Osijek's urban structure, making the river one of the most prominent elements of its identity.

When emphasized in literary texts, the changes in the built environment and the cityscape become elements of the cultural heritage and collective memory of the city and its population. Several literary texts that strongly cover and emphasize the spatial features of the city of Osijek have been published since the 1990s, when the city experienced severe changes in its spatial and cultural urban fabric because of the so-called 'Homeland War'. Vilma Vukelić's *Spuren der Vergangenheit* (A Past Rescued from Oblivion) and *In engen Grenzen* (Narrow Borders) are novels from the first half of the twentieth century, but were first published simultaneously in German and Croatian only by the 1990s, when war was raging in the city. At the same time, a series of urban movements arose. Their aim was to preserve the urban cultural fabric through a number of multimedia projects, including visual materials (photographs and videos) as well as journalistic and literary texts, thematizing the city of Osijek. Among the noteworthy literary texts that have been published since then are the historiographic novel *Unterstadt* (Lower Town) by contemporary Croatian author Ivana Šojat in 2009, Jasna Horvats' novel *Bizarij* from the same year, a series of prose texts by Nenad Rizvanović titled *Sat pjevanja* (Singing Lesson) in 2006, *Trg Lava Mirskog* (Lav Mirski Square) in 2010 and *Trg slobode* (Liberty Square) in 2022, Žarko Plevnik's *Crveni fićo* (The Red Fiat) in 2014, Milovan Tatarin's *Zvijezda baruna Beckersa: Sentimentalna povijest Nutarnjeg grada* (Baron Beckers' Star: A Sentimental History of the Inner City) in 2019, and many more, all of them taking place in Osijek.

This chapter will examine how selected literary texts integrate 'real' urban spaces into their fictional fabric, creating new meaning and (re)shaping the cultural identity of a city that has throughout history been perceived as peripheral, provincial and secondary to its adjacent European metropolises.[1] Many of the abovementioned texts rely on historiography to reiterate the referential,[2] as the descriptive and representative function of the text, but, at the same time, amplify the aesthetics of the described urban spaces, creating a multiplicity of city images that accentuate its individuality, specific lifestyle, identity, image and symbolism. The theoretical foundation of this chapter relies on Deborah Stevenson's notions of the physical, real and imagined city,[3] on Darran Anderson's argument that 'we inhabit our actual cities through . . . personal mythologies',[4] and on Roland Barthes' *Semiology and Urbanism* as well as Lefebvre's notion of space as a social product.Paraphrasing Kevin Lynch, Roland Barthes states that

> *there exists in every city, from the moment when it is truly inhabited by man, and made by him, that fundamental rhythm of signification which is opposition, alternation and juxtaposition of marked and of unmarked elements. Finally, there is a last conflict between signification and reality itself, at least between signification and that reality of objective geography, the reality of maps.*[5]

This opposition and split arise from the difference between the experience of signification and the objective data. This can, in the case of a literary text and the representations of cities in it, be mirrored in the split between the imagined, written city, 'def[ying] time, space and identity', and the real city, which is 'soundly located and constructed within personal biography and the physical world'.[6] The representations of real cities in literature are indeed imagined cities, yet they tend to intersect with the real in that we locate them on our imaginary maps, since it is part of human nature to look for recognizable patterns and relations in what is described and to search for anchors to confirm our own position within a social context. Reading the city as a text and the text as a city produces a multitude of mental maps of the city – both the real and the imagined one – that depend on our personal experience, knowledge, background and connection with it. We 'create cognitive maps of places and spaces according to a vast range of different visual cues associated subconsciously with our own and shared experiences',[7] because 'we inhabit our actual cities through these personal mythologies, walking the ghost trajectories of

Fig. 1. Ornamental details of houses that are falling slowly apart, 'rotting quietly and unnoticed' in downtown Osijek.
Photo: Angeliki Sioli, August 2022.

Fig. 2. Osijek Train Station under reconstruction.
Photo: Angeliki Sioli, August 2022.

earlier events'.[8] In this process we are again contributing to the creation of another layer of socially produced space in Lefebvre's terms.[9]

The city as a narrative is not just 'a moderately polysemic, frugally plural, and partially closed text', which can be conquered via the act of reading (the conquered city as a *texte lisible* (readerly text), but is in fact a *texte scriptible* (writerly text), 'eternally polysemous, triumphally plural, perfectly open'.[10] That is to say, the real city does not exist independently because it is also a socially constructed space, in Lefebvre's terms, but it is rather a construct of various discourses, codifications and significations, very much like a literary text. In the interplay of the city as text and the text representing a city, a multilayered identity is further formed by the subjects that come into contact with it – authors, readers, protagonists, inhabitants – all of them weaving a complex spatiotemporal tapestry of the city's everchanging and vibrant life.

Analysis

The methodology that will be used in this chapter is a close-reading analysis of Vukelić's, Šojat's, Horvat's and Rizvanović's texts, followed by the (re)tracing of the city's walks, mapped according to selected excerpts in order to explore the poetologically assigned meaning(s) of urban spaces described in them.[11] The city will be read as a text and the text as a city. The aim of the chapter is to map out the fictional and the physical city narrated through different textual cartographies that integrate or synthesize the contemporary urban cultural identity map of Osijek. The analysis will show that there are certain reference points that serve as landmarks in mapping out this identity. On the one hand, references to the political and social history of the city during the turmoil of different wars, which caused huge changes in the urban and social fabric (including its multi-ethnic heritage, which is evident in its former sociolect known as *Essekerisch*). On the other are the city's infrastructure, architecture, and its strong connection to nature, which is reflected in the city's multitude of green spaces, such as park facilities and the connection to the river. In parallel, images from Osijek today weave an additional narrative along the narrative of the authors. The images are not meant to be illustrations of the literary excerpts, but rather impressions from the city in its current state that touch on conditions and elements mentioned in the novels.

Social and Political History

Vilma Vukelić's publication *A Past Rescued from Oblivion* is the earliest novel selected for this analysis and can be described as both an autobiographical novel and an urban chronicle of the city of Osijek, mirroring its life at the beginning of the twentieth century in terms of its architecture, infrastructure, spatial positioning within the Austro-Hungarian Empire (as peripheral, provincial), education system, cuisine, language and ethnicity, politics, gender roles, etcetera. It is a retrospective of the author's own life as a young girl and woman living in this provincial town. She refers to different living conditions at different stages of history, evoking the two World Wars as well as an almost ethnographic depiction of the different living conditions of various social groups in the very multiethnic and very multicultural community of Osijek. The memoir goes all the way back to 1904 and even in the description of her childhood years, the author captures the looming social and political turmoil:

> *. . Melanka was laughing at my state of despair. With a derisive expression on her face and in a superior tone of voice, she declared, 'Croatia is not your homeland, even if you write it out a hundred times! You may be a good pupil, but you will still not go to heaven, but to the place where only wailing and gnashing of teeth could be expected. The catechist told us that in class today!'*
>
> *Growing up in the protected environment of my home, I had been unfamiliar with anti-Semitism. I made good friends at school and in the Long Courtyard and we got along perfectly well at all times. I was, of*

Fig. 3. Contemporary realities juxtaposed with past façade elements on Županijska ul (County Street), Osijek. Photo: Angeliki Sioli, August 2022.

Fig. 4. The embankment of the River Drava in the Upper Town, where Vilma Vukelić, narrator and protagonist of *Spuren der Vergangenheit*, used to spend many hours as a child. Photo: Angeliki Sioli, August 2022.

> *course, aware of my Jewishness because I had separate religion classes and did not participate in the religious practices intended for Catholic children . . . I felt entirely at home among my friends and behaved the same as any other child. There was no doubt that Croatia was my homeland. That was what our textbooks were saying. My father also used to say, 'Every person has to love the country in which he was born and in which he lives.' I sang the anthem 'Lijepa naša' . . . in unison with all the others and was annoyed if anyone maintained that Nikola Šubić Zrinski was Hungarian!*[12]

The quote reveals the complexity of the social and political history of the multiethnic community of Osijek at the beginning of the twentieth century. It was comprised of many ethnic groups living in the periphery of the Austro-Hungarian Empire, which could not yet be described as nationalities at the time, but were nonetheless distinct from each other according to the languages they used – German, Slavic, Hungarian and many more – or the religions they followed – Catholic, Jewish, Protestant, Orthodox, etcetera. It was a time of an increasing national awareness, on the one hand, and the expansion of imperialist politics, on the other. This led to great societal changes such as a changing attitude towards the German language, which was until then used as the official language for administration and culture, but was being pushed out with Serbo-Croatian becoming more dominant. Due to historical events surrounding Osijek, such as the resettling of Slavonia by different ethnic groups from central Europe (Austria, Germany, Bohemia, Hungary, etcetera) after the invasion of the Turks in the eighteenth century, multiethnicity has long been one of the city's characteristics. The phenomenon of a coexistence of multiple ethnic groups that remain distinct reached a certain hybrid level in social terms. This means that in the city's past it was impossible to determine a clear ethnic affiliation of a great deal of its inhabitants. This was partly due to the fact that nations were relatively illusive terms at the turn of the century as well as the fact that the inhabitants at that time were usually bilingual, coming from mixed marriages, and were quite mobile in terms of residence over the course of their lives and within the Empire. Such was the case for Vilma Vukelić in her real life, but also for Oto, the protagonist of Rizvanović's novel *Sat pjevanja*, in which, written in the 1980s, the multiethnic history of the city is described as follows:

> *Outside, above the cherry plum trees, the clouds were hovering as peacefully as if it were just daybreak. Oto was on his favourite route towards the old post office and from there on towards the Healthcare Centre and the residential area . . . The Jewish and German citizens used to live in these houses that were now rotting quietly and unnoticed. Oto even knew some kids with Jewish family names, or maybe those were German family names, maybe Jewish-German, most of those family names were difficult to distinguish anyway; they were so similar to each other, if not practically the same.*[13]

Furthermore, Jasna Horvat's *Bizarij*, in addition to the history of the city and the region, also puts forward the Esseker sociolect as an integral part of a culture that is now gone, as nobody uses this sociolect anymore. It was a mixture of spoken languages – German, Hungarian, Yiddish, Serbo-Croatian – reflecting the hybridity of Osijek's population in the nineteenth and the first half of the twentieth century. By incorporating it into her novel, Horvat opens up an archive of the city's memories that now speak – in Barthes' terms – through the novel's characters:

> *– Habidiere! Reidnc esekeriš? [Habe ich die Ehre! Reden Sie essekerisch? / It's an honour! Do you speak Essekerisch?]*
> *– Eseka sajn fajni lajt, fua fi acih joan veat kana kšajt. [Esseker sind feine Leute, vor dem vierzigsten Lebensjahr wird keiner gescheit. / The Essekers are very nice people, nobody comes to their senses before they are forty.]*[14]

Today, even though Essekerisch is not used any more, there are still active Jewish, Hungarian and German minorities in Osijek and the relations with

Austria and Hungary as well as its Central European heritage are nurtured through cultural and educational institutions and events, making up a significant feature of the city's social and cultural life.

As opposed to Vukelić's memoirs, which bear witness to societal changes, Ivana Šojat's *Unterstadt* can be described as a historiographical novel, critically reflecting on the city's history over the course of the twentieth century, especially its political history in the depiction of the turmoil during both Worlds Wars and the Homeland War in the 1990s. Šojat begins by describing the aftermath of the Homeland War in the 1990s in Osijek:

> *Near the station, there was no longer the supermarket in which football fans and students drowned in their beers before leaving for college or returning home, and then staggered and vomited in the trains. Although I had seen it burning on the TV, hit by multiple rocket launchers, I guess, I was still stunned by the void, by the absence of something that used to be there. I stopped for a moment, laid my suitcase down on the cobbled pavement made from yellow, smooth bricks and stared at that void in space.*[15]

In taking the reader on a journey through her family's past and thus through the past of the city, the protagonist Katarina describes recollections of another war that has greatly influenced the city. This time she explains the events from the perspective of her grandparents, Peter and Klara, who lived through the Second World War:

> *It was on Good Friday, 11 April 1941, when Klara was walking with her three-year-old son Antun and passed by the hotel Tomislav, towards the Chapel of Our Lady of the Snow, that war came to Osijek . . . the sky was clear . . . Klara just stood there. She didn't know how to feel, what she was feeling. Everything had changed, turned completely upside-down, as if she had, instead of in her bed, woken*

> *up in the middle of the night, thirsty, in her backyard, in complete darkness.*[16]

Klara's feelings of helplessness, confusion and disbelief arise from the fact that the war had changed not only her life, the life of her family, but also the life of several generations of Osijek's inhabitants, and is indicative of the bigger changes in the social and historical dimensions of the city that follow. The following quote from the novel stands as a site of memory for the grand synagogue in Osijek, which was burned down during the Second World War:

> *And [Peter], as if he stubbornly persevered in his intention to inflame her undefined feeling of disgust, one day, by the end of April, on his way back from his office, he saw the grand synagogue go up in flames in the Komitats-Gasse. He stopped and watched as the high flames licked and then devoured the house of worship of the Jewish, but also in a way, of his own God. He stared into the theatre building which was only two entrances away from the synagogue. Ironically, the theatre would in only two weeks' time stage [Julius] Horst's 'Heaven on Earth'.*[17]

Even though the novel *Sat pjevanja* mainly focuses on the topic of the musical preferences of the main character who, as opposed to his family's expectations and wishes, prefers modern and pop music over classical, its plot is set in Osijek, and reflects its urban life during the 1980s.

The descriptions of the city dominate the first chapter, but are very much present throughout the novel, depicting the city's cultural and urban past and present. Rizvanović's protagonist Oto reflects on the city's history as well, in which the wars have played a major part:

> *When sunbathing on such a sunny day, it felt impossible to Oto that anyone could have ever suffered; it was unthinkable that people and children were*

Fig. 5. Old buildings abandoned in Osijek's Lower Town. Photo: Angeliki Sioli, August 2022.

Fig. 6. Different architectural styles blending in the backdrop of a dramatic afternoon sky. Photo: Angeliki Sioli, August 2022.

> *taken by force, tortured, and killed. Thoughts like these melted away in the rays of the sun, but he wanted to remain aware of them, among the tall buildings and high windows. Maybe it was the Jewish and German spirits returning to have their afternoon tea that had been waiting for them since the day they were taken away. Osijek has often been nothing but a giant railway station, where people and things were coming and going, quickly and forever, until it finally became a city of ghosts when the number of those who went away or were missing surpassed the number of those who stayed. Those who were banished from their homes would later think how lucky they must have been to be able to escape, especially those who did not end up in one of the concentration camps. But they would rarely return after the wars. They were afraid of everything they might find here and they didn't have anywhere to return to anyway. Even though the houses and the buildings were the same, painfully the same, it wasn't the same city anymore.*[18]

Similar to Šojat, Rizvanović also refers to the Second World War and the events surrounding it, such as the forceful deportation of thousands of Jews from Osijek to concentration camps during the war, but also by referring to the *Vertribung* (expulsion) of Germans after the War. Written in the 2000s, but set in the 1980s, Rizvanović's novel symbolically circles around another very traumatic period in the city's history without mentioning it: the Homeland War of the 1990s. The reader, aware of this war, recognizes that history will yet again repeat itself in Oto's and the city's lifetime.

Infrastructure and (Landscape) Architecture

The architecture described by Vukelić in *Spuren der Vergangenheit* dates from the nineteenth century, when the most famous street in Osijek was built, the so-called European Avenue, which is the longest Art Nouveau street in this part of Europe with architectural influences mainly from Vienna and, later, Budapest, especially around the time of the Croatian-Hungarian Settlement in the 1850s and 1860s. The architecture mirrors the social and political position of Osijek as a provincial city, as opposed to Vienna and Budapest, which were the two capitals of the Austro-Hungarian Empire and the main sources of architectural influence. It was only after the Croatian-Hungarian settlement of 1868 that, alongside Hungarian architects such as Ferenc Pfaff, who was the chief architect of the Hungarian National Railway and designed the railway station and post office in Osijek, the Croatian architect Janko Holjac was commissioned to design the courthouse in Osijek. It is precisely because of these politically nuanced changes in the city's development that Osijek today has such a multicultural architectural tradition and cultural heritage. A complex political situation created a variety of architectural styles that are both Central European in their origin and influence, but also inherently local with strong influences from different regional centres.

Šojat's novel *Unterstadt* also strongly underlines the city's infrastructure and architecture, with an emphasis on the lower part of the town still recognizable today:

> *We walked very slowly towards the cemetery in the Lower Town. The cemetery was located on an elevated part of the sandy riverbank, where the River Drava meanders right and where the winds during winter time howl and scream like demons, like the damned souls in hell. Yes, that's what the old townspeople call this place: hell. The Austrian Crown had ordered a cemetery to be erected there, far away from the town at that time. The dead had fled away from the living towards hell, but the city grew and flooded over them like the tides.*[19]

Additionally, Šojat's protagonist Katarina critically reflects on the contemporary attitude towards the cultural heritage dating from Vukelić's time. In her description of the school that she used to attend, Katarina expresses her disbelief at the level of neglect of the architecture that was destroyed in the war and never rebuilt:

First, I set out towards the school . . . I stopped in the middle of Crkvena Street in utter horror. My mouth wide open . . . I stood there in a frenzy and stared at the building that was damaged by shrapnel shells and moisture . . . The people got used to the ruins, to the derelict state, I almost screamed that sentence to myself. In Western Europe, in the civilized world, people organize seminars about the Secession period, they preserve the Secession façades and building fronts as national treasures, and we let it collapse on passers-by, I continued thinking. I was horrified. I was still just standing there as if completely dug in, squeezing my fists and lips, and staring at my old school building. Left only half-conscious by this horror, I tried to get inside this derelict, grey, diseased building. I couldn't. I turned around full circle, tilted my head back, and the street spun around me like a merry-go-round, like a grey roller with only a colourful spot here and there. I was appalled. My face wrinkled like a clenched fist. Terrible: two centuries old, grandiose houses of former craftsmen, traders, lawyers, doctors, professors from the Lower Town as well as warm homes of people thanks to whom Essek [the Austro-Hungarian name for Osijek], even though it was geographically an 'outhouse', was actually a town of true Central European spirit. And now it was all falling apart in front of our eyes.
The skin of these buildings was peeling off, they seemed disoriented, as if they couldn't stand up straight any longer. Blackened from the moisture, resembling old folks with bad backs and aches all over, their roofs bent and black. Probably from the moisture and the financial powerlessness of those whose heads they were still kind of keeping safe. . . . Misery, I was hit right in the middle of my forehead by misery, bluntly, as by a rounded rock. But this misery didn't come from everywhere equally, in unison, but from the houses that were left to rot there so that someone would someday buy an empty plot rather than a house, a burial plot from which another flashy, insanely kitschy construction will arise as an emblem of the arrogance of the nouveau riche*. Squeezed in-between the derelict elderly brick buildings, there were now grotesque red and yellow brick-covered formations with plaster lions erected at the gate entrances to their tiny front yards, with*

> ***poor imitations of disgusting royal pillars at the front doors and in front of rich, heavy drapes, resembling theatre curtains in the front windows.***[20]

On the other hand, Osijek is often nicknamed the 'greenest' city in Croatia and it has more parks than squares. There are 17 parks in Osijek, among which the most famous are the Sakuntala Park, Petar Krešimir IV Park, King Tomislav Park, King Držislav Park and many more. It has the longest river promenade and the biggest zoo in terms of surface area in Croatia. The city is stretched out along the river, which connects the three parts of town: the Upper Town, Tvrđa and the Lower Town. Jasna Horvat, in her novel *Bizarij*, describes 'how lucky Osijek was to have been missed by the Danube by some miracle, but instead to have been spat on in the middle of its forehead by the Drava, a river as whimsical as an Italian opera, so very prone to treacherous whirlpools and flooding.'[21]

Šojat describes the green past of Osijek as well when she writes how Katarina's great-grandparents Viktorija and Rudolf

> ***. . . went steady for a whole year and always walked hand in hand in the green City Garden where they had met for the first time. Every Saturday, they would go dancing in the ballroom situated at the entrance of the Osijek 'Schönbrunn',***[22] ***as the townspeople used to flatteringly call their most luxurious park. Fine ladies and gentlemen, who attended the balls organized here, would arrive in their own carriages. The future Mr and Mrs Meier were miles away and 'off the beaten track' from here, as they had to take the horse tram.***[23]

Peter and Klara, Katarina's grandparents in Šojat's novel, also recollect the city's strong connection to the outdoors, the greenery and nature:

> ***When they didn't feel like going to the theatre, where every season would host and stage up to 40 new performances, Peter and Klara would***

> ***walk hand in hand, slowly to the City Garden, listen to regular concerts of military and firemen orchestras, dance at balls, watch chess and marksmen tournaments, or simply wander around the spacious park and paths . . . Peter would sweettalk Klara on their walks, all the way from Eselsberg [Donkey's Hill] in the City Garden to a part with sitting benches, from where they could see the former Majuri, today's Neustadt.***[24]

The Pejačević Well (*Secesijski zdenac*) is located on the riverbank, next to the promenade, placed very centrally and represents one of the sites often frequented by passers-by on the busy promenade.

Conclusion

Urban space cannot be merely perceived as a product of architecture and urban planning along with the everyday life of its inhabitants over the course of time. It is rather inevitably constructed as a multifaceted and multilayered entity, whose identity is also defined by the narratives of its integral tangible and intangible parts. The tangible city is the physical, 'real' architecture and built environment, while the intangible parts are the flow of time, the utilization and appropriation by its inhabitants, the meaning(s) they assign to sites in the city as well as the culture in its broadest sense that they create and the everyday lives that they lead, and to which the urban environment is exposed. In this sense, it truly becomes a wholesome social construct – in Lefebvre's terms – and maintains the basic dialectic rhythm of signification through narratives and its urban reality – in Barthes' terms.

Vilma Vukelić writes about the three main parts of the city of Osijek, which are the Upper Town, the Citadel Tvrđa and the Lower Town, while Ivana Šojat emphasizes the Lower Town, Nenad Rizvanović describes the Upper Town for the most part, and Jasna Horvat focuses on different parts of the city throughout its history, but also on its broader surroundings beyond the city limits. In addition to covering the geographical, spatial scope of the city, the novels unveil different time periods in the city's history as well. In doing so, they map out a broad sociocultural and historical-political panorama of the city, often as a critical reflection on all the major elements defining its identity in the form of textual maps, with spaces to employ one's own imagined city where the real has not artistically been mapped out.

1 Budapest is only three hours away by car and Belgrade two and a half hours.

2 According to Roman Jakobson, there are six functions of language, among which there is a referential function that refers to the context outside of language, which is the extratextual context that has a certain value attributed to it (true or false, or real or unreal).

3 Deborah Stevenson, *Cities and Urban Cultures* (Maidenhead: Open University Press, 2003).

4 Darran Anderson, *Imaginary Cities* (London: Influx Press, 2019), 236.

5 Roland Barthes, 'Semiology and the Urban', in: Neil Leach (ed.), *Rethinking Architecture: A Reader in Cultural Theory* (New York: Routledge, 1997), 158-172: 160.

6 Stevenson, *Cities and Urban Cultures*, op. cit. (note 3), 113.

7 James Clifford Kent, *Aesthetics and the Revolutionary City: Real and Imagined Havana* (Cham: Palgrave Macmillan, 2019), 1.

8 Anderson, *Imaginary Cities*, op. cit. (note 4), 236.

9 Henri Lefebvre, *The Production of Space* (Oxford: Blackwell, 1991), 26.

10 Džerald Prins (Gerald Prince), *Naratološki rečnik* (Belgrade: Službeni Glasnik, 2011), 32.

11 The term 'poetologically' refers to a specific poetics of an author and the way an author constructs their literary texts.

12 Vilma Vukelić, *A Past Rescued from Oblivion* (Victoria: FriesenPress, 2020), 71.

13 Nenad Rizvanović, *Sat pjevanja* (Zagreb: Profil, 2009), 15. Translations of quotes from Rizvanović's, Šojat's, and Horvat's novels have been done by the authors for the purposes of this paper.

14 Jasna Horvat, *Bizarij* (Zagreb: Ljevak, 2009), 39.

15 Ivana Šojat-Kuči, *Unterstadt* (Zaprešić: Fraktura, 2009), 9-11

16 Ibid., 198.

17 Ibid., 203.

18 Rizvanović, *Sat* pjevanja, op. cit. (note 13), 15.

19 Šojat Kuči, *Unterstadt*, op. cit. (note 15), 304.

20 Ibid., 216-218.

21 Horvat, *Bizarij*, op. cit. (note 14), 23.

22 Schönbrunn in Vienna, as one of the biggest and most beautiful parks in Europe, was at the time the ideal example of landscape architecture in an urban environment.

23 Šojat Kuči, *Unterstadt*, op. cit. (note 15), 28.

24 Ibid., 140.

A Travel Captured in Correspondence

Preparations for the Training School The Planned, the Unplanned, and Everything in Between, Kamza and Tirana, Albania

Dorina Pllumbi and Willie Vogel

The COST training school *The Planned, the Unplanned, and Everything in Between* took place in Tirana and Kamza on 24, 30 and 31 March 2023. Its topic stems from the DNA of the two hosting cities, their commonalities, but more evidently, their contrast and contradictions. Tirana developed organically until 1920 when it was declared the capital of Albania. Since then, planning ambitions to give the city an official face started to appear as attempts to represent the country, expressing the ideologies of the political regimes that Albania has gone through. Planning projects for Tirana during the rule of Ahmet Zogu (1922-1939) prepared the stage for the colonial projects during the Italian occupation (1939-1943), which sought to give the capital a Western appearance. The communist (state-socialist) regime (1944-1991) envisioned Tirana as the 'city for the new [socialist] man' and contributed extensively to giving it a new character. Today, three decades after the fall of the communist regime and with a new neoliberal regime consolidating, the city resembles a palimpsest of erasure and overwriting, where visible and invisible, planned and unplanned traces overlap.[1] Kamza stands in complete contrast to Tirana: it is a city constructed by its inhabitants during the last three decades of political transition that followed the collapse of the communist regime. It was co-constructed as a result of a migratory wave of families from remote areas in the northeastern part of Albania that settled on the outskirts of Tirana.

While Kamza is probably unknown to most of the participants, Tirana has actually started to appear in the architecture media as the city is transformed by recent projects involving renowned architects, including MVRDV, OMA, Stefano Boeri, Archea Associati and BIG. The ambition for a Bilbao Effect has arrived in this long-forgotten city in the Western Balkans. For this training school, however, we are more interested in other stories, the ones that reveal the capacity of minor agencies to claim and arrange everyday life in these cities.

This exploration of how the planned and unplanned intersect within these two cities, how these concepts shape each other, gives a sense of the power relations that enable this process. As a method of exploration we combine psychogeographic walks and ethnographic film. During an intense research-creation process of *embodied exploration*, we immersed ourselves collectively in the local realities in these cities, with the aim of crafting stories of *commoning practices* and *material unrest*.

Willie is the only one in the organizing team who was not born and raised in Albania. She is visiting Tirana, Kamza and the surrounding areas for the first time, and will be staying there for a week.[2] The aim of her visit is to test the method of video-making to capture the dynamics of urban encounters. The focus would be a reading of the *material unrest* in/on these terrains, a concept proposed by Dorina as a characteristic of the current fast pace of spatial and material changes in the area. Dorina, who used to live in Tirana and now is located in the Netherlands, initiated the training school and has been studying these fast-changing cities over the years. By sharing our daily correspondence with the reader here, we want to transmit a glimpse of Willie's encounter with the two cities and situations of thoughts exchanged between the two of us as organizers of the training school. Diana Malaj, who is a research and co-founder of the activist Grupi ATA based in Kamza, joined the organizing team of the training initiative subsequent to Willie's visit and the exchange of communications is documented in this correspondence.

Date_22.12.2022 _ Arrival

Willie [W] Dear Dorina, I have arrived in Tirana, your city. I took a taxi from the airport to the apartment. Driving on an empty motorway with flat grassland on both sides and mountains in the back, I had a conversation with the driver. He doesn't live in Tirana, it's too expensive and there's too much pollution according to him. You warned me about the pollution, and after settling down and going out to have something to eat, I immediately have to agree. Also, the construction sounds you mentioned are very prevailing. Almost everywhere you walk, buildings and roads are under construction, and the air is thick with cement dust and exhaust fumes. There are few main access roads in the city centre, and these are always full of cars. In their text 'Tirana Visible and Invisible', Rosen and Musaraj refer to the materialisation of the city as the *betonizim* by the 'concrete maffia'.[3]

Dorina [D] Dear Willie, good to hear you arrived in Tirana. Subconsciously, I feel the urge to explain the city to you who sees it with the foreigner's eye, so you do not judge it right away. But I will refrain from that as I want you to have the full freedom of your own experience of encountering Tirana. It is the place I miss the most while living abroad. It is true that Tirana gives its inhabitants a hard time, but many cities do, right? You will see that there is a continuous struggle to improve, the aspiration and the energy is there. In the process of transitioning, we celebrate the gains and mourn the losses. I know this will sound pretty romanticized, but the concern among many that have Tirana in their heart is of the city losing its soul.

[W] The first encounters with the city reminded me of Istanbul, maybe not so odd considering its history, right? In Tirana, the bustle on the streets late at night, the many coffee shops, how packed it is, but also the city layout seems to be an amalgamation of a bazaar city and a Mediterranean culture of living outside. The streets of the neighbourhood Don Bosko contain quite some similar looking concrete apartment blocks. When were they built? How was the city developed in this area and similar ones? Tomorrow I plan to go to Kamza, the adjacent city, where your friend Diana will show me around.

[D] I totally understand flashback memories coming to you from Istanbul. Indeed, in Tirana you see a mixture of influences. The inner city was an Ottoman-influenced town with its bazaar, but in the *mahalla* (neighbourhoods), the inner roads between the houses were not curated like the façade streets. The inhabitants would give much more attention to the interior of their wall-fenced yards, which were usually semi-private spaces of gathering; they can be considered commoning spaces in the city. On the other hand, the living in the street indeed comes from the Mediterranean characteristic. Here, influences from the East and the West entangle. As you know, Albania had an immense influence from Italian culture as well, not only during its occupation, but also during the totalitarian regime that followed. People could listen to Italian radio stations through frequencies that would enter the territory, which had a huge impact on Albanians who wanted to keep some connection and dream of the Western world. *Xhiro (la passegatta / strolling)*, as it is called in Albanian, was also an important ritual during totalitarianism, and interestingly enough, the place for it to happen was the main colonial boulevard, which was built in times of Italian occupation. The Albanian writer

Ardian Vehbiu has written extensively both about the influence of the radio during times of isolation, but also about the ritual of walking on the main boulevard.[4] Also, New York-based Albanian historian Elidor Mëhilli in his piece called 'Socialism with a Fascist Façade', he explains how the monumental 'fascist buildings' of the boulevard were suitable for the totalitarian state-socialist regime that followed.[5] I will propose these texts as readings for our training school. During the training school, Arba Bekteshi will talk about the culture of walking in the city, and she will explain how she used it as an exploratory method in her own work.

Instead, the area of Don Bosko where you are staying, as many other areas outside of what is known as the (inner) ring, were urbanized after the socialist regime collapsed and when Tirana expanded because many people were free to move and to live in the city. At first, mostly one-family houses appeared, and then apartment buildings, or apartment blocks, took over.

[W] It is wonderful to read your affection for your city. It is something I could read through the line of the contemporary poet Lleshanaku (2018). Although she does not write specifically about Tirana, some of her writings helped me to understand the ambiguous affection towards your city and country. For example, in 'Cities' she writes about how every city is 'more or less the same', but then continues with specificities regarding her own experiences.[6] What comes through is that although there are similarities, each sameness is different by details of the lived experience built with historical and social layers.

Date _ 23.12.2022 _Kamza

[W] I travelled by foot through the self-made settlement of Kamza. Some of the houses are big and spacious, yet most of them remain unfinished. A well-known example are the outside staircases as unrealized dreams of parents wanting their house to grow along with the family, vertically, stacked on top of eachother (Fig. 1). On the main streets, connecting Bathore – one of the neighbourhoods – to the centre of Kamza, I found many little shops selling different building parts and materials. From all sizes of sinks to second-hand window frames, everything you could imagine to build your house with, is available in these small shops. It is an interesting phenomenon, as they are not only tapping into the common pool of resources and recycling them, it also gives agency to the inhabitants since they can extend, change and adapt their house the way they wish. It prompted me to think through an alternative, playful aesthetic in which the innovative, practical and communal effort weigh much more than coherence, alignment or proportion (to name just a few aesthetical criteria we use to value architecture). It reminds me of the plea by architect and educator Jeremy Till in which he warns that architecture as a practice is ruled by specialist artisans who set up their own problems by creating static objects rather than performing a much more needed fluid practice. He states that: 'The creative brief is about negotiating a new set of social relations, it is about juxtapositions of actions and activities, it is about the possibility to think outside the norm, in order to project new spatial, and hence social, conditions.'[7]

[D] These small shops that sell tools, building parts or accessories are ubiquitous, and stand along with grocery stores, cafés, barber and tailor shops. Construction in Kamza is an everyday activity that merges with life itself. To live in Kamza still feels like living on a terrain under construction, where everyone participates in its making, although it has been illegal and prohibited by law since 2014 to construct without permission. ALUIZNI (The Agency for Legalization, Urbanization and Integration of Informal Areas and Buildings) was a governmental agency that used areal photographs of the entire territory of the Republic of Albania to understand when the construction was made in order to legalize it or not. The first aerial photographs were taken in the year 1994, and later in 1999, 2001 and 2007. Although as a process it might sound fair on

Fig. 1. Self-made home. Photo: Willie Vogel, Kamza, Albania, 2022.

paper, the legalization of buildings has often been arbitrary, and used as a tool to capitalize on electoral votes, often through unmet promises. The banning of construction has operated in waves, as the state has sometimes applied strict rules from fines up to imprisonment for construction without permission, and sometimes has tolerated the construction before the elections. The use of aerial photography by the state has also influenced the form and process of construction. As you might have noticed in Kamza, some of the houses have their roofs completed, so the house looks finished in the aerial photography, whereas the construction inside the houses is actually still ongoing. Of course, the application for legalization was not only dependent on the aerial view, but other photos of the house would be required to be submitted by the owners. Those extra elements would be easier to be substituted or negotiated with the state officials at some other moment, which often would be the start of a negotiation through corruption.

The aspiration of *becoming* is part of the landscape, although the agency of the inhabitants has shrunk considerably and the time of full autonomy of communities and families over the territory is coming to an end. Small-scale constructions are in Kamza's DNA, but upon closer observation it is possible to read the role of the state in the process, often not as an entity that wants to improve the life of the citizens, but as a superstructure that operates with the purpose of regaining control over the territory, while in a way becoming a threatening force.[8] The dilemma is whether this newly configured state will recognize the struggle and the capacities of the communities to self-organize and create a city from scratch, or reinforce the fabricated stigma on these areas. Unfortunately, so far, we have seen the latter happening, when those in power label these areas as illegal, abusive, cancerous, informal, therefore keeping the inhabitants outside of legal rights.[9]

I'm curious, why did you start your exploration in Kamza and not Tirana? Usually it's the other way around.

[W] My start of the exploration from the peripheral areas rather than from the centre is related to my interest in communal living, especially in relation to material resources, which is often more explicit in these areas. For quite a long time now I've been interested in the materials used to build urban settlements. Why are certain materials standard and others abandoned? How is the fabrication and organization behind these materials structured? In a way the material assemblages of a city express the cultural, political, economic and environmental structures of society. By thinking through assemblages, through the many networks material holds, we can maybe better understand what 'writes' the city. It's like how Anna Tsing follows one specific mushroom, but by doing so unravels world politics, global environmental issues and cultural specificities.[10] You told me that after the fall of the communist regime people from all over Albania moved towards the capital with the prospect of finding economic luck. Since the government was not prepared for this large migration, people had to organize themselves. Kamza is one of the great examples of this effort. Cow stables were transformed into human homes, as your friend Diana told and showed me. I wanted to see this phenomenon with my own eyes. Also because it has been criticised a lot by, among others, West European architects operating in Tirana. The well-known Belgium office 51N4E called this a 'falling victim to cancerous illegal settlements. People were building everywhere: on rooftops, in courtyards, parks and riverbeds'.[11] With these kinds of stigmas I can only imagine gruesome futures.

[D] Exactly. There is a lack of recognition of inhabitants creating things themselves, their own attempts to improve their material conditions, the way that communities are created along with the co-creation of an urban settlement – Kamza became the fifth biggest city in Albania.

It is remarkable that these urban formations, which emerged in a time when the state was almost absent, were labelled as illegal. A problem that comes with this labelling and reproducing a stigma, defining them as ugly, disastrous, an anomaly, is that it shows how the professionalization of our (architecture and planning) disciplines is becoming detached from the material culture of the people and communities they are supposed to serve. This is indeed easily recognizable in Kamza, when the inhabitants, besides having to arrange their lives without any institutional support, also had to cope with this stigma, and a lack of professional interest in their needs. Instead of acknowledging the capacity and the situated knowledge that these communities produce and operate with to be able to create these settlements, instead of looking into this immense capacity and empowering it, the professional looks at such forms of living with contempt. This is a widespread problem that is not only encountered in Albania, and in general the issue is kept outside of the discipline of architecture.[12] Now, within academia, we are hopefully speaking about changing the mindset and seeking the cooperation of our discipline with other disciplines that study society from a cultural point of view, like anthropology or cultural studies. This will help us as architects and planners to connect better with reality.

[W] What surprised me was the antagonism of the young inhabitants of the neighbourhood. For example, I had a conversation with a young guy, aged 12 or so, and while he was standing next to his grandmother who made such an effort to build and sustain their community, he told me that he disliked his house and expressed his wish to move abroad. Something common in these neighbourhoods where there is an extensive migration to England. People dangerously cross the North Sea in small boats to try to get asylum or use the registration period to work and earn some money to bring back home. In almost all families there is one member who moved abroad. Yet, those who stayed had a robust, powerful attitude and worked to improve their country from within.

[D] As an Albanian that has emigrated herself, I understand the inner call to take that path as an escape route. Many have left, but the connection to your family, your culture, to your place is still very strong. Those houses you see in Kamza and other areas in Tirana, for example the 5 Maji neighbourhood along the river, are a material witness of this connection. Most of them were built with money earned abroad. These areas are a materialization of many sacrifices. And as belonging to a diasporic country, that's how each of us contributes with their own 'brick' to construct something, a house for the family, a collective community archive, a chapter in a book, a protest in the street, an article in a magazine . . .

[W] The whole morning I've been strolling around with Diana. In the afternoon she took me to a theatre play in the forest set up by the collective Grupi Ata, an activist group of which she is a member. It is such a wonderful initiative. The organization is based in a normal apartment in Kamza where they have been hosting a great number of activistic events involving citizens. The play I was invited to was a recapitulation of the community resistance against a meat company that wanted to tear down their own grown forest. It was performed by three youngsters from Kamza and the audience consisted of other activists or people from the targeted neighbourhood. From some freestanding houses we were brought to their little forest next to the riverside. With the splash of water in the background, grandmothers, mothers with children and old men sat down and watched. The compassion and anger was present when an old lady started to mingle with the play and was willing to start an argument with the actor playing the mayor (Fig. 2). Even if I didn't speak the language and couldn't capture the jokes it was such an empowering scene.

[D] In relation to the mainstream tendency of the youth to leave, as you say, you met yourself with people from Grupi ATA, a grassroots form of commoning that shows attempts to do the opposite. They aim to connect with the place in a profound and meaningful way, to weave a community

Fig. 2. A play by Gruppi Ata.
Photo: Willie Vogel, Kamza, Albania, 2022.

that shares the struggles of living in a city like Kamza and still go through the challenges together. As an interdisciplinary collective, they conduct activism through art and research, and are working on a new understanding of their urban reality. As you saw, during their theatre performances, unexpected places in the city become improvised stages of art and activism. Also, as Diana may have shown you, they periodically do fieldwork for their Laboratory of Urban Anthropology, in which I have participated. This annually organized laboratory is an invitation to meet the city differently, through ethnographic encounters, together with others that have an interest in participating. Beyond this, they offer activist and legal advocacy for environmental causes in support of communities, like the case of Zall Gjocaj to protect the river from a hydro plant that puts water in pipes, taking it from the community that relies on it for living.[13]

[W] On this note I want to express my joy to have met these wonderful people. Coming from a Western privileged position, growing up in a small town between the capital of the Netherlands and the sea, my economic, cultural and urban environment has been quite stable my whole life. Although having travelled and lived in other countries I am still figuring out what my position is when I move to different places, how much space I can take. I hope that the curiosity and respect for other ways of living came across during my conversations. I did not want to come with facts, nor did I try to research or point to a mere cause and effect situation for the film I will produce. It links to what I have been reading throughout Le Guin's work. She sees that we are often taught (in Western schools) to 'crave objectivity because the subjective is to be embodied, to be a body, vulnerable, violable'.[14] Something to unlearn when travelling.

[D] Also, the work of ATA reminds me of bell hooks' reflection on choosing the margin as a place of radical openness.[15] Their work is a continuation of their parents' struggles and autonomy. It is intergenerational, it is subversive of the stigma, it comes from a place of resistance, the resistance that for years has been silenced by the dominance of centralities of power. The inhabitants of Kamza are seen as *them*, *ata* in Albanian, the 'Others', that are not supposed to have a voice: them, coming from the mountains, the primitives, that aspire to be modern, but that still cannot escape the framework and fate of their tribe. As Pratibha Parma – cited in the same book by bell hook – would say, 'they appropriate this space of marginality as a political act!'[16] We, and everyone that enters that space has to be aware of where they are entering and where they are coming from. For me, my position as an insider and an outsider simultaneously often puts me in dilemmas of positionality. For all of us organizing and participating in the training school, to go there from TU Delft or other well-known European institutions, we have to be careful to not think of ourselves as the liberators. They do not need us for that, they are capable of liberating themselves and they do it every day. We go there to learn through and with them, to make sense of things, to co-produce some situated knowledge that can only come from the *radical openness* of these places. That's how I see the positionality of this training school we are organizing, while I cherish the autonomy of places like Kamza.

Date _ 24.12.2022 _ Tirana

[W] During my first day I learned a lot about the peripheral areas of Tirana and how this capital of Albania turned into this mid-sized European city. It was my second day when I stepped onto the colourful tiles of the main square in the city centre of Tirana (Fig. 3). I was told that the colours resemble all the different parts of Albania – the square symbolizing the togetherness of a nation (to follow this metaphor one should not look too closely since many tiles are dirty and broken already). As you mentioned the city centre itself showed many different time influences.

The transition from Kamza to Tirana is interesting. Either you take one of the main car veins to the city centre, or you walk along the river through

Fig. 3. Main Square, design by N51E4.
Photo: Willie Vogel, Tirana, Albania, 2022.

the self-made neighbourhoods, trying to cross a self-made bridge.[17] As soon as you come into the inner ring you feel the long history of the city. A patchwork of different architectural styles, shops at every corner, higher apartment blocks all indicate that Tirana is a different city.

Maybe it is only now, looking back, that one can distinguish some sort of timeframes. As the previously mentioned article by Rosen and Musaraj, 'Tirana Visible and Invisible', explains so beautifully, the city of Tirana can be historically read through its several architectural articulations. In their case the Bazaar City, the Boulevard City, the Concrete City and the City of Cafes. If we stick to their interpretation for now (although they don't identify settlements like Kamza), I think one of the proposed 'cities' is dominant at the moment: the Concrete City.[18] This kind of city is planned, dominating, economically driven and composed by many non-Albanian architects. To explore this phenomenon I moved from the periphery and the 'unplanned' Kamza to the centre of Tirana. How do you relate to these 'different' cities? And how do you remember the city centre of the early 2000s?

[D] Tirana has a complex and complicated history and material legacy, unfortunately not so democratic. The city we have today is marked by a transformation from an organic development to ambitious planning actions aimed at Westernizing it. As mentioned by many, the city has now become a palimpsest of erasure and overwriting, with planned and unplanned traces coexisting. That is mostly evident in the city centre within the ring. Professional planning in Tirana has often been done violently and at the expense of the unplanned, through shrinking or erasing the agency of inhabitants and minor and less powerful actors in the city. This has been a common denominator of all the regimes that have ruled in Tirana, including the current one. In his book-length essay *Kulla e Sahatit* (the Clock Tower), Ardian Vehbiu speaks about how during state-socialism Tirana was transformed from a city of artisans to a city of professionals and bureaucrats. He also describes how the city centre has been used as the scene for a political theatre of symbolisms, of influences and for cryptic communication signals.[19] Something similar is happening nowadays with an allegedly apolitical design for the central square, or with nationalistic symbols in tower façades that aim to distract the discussion from more important questions that would help understand where the pressure on the city comes from. A pressure that is usually justified in the name of development and progress. But my question is whether progress can arrive without democracy. Can progress come through violence? Is that real progress?

Date _ 25.12.2022 _ Tirana

[W] I made my way to the neighbourhoods next to the boulevard (Fig. 4). Self-made villas are under threat of being torn down and replaced by the white, supposedly green, urban plan of Boeri. It was a good site to film the main theme of my investigation: material unrest. There was a constant noise of construction sites, in which buildings were being demolished or rebuilt. There were spraypainted texts on the metal sheets protecting the new buildings showing the resistance to these transformations. I know that many protests have taken place here, but nothing succeeded to withstand the political incentives (Fig. 5). The state of unknowing is the main struggle people have. They don't understand why this transformation is happening, when their house will be next to be demolished and where they have to go. We might call this short period of transformation and reordering a shifting of baseline syndrome. The term comes from the field of geology and is used to address the changing of the environment in such a way that we forget how it looked before and thus privilege some assemblages over others.[20] Albania is executing a huge metamorphosis and this is mainly initiated, visible and brought about through matter. Where ideologies differ it is material that matters, that enforces statements.

Fig. 4. Boeri redevelopment. Photo: Willie Vogel, 5 Maji Tirana, Albania, 2022.

Fig. 5. A sign of protest against the Boeri redevelopment. Photo: Willie Vogel, Tirana, Albania, 2022.

Moving through the city I was drawn to the concrete city since this is so present. This material is widespread because it is relatively easy to make since the infrastructure and market are in place. Yet it is damaging in many ways. Taken from the riversides, whole ecosystems are transported to the periphery of Tirana to be mixed with cement and aggregates. Poured in the ground and rising up to the sky, concrete establishes a mark for many years. When new ideas have to be concretized and old buildings have to go, the waste materials are dumped into the river again, functioning as foundations for a new ring road. In the best case scenario if the loop is closed, the material value has gone through many stages. The research has given me several insights into these stages and explained to me quite some aspects of a country and its inhabitants. I can't wait to share these with a larger group and discuss other findings during and after the training school!

With special thanks to our conversation partner Diana Malaj (Activist and PhD candidate Law, Graz University, from Albania living in Kamza) who became a substantial part of the organizing team of the training school.

References

Bardhoshi, N., *Shteti qe i druhemi* (eng. The state we are afraid of), Inaugural lecture within the Laboratory of Urban Anthropology Tirana: LAU, 2017.

hooks, bell. 'Choosing the margin as a place of radical openness'. In *Framework: The Journal of Cinema and Media*, no. 36, 1989, pp. 15–23. JSTOR, http://www.jstor.org/stable/44111660

Le Guin, Ursula K. *Dancing at the edge of the world: Thoughts on words, women, places*. Open Road+ Grove/Atlantic, 2017

Lleshanaku, Luljeta. *Negative Space*. New Directions Publishing, 2018.

Malaj, Diana, *The Story of Their Theater,* Kamza, 2020. https://kosovotwopointzero.com/en/the-story-of-their-theater/
https://www.instagram.com/grupi_ata/

Mehilli, Elidor. 'Socialism with a Fascist Facade', in *From Stalin to Mao: Albania and the Socialist World*, Cornell University Press, 2017.

Novas Ferradás, Maria, and Pllumbi, Dorina. 'Observing the Architectural Stigma of the Ugliness: The Cases of Albania and Galicia'. In D. van den Heuvel, F. Tanis, & S. A. Hwang (Eds.), *The Observers Observed: Architectural Uses of Ethnography: Proceedings of the 8th Annual Conference of the Jaap Bakema Study Centre* (pp. 114-120). TU Delft and Het Nieuwe Instituut, 2021.

Pllumbi, Dorina. Is Tirana's rapit transformation progress or erasure?, 2022. https://kosovotwopointzero.com/en/is-tiranas-rapid-transformation-progress-or-erasure/

Rosen, M and S. Musara, S. 'Tirana Visible and Invisible'. In: Linder, B. (eds) *"Invisible Cities" and the Urban Imagination*. Literary Urban Studies. Palgrave Macmillan, Cham. 2022.

Jeremy Till, *Architecture Depends* (Vol. 55). MIT press, 2009.

Tsing, Anna Lowenhaupt.' The Mushroom at the End of the World'. In *The Mushroom at the End of the World*. Princeton University Press, 2015.

Tsing, Anna Lowenhaupt et al. (ed.). *Arts of living on a damaged planet: Ghosts and monsters of the Anthropocene*. U of Minnesota Press, 2017.

Vehbiu Ardian. *Kulla e Sahatit*, Tiranë: Çabej, 2018.

1 Matthew Rosen and Smoki Musaraj, 'Tirana Visible and Invisible', in: Benjamin Linder (ed.), *'Invisible Cities' and the Urban Imagination: Literary Urban Studies* (Cham: Palgrave Macmillan, 2022).

2 Willie's visit is supported by an STSM (short term scientific mission) of the COST action *Writing Urban Places.*

3 Rosen and Musaraj, 'Tirana Visible and Invisible', op. cit. (note 1), 158.

4 Ardian Vehbiu and Elona Pira run an influential Albanian essay-oriented online magazine, peizazhe.com/.

5 Elidor Mëhilli, 'Socialism with a Fascist Façade', in: Elidor Mëhilli, *From Stalin to Mao: Albania and the Socialist World* (Ithaca, NY: Cornell University Press, 2017).

6 Luljeta Lleshanaku, *Negative Space* (Cambridge, MA: New Directions Publishing, 2018).

7 Jeremy Till, *Architecture Depends* (Cambridge, MA: MIT press, 2009), 169.

8 Nebi Bardhoshi, *Shteti qe i druhemi* (The state we are afraid of), inaugural lecture in the Laboratory of Urban Anthropology Tirana: LAU, 2017.

9 María Novas Ferradás and Dorina Pllumbi, 'Observing the Architectural Stigma of the Ugliness: The Cases of Albania and Galicia', in Dirk van den Heuvel, Fatma Tanis and Sun Ah Hwang (eds.), *The Observers Observed: Architectural Uses of Ethnography: Proceedings of the 8th Annual Conference of the Jaap Bakema Study Centre* (Delft/Rotterdam: TU Delft and Het Nieuwe Instituut, 2021), 114-120.

10 Anna Lowenhaupt Tsing. 'The Mushroom at the End of the World', in: *The Mushroom at the End of the World: On the Possibility of Life in Capitalsit Ruins* (Princeton: Princeton University Press, 2015).

11 51N4E (20 December 2022), *Tid-Tower,* 51n4e.com/projects/tid-tower.

12 Novas Ferradás and Pllumbi, 'Observing the Architectural Stigma of the Ugliness', op. cit. (note 9).

13 Diana Malaj, *The Story of Their Theater* (Kamza, 2020), kosovotwopointzero.com/en/the-story-of-their-theater/; instagram.com/grupi_ata/.

14 Ursula K. Le Guin, *Dancing at the Edge of the World: Thoughts on Words, Women, Places* (Open Roads Media / Grove/Atlantic, 2017), 151.

15 bell hooks, 'Choosing the Margin as a Place of Radical Openness', *Framework: The Journal of Cinema and Media* 36 (1989), 15-23.

16 Ibid.

17 Lorin Niculae, professor at the 'Ion Mincu' University of Architecture and Urbanism in Bucharest and one of the participants in the training school was

inspired to write about lessons learned about this self-made bridge and the way it works as a self-managed and commoning piece of infrastructure. Online: dilemaveche.ro/sectiune/societate/un-pod-si-citeva-invataminte-2259717.html.

18 Rosen and Musaraj, 'Tirana Visible and Invisible', op. cit. (note 1).

19 Ardian Vehbiu, *Kulla e Sahatit* (Tirana: Çabej, 2018). Selected pieces from *Kulla e Sahatit* are to be published in English in *Other Destinations*, a publication supported by the COST Action *Writing Urban Places*.

20 Anna Lowenhaupt Tsing et al. (eds.), *Arts of Living on a Damaged Planet: Ghosts and Monsters of the Anthropocene* (Minneapolis: University of Minnesota Press, 2017), 6.

Views on Delft

Around 1661, Johannes Vermeer painted what has become one of the most famous city views: the *View of Delft*. The city of Delft is depicted from across the water of the River Schie. We see the city as a collection of brick buildings with lower and higher towers, peaking into the sky, and being reflected in the water of the river. The light looks alive: despite the clouds it is bright, setting the buildings of Delft and the riverbank in the foreground in a palpable warmth.

Delft, an intermediate European city in the province of South Holland, between The Hague and Rotterdam, has featured quite prominently in Dutch city narratives, partially thanks to Vermeer's paintings, which showed fragments of both spatial and social characteristics of the city in the seventeenth century. In the same period, biologist Anthoni van Leeuwenhoek experimented with lenses and built a microscope, which led to the discovery of the micro-world of cells and bacteria. The city's small streets, the canals, the church towers and the market squares still remind us of the times of Vermeer and Van Leeuwenhoek. But Delft today, as a centre of trade, knowledge and art, is a very vibrant city, with the University of Technology as one of its most celebrated contemporary inhabitants. The TU Delft is recognized around the world for educating progressive thinkers and innovators in varied engineering fields, while its Faculty of Architecture has raised, and keeps raising, inspired generations of architects and designers.

As Delft is the city where this *Writing Urban Place* network originated, and where many members of the network have lived, studied or lectured, or are still doing all the above, we have asked our Delft-related colleagues for their views on Delft, painting for our readers, in words, their accounts of the sociospatial characteristics of this city, their relationship with the water, their favourite urban places, their personal *Views of Delft*.

A View of Delft: Reflections of Memory and History on Water

Fatma Tanış

The lights of the hanging colourful bulbs blend with the smooth waves of the green canal in Delft. This canal is known as the Schie, a waterway that connects the Maas River to the North Sea through the delta, passing by medieval port cities in South Holland. Delft was known for its trade, brewery and pottery industries. Famous Delfts Blauw pottery has been produced since the seventeenth century: porcelain decorated with scenes from the Netherlands, as well as figurative depictions, can be found on Delftwares and tiles. These small tiles of 15 x 15 cm have travelled to other cities and can also be seen on the streets of Cherbourg in France, for instance.

The branches of the river give a hint about the historical role of the Schie: Rotterdamse Schie, Delfshavense Schie, Schiedamse Schie and Delftse Schie – where I am now. A barge is perpendicularly tied with braided ropes to the quay. Wooden benches are aligned well together with long tables as an extension of a restaurant. Not only does the boat provide an enveloping atmosphere for those who enjoy their cold drinks on warm summer days, but it also urbanizes the canal, just like the other fancy boats anchored permanently on its sides. In one of them, a family is having their dinner. Being at the intersection of canals, that are in fact streets on water, one could say this is another Delft square.

As I looked across the canal, an old vessel caught my eye. It appeared to have been abandoned here for some time. It was reminiscent of the boats depicted in Vermeer's *View of Delft*. Coincidentally, it was also positioned almost exactly where its predecessor was in the mid-seventeenth-century painting. The painting offers a glimpse into history with its depiction of a city wall made of bricks (which likely inspired the name of Zuidwal street), a single arched bridge flanked by prominent buildings, and a canal leading to the city centre, where churches can be seen. The towers of the old and new churches, along with the steep red roofs of houses, create the city's skyline. How powerful a frame it is, making you explore further into Old Delft. How was life back in those days? While wandering in the seventeenth century, a voice brought me back to the moment: *Heeft het gesmaakt*?

Around the Schie

Angeliki Sioli

This is what we call the evening walks with our dog, around the long wide canal that connects Delft and Rotterdam. 'Around the Schie', we usually decide when the wind is not hostile, and Caldonia, our Louisiana bluetick hound who braces any kind of weather, follows willingly. We start at Abtswoudsebrug, the bikers' rotating bridge, and head up north facing the city centre. The first green spot on the right of the route dictates a stop. Caldonia takes in as many smells as possible before adding her own olfactory prints to the place. We continue parallel to the canal, with the water on our left, in front of tall, impressive waterfront multiplexes, until we hit Scheepmakerij. Here the lower single-family homes change the landscape. If their lights are on, glimpses of the residents' private lives are reflected on the water, shedding their light on ducks and occasional rowers below. Our next stop is usually Willemijn's house. Caldonia pulls us forcefully towards her and her husband Maurice when they happen to stand at their entrance door. We stop, we chat, we occasionally have a glass of wine, and we keep walking. A few metres further down the road we get a glimpse of Kapelsburg, the harbour and south water-entrance to the old city. There are benches, an overlook for smokers or young lovers.

Fig. 1. We cross the water over Hambrug.

We turn with the canal and head straight, cross the water over Hambrug (Fig. 1), where Caldonia sometimes stops to look at the ducks gathered around the old steel structure.

Then we start circling our way around the harbour. The expanse of the Schie and the horizon soon take over the view on our left (Fig. 2). When there is sun, every pass here is a golden hour to bask in. Caldonia shares the feeling. It is here where she often stops to do her frantic swirls around herself, pausing only to ask for some caressing. We call it the 'loving spot' and we all crouch down and readily indulge.

The impressive building of Huszár protects our embraces from a distance, knowing we will be walking by its side in a few minutes, and then immediately finding ourselves at the Vermeer spot. This is where Vermeer painted his famous ***View of Delft***. A contemporary public art installation commemorates the historic location but falls short in communicating the power of the view itself, even more of the painting. So do the garbage and recycling bins besides the location marker. Behind the installation lies an open green

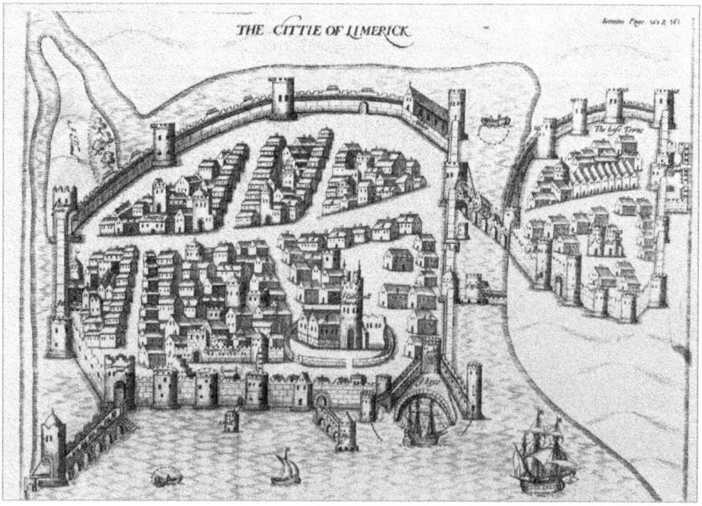

Fig. 2. The expanse of the Schie and the horizon in the evening.

Fig. 3. Nearing the end of our walk we cross Abtswoudsebrug and wave good night to the crooked belfry of Old Jan.

Fig. 4. 'In Delft, 3 March 2020'.

field where Caldonia runs around, unless the weather is too wet or cold. This is our last stop along the way. Soon we find ourselves on the other side of Abtswoudsebrug, where we first met the Schie. Crossing it signals our goodnight to the city, the water, the outdoors. The crooked belfry of Old Jan responds to our waves, or so we want to believe (Fig. 3). The sound of the door locking behind us ends our evening walks. Caldonia discreetly curls up in her bed and soon starts whistle snoring in her unique way. Whether she dreams of the smells 'around the Schie' or her beloved Louisiana back home, is something we will never really know.

Bridging

Aleksandar Staničić

These days I've developed a routine. The first thing I do after getting up is to go to my window on the second floor of the former Physics Department building – now a DUWO students' residence – and just look at how the Sint Sebastiaansbrug is being rebuilt. Before switching on the coffee pot, or even checking my emails, I just stand there for scores of minutes and observe workers swarming the construction site, heavy loaded trucks coming and going down the Kanaalweg, and the new bridge appearing slowly, slowly, in front of my eyes. It is a sublime experience, like constantly reliving Kafka's *The Bridge*, but in slow motion and in reverse.

The canal that the bridge-to-be is trying to conquer is an equally impressive feat of engineering, linking the two important Dutch cities The Hague and Rotterdam. This particular stretch marks the southern border of the old city of Delft and connects the best ice cream shop in town, 'J.H. Beaart ijs' on the north-east bend, with the place on south-west bend, the Zuidkolk, from where Johannes Vermeer painted his famous *Gezicht op Delft* (*View*

of Delft). Across the canal, humbling fortress-like walls of the former power plant are trying to conceal the old city centre that sprawls beyond it, while on the opposite side I can sense – although I cannot physically see it – the heavy presence of the Faculty of Architecture building.
This particular morning is slightly different, though. It is 9:00 a.m. and I am already in my suit, though I don't wear suits that often. There's also a palpable tension in the air, and not the kind that is caused by dismayed citizens trying to navigate their way through the construction site and congested parking lot in order to reach the Vakwerkhuis for their morning coffee. Today I am having the most important interview of my life, in an effort to make long-term personal and professional bridges of my own. What to expect, how will it go? I take one closer look at the site in front of me: foundations are strong, they reach deep all the way to the solid ground; the material is rich and of the highest quality; the supporting structure is well thought-through; the personnel overseeing the work is skilled and experienced; the goals are set high but achievable. One deep breath before I go. Thank you, Sint Sebastiaansbrug.

Evenings at the Koornmarkt and Beestenmarkt

Klaske Havik

I used to live in one of those old canal houses on the Koornmarkt, with eight other students. We were a close group, sharing much of our lives together for several years. In the evenings, usually someone would come up the three stairs to my attic room – a room with big curved wooden beams and small windows on three sides, offering views of the roofs of Delft – and knock on my door: let's go for a drink in town! We would walk, the three, four or five of us, towards one of the nearby cafés': Wijnhaven or Tango. Late in the evening, there was hardly any traffic, and we would walk next to each other in the full breadth of the Koornmarkt street. Our footsteps on the brick pavement and our voices were the only sounds in the street.
Apart from the university, where we spent most of our time, the cafés were important in our everyday life in Delft; they formed a social structure in the city, as they were the places where we often gathered. Each of them had their own crowd. We enjoyed these bars not only as consumers, but also as employees – we worked in kitchens and served on terraces to support our studies. I used to work at Kobus Kuch at the Beestenmarkt, the square that used to be an animal market. Now, chairs and tables occupy the elevated square between the platanus (sycamore) trees from spring until late autumn, and on summer evenings the sound of the chitter and chatter of people fill the space between the trees. The most notable moments at the Beestenmarkt were those late summer nights. After the closing hour of the bar, after the last guests had departed, I would close the wooden window blinds at the façade and clean the terrace, stacking chairs and tables. Suddenly, that space between the platanus trees was mine alone, the square was silent, breathing night.

Savouring the Streets

Holly Dale

'Do you still have some space for dessert?' I ask, hoping he will say yes.

It is late May, and the young leaves on the trees are unravelling above us. The old trees stand tall between the road and the canal on the Voorstraat, the low evening light dances between the leaves and onto the water.

As we approach the Poelbrug, I can see the queue of people crossing over the bridge. At the front of the line, I recognize the flag of De Lelie blowing gently in the breeze. People wait eagerly, midday or dusk, from May to October for De Lelie's homemade ice cream. On a hot day, the queue can be so long it would cross the Voorstraat, go over the bridge, extend through the small square beside the Oude Kerk and end down the narrow alley behind it.
It is still early in the year, so we can join the queue in the square at the end of the bridge. We stand encased by brick all around us, the brick of the monumental old church to our back, all dishevelled and wonky. The straight and structured brick patterns on the ground flow over the water to the other side, meeting modest shops with small apartments above. At the base of the shops, the brick folds up the walls in different shades of red, each shade revealing a different moment in time.

There is a calm excitement around; we watch groups of people moving in and out of the city centre. Groups of students laugh and holla as they cycle by, friends piled up on their bikes. The old bike frames shake and rattle as they roll over the brick streets. The sound of rolling suitcases echoes as tourists make their way wearily to the train station. A family carrying sleeping children gently walks home from dinner.

We are nearly at the front of the queue, and I am standing on my tiptoes to read the flavours in the small shop front. 'Which flavour will you pick?'

A Garden of Techne

Willie Vogel

Two palm trees form a gate. While going through, the smell of lavender meets you. A bit further, two old ticketing ladies greet you. Some small ceramic and metal works are exhibited just before you enter the Botanical Garden. The 2.5 hectares of diverse greenery is situated just outside the waterways enfolding the city centre of Delft, between the old university buildings. Initiated as a 'Cultural Garden for Technical Crops', it makes me wonder what could be so 'technical' about crops. In the greenhouses, a technical invention themselves, a wide variety of cacti and jungle plants are grown. Some of them get a little usage explanation at the end of the route. Reading technical as *techné* – as a craft or making – this botanical garden is the result of a long careful act. I look at the gardeners with their wheelbarrows, spades and shovels as extensions of themselves. Do their craft and knowledge, plus the crops, form the technicity of this cultural garden?

Herbs, flowers, trees and mosses all have nametags. The same goes for a big rosemary plant, some different varieties of sage and some types of mint. Around the little pond, it is serene and some chairs invite you to sit down. This relatively small garden, an oasis during warm summers, does not only teach the gardeners the *techné* of maintenance. Even I learned, while coming here regularly during study hours or on weekends, a certain craft of pause and stillness. Maybe the Garden of Technical Crops initiated by Gerrit van Iterson in 1917 is in fact not merely related to the 'technical' university. Perhaps this cultural garden is the place where technology is not only seen as mechanical equipment, but allows us to reflect on the *techné*, skills and craft, that technology brings in the dynamic interaction of our bodies with our environment.
With fresh cheeks and some space in my mind, I leave the garden. I greet the gardeners, the ladies at the entrance and take a little branch of lavender with me.

A Wooded Spatial Sequence: Verzetstrijdersbuurt

Saskia de Wit

Besides the walk from the train station to the campus, I don't really know Delft that well. So when I visited the Verzetstrijdersbuurt, a large residential area from the 1960s, very similar to any other housing area built in the Netherlands in the same period, I was kind of lost at first. It could have been anywhere. Only when I stepped away from the streets to explore it from the margins, a sequence of loosely defined courtyards at the backside of the low-rise housing, did its unique qualities unfold. I was surprised to discover that I could walk from one green space to the next, only occasionally encountering the formal traffic spaces. This green

structure is the realm of pedestrians and animals, separated from the functionally determined urban space. Surrounded by garden fences and sheds, low and inconspicuous, these spaces are defined by the mature trees inside, which, rather than forming a ubiquitous green blanket, provide distinctive spatial, formal and experiential qualities to each individual space.

In one courtyard I found myself on a field framed by a back street and garages, under a 'ceiling' formed by a regular grid of plane trees. After crossing the Wilhelminalaan, with its short 'colonnade' of alder trees, a second courtyard was framed by a 'bosquet' of dense shrubs below a mixture of trees: a living wall enclosing an introverted outdoor room. Next to it a 'thicket' of mixed trees and tall shrubs forms a closed wall from the outside, but unlike the bosquet it is dense and impenetrable on the inside, providing shelter to blackbirds, sparrows, tits, hedgehogs, mice, spiders and all sorts of other non-human species, complementary to the bosquet in terms of spatial experience, use and accessibility. A narrow bridge crosses the water line that divides this neighbourhood from the next. On the other side of the bridge a line of alders and birches forms a loose and transparent 'curtain', in dialogue with the impenetrable thicket on the opposite bank.

I could still perceive the traces of the original design: an alternation of tree lines and squares of trees around an open centre. But 60 years later this simple spatial construction has diversified into a gradient from clear to ambiguous, from simple to diverse. The (probably unintentional) effects of different expressions of growth and maintenance has led the canopy to close and develop into a roof in the northern courtyard, joining with the underlayer and developing into a wall in the southern courtyard, forming a diverse and specific spatial sequence with a rich palette of social and ecological possibilities.

Westerkwartier

Jorge Mejía Hernández

At first, I thought our next-door neighbour didn't really want to move here. Probably that's why she was a bit grouchy for some time, complaining about our 'Spanish parties', as she called them. Then I noticed she'd become friends with the other old woman across the street, and she never complained again. Now she receives our mail when we're not home. That other older lady across the street takes care of the kid who lives with his mom. Like most children here he goes to school on the other side of the outer canal, as it's called. You see them all leaving around eight to be there on time, quarter past; turn the corner, cross the bridge, left turn again, and into the square in front of the school.
While my mom remembers many things of the year they spent in Delft back in the 1960s, my dad says that his most beautiful memory was seeing how loved Dutch kids were. 'He's right,' I think on that square. Probably that's why it broke my heart to see the woman from a few houses down the street bald after her chemo. 'She's so young, so sweet, so decent,' I thought, 'and her kids are so small.' Her husband is a schoolteacher, I've heard. Not sure what the guy next to them does for a living, but he organized everyone to buy a long ladder to fix the roofs and clean the windows, and then made sure that the municipality did not cut our beautiful trees. This is the only street with trees in the western quarter, as it's called.

Our Chilean neighbours also have long lunches in their backyard on summers, and there's a new, much younger couple at the end of the block who throws real parties at night. The man looks South Asian, so I wonder what our next-door neighbour calls their gatherings. Our street was built in the late 1930s, so almost a century ago, and is named after a Carthusian monk, as there was an old charterhouse here. Recently a few men came and changed the whole sewer system in just a few weeks. They found some ruins of the old monastery and had to call an archaeologist from the municipality. Now we have brand new brick herringbone pattern pavement on the street, and neatly done sidewalks paved with concrete tiles. While the construction was going on, all the boys in the street stared for hours out their windows. Besides my neighbours' love for their kids, it might be that my most beautiful memory of Delft is seeing men do simple things very, very well.

1536
1632
2023

Elena Perez Guembe

While waiting for a friend in the enchanted Delft, I read on a façade 1536, and my mind starts flying. I am suddenly transformed into a passer-by, standing in the middle of the street, who curiously looks at the inauguration of a recently finished building. Not without feelings of estrangement I try to understand what I see. Perhaps a bit 'too new', or a bit 'extravagant'? . . . All is fine. There are many forms of being in the world and not all will be known to me. Thank God! Isn't this side of life fascinating? I look at the corner, trying to find something more familiar that would make my imaginary me feel at home. I see the entrance to the main square, and visualize a market, cows, shit, and mud, wet and cold. I see strong women lifting buckets, pouring milk with love. The same ones Vermeer would have been acquainted with since he was a kid. A little two floor brick building is bowing towards the street, kindly inviting me to enter. His hat is similar to mine. I gently bow my head back at him with a smile, lifting my hat a tiny bit entering into the multitude with joy.

Witold Rybczynski says that during the Dutch Golden Age, people used to dress like their grandparents. Calvinism was the state religion and exercised a major influence on everyday life. They 'admired saving, frowned on conspicuous spending and naturally evolved conservative manners'.[1] So Vermeer, who was born around a hundred years after 1536, might have dressed like my imaginary me. Perhaps he was even my height. The people in his paintings, portrayed with so much love, look small and 'fatty'. Not because they were, but according to Rybczynski, because of the many layers of clothes they used to put on themselves. Dutch people know how to dress for the cold weather. All the same, they look strong and 'squarish', more connected to the earth and most likely to the farming life. Home doorframes from paintings and from my little brick building friend also seem to be much smaller than current Dutch standards. Some men of today are thin and long, like giant reeds flowing in the wind. Now everything seems to be more fluid. I look at what seems to be a self-portrait of Vermeer. He looks quite flamboyant to me though.

The exhibition of Vermeer at the Rijks was sold out months ago. The system crashed when they opened the tickets sale.

'He's a popular guy,' a Dutch artist friend tells me.
'In general, I think Dutch people are very much into art,' he continues.

'But Rembrandt died poor!,' I replied, amused.
'Because he was out of fashion. Dutch are very much into fashion.'
(joyous laughter)
'You know all about it. You are a very glamourous man.'
'Haha! Lucky that nobody can smell my underwear'
(crazy laughter)

I think I am starting to understand this culture . . .

1 Witold Rybcynski, *Home: A Short History of an Idea* (New York: Viking, 1986), 54.

The Joy of a Sand Street in Delft . . .

Dorina Pllumbi

Often, going to the playground means carrying a bag of earthmover toys with us. Lissus, my almost-four-year-old, thinks the little yellow excavators, dump trucks and bulldozers are fun to play with.

'I am a *punëtor,*' he says, in his special language blend, while excited, continuing to dig in a sandpit with his green helmet on. Excavating sand, loading and unloading. What a joy!

On a sunny day of winter, on our way to Olofspark to meet Ariana, his dear friend, we noticed that suddenly, the entire Singelstraat – a typical brick street in Hof van Delft – had turned into a huge prolonged sandpit.

'Wow, what is happening here mom? Wow!'

Other kids that live around are enjoying the exceptional situation.

It is afternoon, and the big excavators are resting after a long workday, but the little earthmovers, operated by little hands, have just started to load and unload some sand here and there. A woman standing on the door of her house looking towards the street tells me that this has been going on already for some days. Her two toddlers are playing with shovels and trucks. She carries her third child in her arms, a cute little baby of a few months.

'They love it,' she says happily looking at her sons. 'I know they will remember these special days. And will miss it when all this will be finished.'

In a city where everything is clean and in order, this is uncommon. Although as a parent, I should normally be concerned with safety first, I must say that I appreciate the openness of this 'construction site'. No impenetrable fences or bold signs to keep us away. It feels as if it was done on purpose; an invitation for all the kids in the neighbourhood to get together. A joyous moment for the little ones to learn and play, and for grownups to socialize while looking at the happy little excavators loading and unloading sand. This brick replacement event, instead of being a burden to the neighbourhood, as one might think, is actually a chance to celebrate change and maintenance as part of life, where kids can participate with their felicity.

'Mom, my three cities are New York, Tirana and Delft,' says Lissus on our way back home.

'In New York, there are big towers and bridges. In Tirana, there are mountains of fruits in the streets. But in Delft there are clocktowers, canals and bricks. And sand streets with big and small excavators.'

Dear Colleagues,

Jeremy Hawkins

I have to say I was very pleased to have the chance to read your draft of 'Views of Delft', in part because the city has become dear to me over the past couple of years, but also for the pleasure of reading such a collection of personal *Delftse verhalen*. To start with the frame and scope of the overall piece, I think the opening, which superimposes Vermeer's painterly artifact with the lived experience of contemporary Delft, is both vibrant and effective. As a reader, it allowed me to consider a projection into the past, a feeling for representation and aesthetic appreciations of the city, as well as the use of perspective as a device that would carry me through the text. Thanks to this frame, a text in many voices seemed not just as one possible approach among others, but as perhaps the necessary one. What if Joyce had written *Dubliners* about Delft instead?

The range and variety of perspectives throughout the ten sections are broad, but I felt guided by recurring motifs and juxtaposed images that lend to a supple connectivity in the text between sections. I'm thinking, for example, of the frequent appearance of brick, from the ambiances it sets against an evening walk among students in Klaske's recollection, to the mineral flows in Holly's walk, down to precise design patterns, such as when Jorge admires fine workmanship materialized in a herringbone pattern. Oh, and let's not forget how Dorina's piece brings us to what lies beneath the brick!

Of course, it may come as no great surprise that the most prevalent apparent building material in Delft would play a strong role in a text, even if there wasn't a single architect among us. But part of why I think it works well is due the fact that I was not reading about the Platonic form for 'brick', but rather that each mention is specific, situated and embodied, giving a sense of the particular where otherwise it might just be a material category. This connects to my main thought: the strength in this text is the way that each section offers up particularities of the lives and practices that make you all *Delvenaars.*

I read with a particular thrill for the moments of surprise, the particularities and eccentricities, and the details that make each section unique and individual. Because, in the end, I recognize the Delft I have recently come to love in each and every part of the text, but in a way that has everything to do with these being your specific experiences rather than my own. It's the texture of your experiences that allows me to relate my own. Or maybe another way of putting it is in George Saunders's words, where he says, in discussing a story by Donald Barthelme, that 'the real work of the story' is to 'give the reader a series of pleasure-bursts'. Naturally, you do much more than that in this text – you open up a sense of today's spatial practices in Delft, you share the ways in which you understand and live the city, you make an argument for its relevance in the (European) imaginary, you add to the aura of Vermeer's painting, you start to populate the city's landscape, you construct meanings that don't make it into either the guidebooks or the history books – but I'd like to underline the importance of the pleasure your stories bring, especially with that pleasure being almost entirely coextensive with knowledge production. Whatever I may have known before about Delft, the pleasure of discovering the unexpected-and-yet-familiar situations through your particular visions has definitely informed my understanding of the city. I never stopped for ice cream!

So, if I have any constructive criticism, it would only be to say I could even imagine a few more of these kinds of personal, individual, particular, eccentric and even weird perspectives emerging. Oh, and an observation rather than a criticism, is that I found it really intriguing that so many of the sections make it implicit (and sometimes explicit) that the speaker is from an 'elsewhere' that would stand in strong contrast to Delft, but that the *mise-en-mirroir* was scrupulously avoided. This text brought me back to Delft but in ways that were new to me, and which felt generous in how they share your experiences, your favourite haunts and your thinking. A 'loving spot' indeed!

Klaske Havik – *Action Chair* – is professor of Methods of Analysis and Imagination at the Faculty of Architecture and the Built Environment, Delft University of Technology, the Netherlands. She studied architecture in Delft and Helsinki and literary writing in Amsterdam. She has developed a distinct research approach relating architectural and urban questions, such as the use, experience and imagination of place, to literary language. Her book *Urban Literacy: Reading and Writing Architecture* (2014) proposes a literary approach to architecture and urbanism. Havik initiated the platform *Writingplace* and organized the conference *Writingplace: Literary Methods in Architectural Research and Design* (2013). The resulting book *Writingplace: Investigations in Architecture and Literature* was published in 2016. Klaske Havik was editor of *de Architect* and *OASE*, and initiated the *Writingplace Journal for Architecture and Literature* in 2017. Havik's literary work appeared in Dutch literary magazines, her poetry collection *Way and Further* (2021) appeared in English with RightAngle Publishing.

Susana Oliveira – *Action Vice Chair, WG1* – is an associate professor at the Faculty of Fine-Arts, Lisbon University, Portugal, where she teaches Drawing, Illustration and other courses. She studied Fine-Arts, has an MA in Aesthetics and Philosophy of Art and a PhD in Communication and Culture and published several articles and books on visual culture. She co-organized the 1st International Conference on Architecture and Fiction – Once Upon a Place, Lisbon 2010, published in book format in 2013, and was a co-proponent of the Writing Urban Places network. She was a visiting scholar at the GSAPP – Columbia University NY in 2014, with postdoctoral research in Architectural Imagination in Fiction Literature, a subject she continues to pursue, namely within Graphic Representation, Book History and Culture and Word & Image Studies. She also works as a freelance illustrator and has published over 25 youth and children's books.

WG1 abstract

The essay departs from the question: How can stories be used for the development of cities?

In response, a theoretical framework is delineated that recognizes the built environment as a model that is both telic (a vision of a possible future) and technical (the means required to attain that future). By adopting this framework, the essay approaches the city at the scale of everyday, ordinary planning, rather than at the scale of 'cosmic crisis'.

In line with that approach, the essay shows how stories can be useful to develop cities given their ability to encourage and foster sympatry, understood as the quality of environments where different (even adversarial) species coexist. Different individuals simultaneously use and offer different resources to the environment they share, and some of these resources fall within the category of 'understanding'. This final category is captured in a series of micro-narratives about the city, which are then evaluated in relation to three distinct technologies that can be seen as common to buildings and stories, namely: sense, sequence and proportion.

Jorge Mejía Hernández – *Leader WG1* – graduated as an architect in Colombia, and received a PhD form Delft Unoversity of Technology, where he teaches design studios and researches with the section Methods and Matter as an assistant professor. He is a member of the Delft/Rotterdam-based research group Architecture Culture and Modernity, where he supervises PhD candidates from the programme Architecture and Democracy, and also acts as science communications manager for the EU-funded COST Action *Writing Urban Places*. Mejía participated in the design of the 'Balcony' exhibition, part of the 2014 Venice Biennale, and designed the San José de Castilla high school in Bogotá.

Onorina Botezat – *Co-leader WG1* – is Director of the Center for Linguistic and Intercultural Research and Associate Professor Ph.D. at the Faculty of Foreign Languages and Literatures, *Dimitrie Cantemir* Christian University in Bucharest, Romania. Her main fields of interest and research are Imagological and Cultural Studies and Legal Terminology. She is the author of *Dictionary of Legal Terms, Romanian-English and English-Romanian* (2011), *The Image of the Foreigner in the National Literature* (2016), co-author of ESP and FSP courses, and editor of the Annals of "Dimitrie Cantemir" Christian University Linguistics, Literature, and Methodology of Teaching. Her last book is *Mapping Cultural Identities and Intersections: Imagological Readings* (2019, Cambridge Scholars Publishing, co-editor with Mustafa Kirca).

WG2 abstract

This article will discuss the conditions that define the intermediate European city at the beginning of the twenty-first century: the mid-size, other or secondary city as it many times appears in the relevant bibliography, although these terms fail to capture its full potential. We argue that the intermediate European city cannot simply be defined by parameters like population number, territorial extension, or other forms of scale. Instead, we propose an interpretation through categories of conditions from various scientific disciplines covering different perspectives, as provided by our network members. These conditions suggest a systematization of phenomena commonly manifested in the urban contexts under examination. The article aims to get closer to defining what an intermediate city is or is not, concluding with the concrete illustration of seven selected conditions: scale as a commodity, gravity, perceptual coherence, open-ended image, walkable distances, parochial realm and against fragmentability.

Angeliki Sioli – *Co-leader WG2* – PhD, is an assistant professor at the Chair of Methods of Analysis and Imagination at the Faculty of Architecture and the Built Environment at Delft University of Technology in the Netherlands. She is a licensed architect, holding a PhD degree from the History and Theory Program of McGill University, Canada. Her research seeks connections between architecture and literature in the public realm of the city, focusing on aspects of embodied perception of place in the urban environment. She has edited the volume *Reading Architecture: Literary Imagination and Architectural Experience* (Routledge, 2018) and she is currently working on a collection of essays dedicated to sound and acoustic atmospheres of architecture. She is the co-leader of Working Group 2 in the COST Action *Writing Urban Places,* working along with the group's members to create a strong, contemporary and interdisciplinary theoretical context for the study of mid-sized European cities.

Sonja Novak – *Leader WG2* – PhD, is currently assistant professor and chair of German Literature at the Department of German Studies, Faculty of Humanities and Social Sciences in Osijek, Croatia, where she teaches History of German Literature and courses on Literary Theory at undergraduate (BA), graduate (MA) and postgraduate (PhD) level. She conducts her research in the humanities within the research field of Philology and her area of expertise is Literary Theory and History of Literature. Current research topics cover comparative literature, contemporary fiction and drama, with special emphasis on German and Croatian literature. She joined the COST Action *Writing Urban Places* to explore literary heterotopias.

Giuseppe Resta – *Co-leader WG2* – is a Researcher at the Faculdade de Arquitectura da Universidade do Porto (PORTofCALL project). He previously held teaching positions in Istanbul, Ankara, Bari and Tirana. He is the owner and curator of Antilia Gallery (IT) and co-founder of the architecture thinktank PROFFERLO Architecture (IT-UK). His latest monographic books are *Journey to Albania: Architectures, Expeditions and Landscapes of Tourism* (Accademia University Press, 2022) and *Jean-Christophe Quinton: A Few Houses and Shelters 2002-2021* (Libria, 2021). His research on architecture and the city is focused on the relationship between space and power, and on adaptive reuse via artistic practices. Resta is a co-leader of Working Group 2 in the COST Action *Writing Urban Places.*

WG3 abstract
Urban narratives offer a situated, experiential and subjective window into urban places. They come in spoken, visual and written forms and can be queried through a variety of approaches and methods. This contribution draws on the work of WG3–Methodological Framework of the COST Action–*Writing Urban Places* and reflects on the quest to find and bring together different methods and approaches to unearth, understand and retell urban narratives.

We begin this essay by contextualizing the growing interest in narratives within the multidisciplinary field of urban studies and acknowledging the need for methods and approaches to find, analyse, represent and construct such narratives. Following this introduction, we briefly describe the task of WG3 and broadly present the range of methods that were collected as well as the interesting outputs that were produced, including a special issue in a journal, an interactive and iterative online platform, an international digital conference, a book with around 50 methods and assignments, and a set of postcards to disseminate them.

Subsequently, we reflect on this process and discuss the way in which: it helped visualize the often hidden spaces/sites/places where narratives can be found; it unsettled our understanding of what constitutes an urban narrative as well as a method and what these methods are for; and it illustrated the potential of narratives as a medium not only to unlock and generate situated, subjective and experiential knowledge about urban places, but also to mobilize ideas that may even shape urban futures.

Carlos Machado e Moura – *Leader WG3* – is an architect (FAUP, 2006), postgraduate in Architectural Heritage (CEAPA-FAUP, 2013), PhD candidate (PDA-FAUP/FCT, 2015) and integrated researcher at the University of Porto (CEAU-FAUP). He currently lectures at the Faculty of Architecture of the University of Porto (FAUP) and the School of Art, Architecture and Design of the University of Minho (EAAD), and is deputy editor-in-chief of *J–A Jornal Arquitectos* (2022-2024). Carlos is also a researcher of the project (EU)ROPA Rise of Portuguese Architecture (CES-UC), and the author of books like *Building Views* (Circo de Ideias, 2017) and *Casas Quinhentistas de Castelo Branco* (CMCB/Argumentum, 2008). Alongside his practice as an architect with MAVAA, Carlos co-organized several initiatives about drawing and was assistant curator of the 'Physics of Portuguese Heritage' exhibition (DGPC, 2018-19) and Open House Porto 2016. His work has received several awards and recognitions, including Premio Architettura Toscana 2022, Prémio Távora 2020, an honourable mention by Premio Architetto Italiano 2020 and the award of merit of AZ Awards 2019.

Dalia Milián Bernal – *Co-leader WG3* – is a doctoral researcher and lecturer in the School of Architecture, Faculty of the Built Environment at Tampere University in Finland. Her background is in the field of architecture and her current research focuses on the temporary uses of vacant and abandoned urban spaces in the context of Latin America. Delving into online arenas, following several cases and applying different analytic methods of narrative inquiry, she aims to explain why temporary uses develop across Latin American cities and to unearth their deeper meaning. Currently, she teaches sociospatial aspects of sustainable architecture, critical urban theory and, since 2019, she coordinates the IFHP Urban Planning and Design Summer School in Finland. She is the co-founder of the collective-blog *Interrogativa*, a platform that discusses diverse urban processes through the perspective of women and their experience of urban space.

WG4 abstract

Fieldwork within the COST Action *Writing Urban Places* aims to research the possibilities of interdisciplinary narrative practices in understanding and activating urban contexts in European cities. As a way to sustain and foster the meaningfulness, appropriation and integration of places and their communities, it intends to reflect and test its concepts and methodologies in reality. Fieldwork bridges the link between investigation and practice, knowledge and performativity, thinking and doing. Gathering expertise of diverse disciplines, from the social and human sciences to urbanism, architecture and art, fieldwork is debated in the context of the spatial practices, with their critical and aesthetic dimensions. By visiting places (Almada, Limerick, Tallinn, Osijek, Tampere, Çanakkale, Skopje, Tirana, Delft) and sharing knowledge, collecting existing narratives and implementing new ones, crossing local inhabitants and international participants, fieldwork activities allow for a deeper involvement in physical and social contexts and an active engagement with communities and stakeholders.

Luís Santiago Baptista – *Co-leader WG4* – is an architect, researcher and curator. He is an assistant professor in the Department of Architecture of Lusofona University (ULHT), Lisbon, and School of Arts and Design (ESAD-CR), Caldas da Rainha, Portugal. He holds a master's degree in Contemporary Architectural Culture from the Faculty of Architecture of the Technical University of Lisbon (FA-UTL), and is a PhD candidate in Architecture and Urban Culture at the School of Architecture of the University of Coimbra (DARQ-UC). His research interests are contemporary theory of architecture and urban culture. He is working group leader in the European project COST Action *Writing Urban Places*. He develops a multifaceted activity encompassing professional practice, teaching, criticism, curatorship and publishing. He was the winner, with Maria Rita Pais, of the FAD Award of Theory and Criticism 2020 with the book *Journey into the Invisible.*

Slobodan Velevski – *Leader, WG4* – is holding a PhD in Architecture and Urbanism. He is an associate professor at the Faculty of Architecture in Skopje, N. Macedonia. Previously he graduated in Skopje and concluded his master studies at Dessau Institute of Architecture in Germany. In 2018, with Marija Mano Velevska, he co-curated the exhibition 'Freenigspace', representing the Republic of Macedonia at the 16th Architectural exhibition of La Biennale di Venezia. His academic and design interests are mainly focused on research that explores the scale and complexities of architecture and urban design.

FIELDWORK

LIMERICK abstract

Extra Muros: Urbanity from the Outside

Michael G. Kelly and Anna Ryan Moloney

The Walls of Limerick are a recurrent motif in textual treatments of Limerick city and its specificity in Irish and international contexts. The reference functions as a synecdoche for the city as a besieged place at key moments in the history of the island. The Walls function as vestigial reminders of Limerick's position as a mid-sized 'regional' city within a fully European history, and of its status as a major urban site of colonial and post-colonial interactions and hybridizations.

There is a parallel sense in which Limerick has, through modern Irish history, been cast in the role of an urban 'other' within the social and economic politics of the independent Irish state. Associations of urban deprivation and dysfunctionality have frequently been mobilized in a national context to make of Limerick a kind of counterexample, an urban reality paradoxically *extra muros*, as far as national political agency and intentions have been concerned.

Our essay draws together examples of an urban imaginary rooted in an ancient urban history and permanently *extra muros* – profoundly urban(ized) and yet constantly revisiting the process of asserting a collectively shared 'right to the city'.

Michael G. Kelly – *WG2* – is a professor in the School of Modern Languages and Applied Linguistics at the University of Limerick (Ireland), where he is also director of the Ralahine Centre for Utopian Studies. He is the author of a study on the relations of utopia and modern French poetry, *Strands of Utopia: Spaces of Poetic Work in Twentieth-Century France* (Legenda, 2008/Routledge, 2020) and has published widely in both English and French on a range of topics in modern and contemporary French and comparative literature. Recent work at the intersection of literary urban studies and utopian studies includes the editorial projects 'Urban Utopics' (Special thematic issue of the *Forum for Modern Language Studies* Vol. 59.1, January 2023) and *Utopia, Equity and Ideology in Urban Texts: Fair and Unfair Cities* (Palgrave Macmillan, 2023).

Anna Ryan Moloney – *WG4* – is an associate professor at the School of Architecture, University of Limerick, Ireland, where she follows interests in landscape, writing, drawing and photography through her teaching and research. She holds a BArch from University College Dublin, a PhD from the Department of Geography at University

College Cork, and has recently completed an MA in Creative Writing at the University of Limerick. She practised with Grafton Architects in Dublin, and was editor of the journal *Building Material*. In 2016, Routledge published her book *Where Land Meets Sea: Coastal Explorations of Landscape, Representation and Spatial Experience*. Recent essays have been published in a range of venues, including *The Coastal Atlas of Ireland* (Cork University Press), and have focused on architectural thinking on the coast, topography and spatial experience, writing methods, spatial literature and Tim Robinson.

PORTO abstract

Campanhã Collage. Stories from the City's Edge

Carlos Machado e Moura and Eliana Sousa Santos

Campanhã, the easternmost parish of the city of Porto, Portugal, is a land marked by problems of social and territorial cohesion, fractured by large-scale rail and road infrastructures, an area still torn between its past of rural tradition and the increasingly visible features of middle-class modernity with cosmopolitan aspirations. Campanhã Collage provides a kaleidoscopic overview of this area through four contributions based on the work of different projects with distinct methods, agendas and outputs, some of which focused on specific parts of the parish.

StreetArtCei, the first case, applies its method of digitally mapping street art routes to Campanhã, expressing specific cultural geographies and serving as a barometer of the city's changing spaces. The Atlas of Literary Landscapes, the second case, proposes a collection of textual excerpts documenting the railroad and the Campanhã train station through Portuguese literature. The third case, The Worst Tours, an initiative of walking tours that offer a critical perspective of the city apart from mainstream routes, discusses and envisions possibilities of transformation. Its contribution includes coloured hand drawings, photos, and a poetic text, focusing specifically on Freixo, the riverfront area of Campanhã. Finally, A Drift in vacant Campanhã recounts the experience of URBiNAT, a project aimed to design opportunities to co-create an inclusive public space in these underutilized areas, together with local citizens and stakeholders.

Despite the evident differences in the nature of these projects, the juxtaposition of these stories and accounts provides alternative views of the fragmented territory of Campanhã. It also conveys a spatialized description of several of its multiple problems and possibilities. While not offering a comprehensive reading of this part of the city, the methods and fieldwork experiences used testify to the rich potential of each medium and allow for the construction of new meaningful itineraries.

Carlos Machado e Moura – *Leader WG3* – *(p. 337)*

Eliana Sousa Santos – *WG2* – is an architect, researcher and an assistant professor of Architecture. In 2017, she was awarded the Fernando Távora Prize and has since been publishing her travel essays in the press. She was the curator of the exhibition 'The Shape of Plain' (Gulbenkian Museum Lisbon 2016-2017), an associate project of the Lisbon Architecture Triennial 2016. In 2013-2014, she was a visiting postdoctoral research fellow at Yale University, and currently is a researcher at Center for Social Studies, University of Coimbra, and an invited assistant professor at the Department of Architecture and Urbanism at ISCTE-IUL. She has a degree in Architecture awarded by the University of Lisbon, a master degree from the University of Coimbra and a PhD from the London Consortium, University of London. She joined the COST Action *Writing Urban Places* to explore narratives of place and writing historical essays as travel diaries.

TALLINN abstract

Stories of Pictures and Pictures of Stories

Jüri Soolep

One can say: a picture is worth a hundred words, but if the hundred words contain a story, then this story is also worth a hundred pictures. We also see old pictures with new stories and old stories with new pictures. All of this is fascinating as stories and pictures create and build meanings, both old and new. The meaning continua, sometimes thousands of years old come to us in the form of stories and pictures.

This article examines some of Tallinn's local stories. The first is about an archetypal flood, as the beginning and end of the Lake Ülemiste. The second deals with the Medieval Town Hall Square in the format of an artificial fairy tale and explains how marzipan came to be used. The third is a sinister geopolitical story, or to be more exact: a whole knot of stories spawned by the Red Army monument known as the Bronze Soldier.

We look at these stories through the language of images and films. The old and new images tell us about the history and future of these stories in the most imaginative ways.

Jüri Soolep – *WG4* – received his diploma in Architecture in Tallinn (1986), where he also was professor and dean. He has been a professor at the NC State European Center in Prague, Czech Republic and a guest professor at the Umeå School of Architecture, Sweden. He was the rector of the Nordic Academy. Soolep has lectured at the universities of Tartu, Oulu, Porto, Cork, Portsmouth, Liverpool, Halle and Hosei Tokyo. He is on the editorial board of the journal *Ehituskunst*. He was a member of steering boards for Strong Research Environments ResArc and Making within Swedish Research Council Formas grant.

Since 2001 he has been partner and lead architect in the architecture studio AB Medium. Most of his designs have been built in Pärnu and Tallinn. His most recent book is *Architecture, Imagospheric Horizon and Digital Universe* (https://soolep.ee). His current field of research include studies in the representational systems of architectural phenomena, innovation and composition in the Digital Age.

TAMPERE abstract

Co-Constructed Narratives of the Grassroots in the City: Narrating Hiedanranta

Dalia Milián Bernal, Elina Alatalo, Jeremy Allan Hawkins and Panu Lehtovuori

Hiedanranta is a former industrial complex located on the shores of lake Näsijärvi in Tampere, the second largest city in Finland. Currently, the area is inhabited by diverse cultural actors that work on individual as well as collective projects and who have also appropriated the buildings and surrounding areas, physically transformed them and provided them with new uses, while unleashing other, often political, processes. It is the work of these actors on the territory that renders this site's special, haptic and creative character. Notwithstanding, the area is currently undergoing a dramatic transformation. Due to a large urban development project, the material substrate of the site as well as its internal social dynamics are rapidly changing, already seeing some cultural groups being permanently displaced. It is within this context that the COST Action team in Tampere organized a workshop to gather, understand and retell the stories of different cultural actors working on the site by employing different participatory visual and narrative methods.

In this contribution, we explore Hiedanranta through six co-constructed narratives. These narratives bring together visual material and poetic practices as well as long narrations of personal experience that shed light on the lives of these cultural actors as they unfold in and relate to Hiedanranta. By bringing these narratives to the fore, we aim to challenge objectivist and positivist forms of generating knowledge about urban places by taking narratives of personal experiences as legitimate sources of knowledge seriously, recognizing that knowledge is both situated and subjective; to deploy co-constructed narratives of a site as a form of subjective representation of a place that counters abstract representations of space; to illustrate the way in which the grassroots are also shaping plans, policies and spaces and therefore should find a place in theoretical planning discourses. Most importantly, through these narratives we hope to keep the stories of Hiedanranta alive before, like the old factory buildings, these are forever erased.

Dalia Milián Bernal – *Co-leader WG3* – *(p.337)*

Elina Alatalo – *WG4* – is an architect and doctoral researcher in Environmental Policy at Tampere University, Finland. Her recent research has concentrated on new forms of urban activism, getting vacant spaces back into use and developing sustainable urban neighbourhoods. She is specialized in creating experiments with citizens. Currently she teaches in and coordinates Climate University (climateuniversity.fi) in Tampere, which offers multidisciplinary courses for those who want to make the sustainability transition in society real. She is a co-founder of the Insurgent Spatial Practices collective (research.tuni.fi/insurgentspatialpractices), which explores the valuable knowledge that alternative cultures develop, for example by combining methods from art and research.

Jeremy Allan Hawkins – *WG3* – is a poet and lecturer at the Strasbourg School of Architecture in France, where he is a member of the AMUP research laboratory and contributes to teaching and research on design narratives, architectural writing and poetics. He is a doctoral candidate in Creative Writing at the University of Glasgow, studying situated writing practices and knowledge production in spatial design contexts. He is the author of the poetry chapbook *A Clean Edge* (BOAAT, 2017). His writing has been published widely in Europe and the United States and has been selected for inclusion in the *Best New Poets* anthology series, as well as the extended programme of the 2018 Venice Architecture Biennial. His research interests include creative writing as spatial practice, material poetics, practice-based research and knowledge production in urban design.

Panu Lehtovuori – *WG4* – is a professor of Planning Theory at Tampere University, School of Architecture. Before the current position, he was a professor of Urban Studies at the Estonian Academy of Arts in Tallinn. Lehtovuori's research interests focus on contemporary forms of public urban space, new urban design approaches and the resource efficiency of the built environment. Lehtovuori regularly partners with Livady Architects, one of Finland's leading experts on heritage evaluation and conservation; SPIN Unit, a transnational research group combining art and science for urban studies and advanced data solutions; and Nordic Urbanism, a start-up in continued professional education and urban consulting. His recent publications include 'Drivers of Global Urbanization: Exploring the Emerging Urban Society', in the Routledge *Handbook of Henri Lefebvre, the City and Urban Society* (co-written with J. Tartia and D. Cerrone) and 'Temporary Uses Producing Difference in Contemporary Urbanism', in *Transience and Permanence in Urban Development* (co-written with S. Ruoppila).

ÇANAKKALE abstract

Travelogues of a Sentimental Journey through Çanakkale, Turkey

Giuseppe Resta and Sonja Novak

Çanakkale is a mid-size city on the Dardanelles Strait. It is generally known as the Second World War battleground of the Gallipoli Campaign, when the British Empire and France failed to capture Istanbul as the Ottomans used geographical features to their advantage. Çanakkale also sits in the region that is believed to be the same as ancient Troy, whose destruction is featured in Homer's *Iliad* and *The Odyssey*. Until the late nineteenth century, the Trojan War was considered to be a fictional event, but then pioneer archaeologist Heinrich Schliemann followed Homer's geographical descriptions and identified Hisarlık Hill with the help of Frank Calvert as the site of the ancient city. The site is now UNESCO World Heritage, but the line between myth and reality is still blurred. The case study of Çanakkale will thus expand on the grey area of the city's contemporary physical condition and the mythological potential of its underlying urban narrative as a place of epic significance, a place in which fictional stories overlap with the physical description of the urban and natural environment. The multitude of meanings and symbolism assigned to the city and region of Çanakkale thus prove to be fruitful grounds for the exploration of travelogues' potential as a subgenre of travel literature that sways between myth and reality, as was shown in the workshop The City and the Myth organized 18-20 July 2022 with the support of the COST Action *Writing Urban Places*.

Sonja Novak – *Leader WG2 – (p.335)*
Giuseppe Resta – *Co-leader WG2– (p.335)*

SKOPJE abstract

Skopje Brutalism Trail: Rebuilding Social Fabric through Architecture and Performance

Marija Mano Velevska, Slobodan Velevski, Aleksandar Staničić, Blagoja Bajkovski

The article reflects the city of Skopje from the perspective of the workshop Skopje Brutalist Trail held in late September 2022 as a part of the activities focused on fieldwork within the COST Action *Writing Urban Places*.

The workshop departs from the general topics of brutalist architecture and solidarity, both highly relevant and related to the city and its culture. The idea of the workshop is to offer a new viewpoint by means of civic participation and activism in order to reassess forms of solidarity in the process of community building. The workshop engages creative writing and performing arts to develop urban narratives that link architectural legacy, *in-situ* findings and memories of people and places, juxtaposing past, present and future narratives.

Reflection on the theme and the workshop experience

Holly Dale

The chapter also includes a reflection on the theme by Holly Dale, from the stance of a participant in the workshop and a researcher on the topic of literary methods in understanding, performing and creating urban scenarios. The review highlights how these literary methods can help drive the development of heritage conservation to reflect past inconsistencies, integrate contemporary values and develop approaches to ensure more inclusive futures.

Marija Mano Velevska – *WG4* – has a PhD in Architecture and is an associate professor at Ss Cyril and Methodius University, Faculty of Architecture in Skopje, N. Macedonia. Besides teaching a course in Architectural Design, she co-leads the master studio in architectural urbanism entitled Growth 2.0. She is the editor and co-author of several books, including *Conversations*, which embodies a series of interviews with eminent architects and educators. With active participation in numerous workshops, seminars and conferences, concerning both the academia and the practice in architecture, the focus of her work refers to teaching and learning architecture by combining design practice and architecture theory.

Slobodan Velevski – *Leader WG4* – *(p.339)*

Aleksandar Staničić – *WG4* – is an architect and assistant professor at the Faculty of Architecture and the Built Environment of Delft University of Technology. Previously he was a Marie Curie postdoctoral fellow at Delft University of Technology (2018-2020), a postdoctoral fellow at the Aga Khan Program for Islamic Architecture at MIT (2017-2018), and a research scholar at the Italian Academy for Advanced Studies, Columbia University (2016-2017). His most recent work includes the edited volume *War Diaries: Design After the Destruction of Art and Architecture* (University of Virginia Press, 2022) and numerous research articles in various journals, including *The Journal of Architecture, Footprint* and *Architecture and Culture.*

Blagoja Bajkovski – *WG4* – is a teaching assistant at the Faculty of Architecture at Ss Cyril and Methodius University in Skopje. He finished his PhD in Italy at Mediterranea University of Reggio Calabria on the topic *Operative Atlas of Brutalist Skopje: A Graphic Biography of 15 Architectures.* His main research strands developed in the last years are focused on the interdisciplinary approach to Skopje's brutalist architecture. In 2018 he participated at the 16th architecture exhibition of La Biennale di Venezia with the project SKOPJE DESTRATIFICATION '29'65sk14.

Holly Dale – *WG1* – graduated in 2020 from Delft University of Technology. While at Delft, she researched an alternative 'open' architectural approach that encourages intimate narratives to flourish in the city. After graduation, Holly co-founded RARE Collective, a space for interdisciplinary collaborations exploring values within artistic and scientific processes. Holly has worked at leading architectural practices in the UK, Australia and the Netherlands. Currently, she works in Amsterdam with a focus on sustainable design and teaches Architectural Design in the chair of Methods of Analysis and Imagination at Delft University of Technology. Through research projects and teaching within the chair, distinct methods are developed for producing, using and understanding the built environment.

ALMADA abstract

The Other Margin

Luís Santiago Baptista and Susana Oliveira

Almada, which is both a city and a county located on the south bank of the Tagus River and part of the Lisbon metropolitan area, has a unique identity that is influenced by both its proximity to and separation from Lisbon. This so-called 'other margin' was built on the productive base of the agricultural and fishing industries, the military and quarantine infrastructure, the burgeoning tourist industry on the Atlantic waterfront, the significant naval shipyard presence on the riverfront, the communal associations and cooperatives in the towns, and the expanding suburban condition throughout the entire territory. Almada is depicted here from various angles using various ways of representing its people, places, events and narratives that were taken from literary, artistic, architectural and documentary sources like books, illustrations, models, photos and movies. The urban narratives of Almada are replayed, alternating back and forth between past and present, memories and reality, the written and the visual.

Luís Santiago Baptista – *Co-leader WG4 – (p.338)*
Susana Oliveira – *Action Vice Chair, WG1 – (p.332)*

OSIJEK abstract

Mapping the Fictional and the Physical City: The Spatiotemporal and Cultural Identity of Osijek, Croatia
Sonja Novak and Angeliki Sioli

Because of its status as the fourth largest city in Croatia, Osijek is considered an intermediate European city. It is the administrative, economic and cultural centre of eastern Croatia, located on the River Drava, and has a rich, multicultural history that is reflected in its tangible and intangible urban identity. It is famous for its historical Fort Tvrđa and its European Avenue, the most representative street of Austro-Hungarian Secession architecture, but also for its specific sociolects that have been a part of its everyday life. Within the COST Action *Writing Urban Places: New Narratives of the European City*, Osijek was host to the doctoral training school 'Urban Chronicles in Empirical Context' (April 2022) and a short-term scientific mission to investigate the 'other' perspectives of the city (August 2022). As events that fostered the training, research, and the networking of international and national young researchers, doctoral candidates and members of academia, they helped to raise awareness of the notion of urban identity of a city as a complex of its physical (geography, architecture, infrastructure) and ephemeral manifestations (literature, culture, history) through time. As such, the events functioned as an outreach, linking the involved participants to their own responsibilities to the city as potential and future policymakers. The following chapter focuses on elements of the city of Osijek as presented through the literary point of view of local authors from the mid-twentieth to the early twenty-first century.

Keywords: Osijek, urban cultural identity, literature, architecture, literary built environment

Sonja Novak – *Leader WG2 – (p. 335)*
Angeliki Sioli – *Co-leader WG2 – (p. 335)*

TIRANA abstract

A Travel Captured in Correspondence
The Planned, the Unplanned, and Everything in Between
Dorina Pllumbi and Willie Vogel

The text offers a glimpse into the conversation between two of the three organizers behind the training school titled 'The Planned, the Unplanned, and Everything in Between' held in Tirana and Kamza in March 2023. Three months before the training school, the two correspondents, Willie, visiting Albania for the first time through an STSM, and Dorina, temporarily located in the Netherlands, exchange daily thoughts aiming to interpret the two cities' urban situations and sociopolitical conditions. Albania's historical position at the edge of Europe has seen a remarkable shift in recent times, turning into an emerging discovery. Simultaneously, a burgeoning self-awareness of subverting narratives of representation has begun to take root among the Albanian youth – a phenomenon that adds depth and complexity to the ongoing dialogue. The transformation of the cities and the country is explained as multivocal while acknowledging protests, loss and destruction as part of a glorified urban project.

Dorina Pllumbi – *WG2* – is an architect and a PhD candidate in the Faculty of Architecture and the Built Environment of Delft University of Technology, the Netherlands. Her research interest resides in studying practices of commoning as material and spatial engagement in realities of political transition. Her particular focus is to understand the role that commoning practices have played in Albania during the transitional period from a totalitarian state-socialist regime to a recently consolidating neoliberal one. Currently, Dorina is a visiting scholar at Parsons School of Design in New York City.

Willie Vogel – *WG1, WG2* – graduated in 2020 from Delft University of Technology. In her final project she used narrative tools to research the feeling of being at home through scales. After graduating she moved to Berlin where she is finishing her double degree bachelors in Philosophy with a thesis on Ecophilosophy and New Materialism. She works parttime in a start-up with Sophie van Riel and Italo de Vroom to develop the graduation project further under the name Studio Makadam. She also works parttime in the start-up Studio Inscape, where she merges her philosophical interests with (architectural) design together with Eileen Stornebrink and Charlotte von Meijenfeldt. Finally, she is involved in the network as research assistant for the chair Methods of Analysis and Imagination at the Faculty of Architecture and the Built Environment of Delft University of Technology.

DELFT abstract

Views on Delft

Fatma Tanış, Angeliki Sioli, Aleksandar Staničić, Klaske Havik, Holly Dale, Willie Vogel, Saskia de Wit, Jorge Mejía, Elena Perez Guembe, Dorina Pllumbi and Jeremy Hawkins

Around 1661, Johannes Vermeer painted what has become one of the most famous city views: the *View of Delft*. Delft, an intermediate European city in the Netherlands, located between The Hague and Rotterdam, has featured quite prominently in Dutch city narratives, partially thanks to Vermeer's paintings, which showed fragments of both spatial and social characteristics of the city in the seventeenth century. As Delft is the city where this Writing Urban Place network originated, and where many members of the network have lived, studied or lectured, or are still doing all the above, this contribution collects their views on Delft, painting for our readers, in words, their accounts of the sociospatial characteristics of this city, their relationship with the water, their favourite urban places, their personal views of Delft.

Fatma Tanış – *WG1* – is the coordinator of the Jaap Bakema Study Centre at the Nieuwe Instituut, Rotterdam and lectures at the Faculty of Architecture and the Built Environment, TU Delft. Prior to Delft, Tanış trained as an architect in İstanbul and Stuttgart. She holds Master's degrees in Architectural History (ITU) and Conservation and Restoration of Cultural Heritage (MSFAU). Having a particular interest in the in-between realm, she has explored the specificity of port cities through the notion of cosmopolitanism in her doctoral dissertation titled *Urban Scenes of a Port City: Exploring Beautiful İzmir through Narratives of Cosmopolitan Practices* (2022). Her other publications include *Spatial Stories of İzmir* (2020); *Space, Representation, and Practice in the Formation of İzmir during the Long Nineteenth Century* in *Migrants and the Making the Urban-Maritime World: Agency and Mobility in Port Cities, c. 1570–1940*, eds. Christina Reimann, Martin Öhman (New York, London: Routledge, 2020); and a themed issue *Narratives #1: Mediterranean and Atlantic Cities* (2021).

Angeliki Sioli – *Co-leader WG2 –* *(p. 335)*
Aleksandar Staničić – *WG4 –* *(p. 349)*
Klaske Havik – *Action Chair –* *(p. 332)*
Holly Dale – *WG1 –* *(p. 350)*
Willie Vogel – *WG1, WG2 –* *(p. 353)*

Saskia de Wit – *WG2* – landscape architect, is an assistant professor in the Section of Landscape Architecture, Delft University of Technology, the Netherlands. She holds a master's degree from Wageningen University and a PhD from Delft University of Technology. She combines teaching and research with practice at her own firm *Saskia de Wit tuin en landschap*. Her research focuses on the garden as a core concept of the field of landscape architecture, as expressed in her recent publication *Hidden Landscapes* (2018), which ties the concept of the enclosed garden as an expression of landscape to contemporary metropolitan developments. She uses the concept of the garden as a lens for research into perception of place, sensory landscape qualities and contemporary notions of nature.

Jorge Mejía Hernández – *Leader WG1 –* *(p. 333)*

Elena Perez Guembe – *WG4* – is a licensed architect, currently undertaking a PhD at TU Delft in the Netherlands. Elena has worked in the offices of Zaha Hadid, Rafael Moneo, and Nicholas Grimshaw. Her work has been exhibited at the 2018 Venice Biennale as well as at the 2019 Lisbon Triennale. Her design work and writing has been published internationally: DeArq Magazine (Colombia), Hipo-

Thesis (Spain), Global Art Affairs Foundation (La Biennale di Venezia), Routledge (UK/USA) and others. After teaching at Rensselaer Polytechnic Institute's (RPI) School of Architecture in Troy, New York for several years she moved in 2021 to TU Delft (Netherlands) as a PhD researcher. Her interdisciplinary research "Architectures of Care. From the Zapotecs to the Cosmos" combines critical thought and praxis through hermeneutics and material culture as architectural discourses.

Dorina Pllumbi – *WG2 – (p. 353)*
Jeremy Allan Hawkins – *WG3 – (p. 345)*

COLOPHON

Writingplace, Journal for Architecture and Literature

#8+9 SPECIAL ISSUE

Writing Urban Places. New Narratives for the European City

This publication is based upon work from COST Action CA 18126 Writing Urban Places, supported by COST (European Cooperation in Science and Technology).

COST is a funding agency for research and innovation networks. Our Actions help connect research initiatives across Europe and enable scientists to grow their ideas by sharing them with their peers. This boosts their research, career and innovation. **www.cost.eu**

Editors of this issue:
Klaske Havik
Susana Oliveira
Jorge Mejía Hernández
Holly Dale

together with: Onorina Botezat, Sonja Novak, Angeliki Sioli, Giuseppe Resta, Carlos Machado e Moura, Dalia Milián Bernal, Luís Santiago Baptista, Slobodan Velevksi

Copy editing: D'Laine Camp

Design & cover:
Studio Sanne Dijkstra

Publisher:
Marcel Witvoet, nai010 publishers in collaboration with TU Delft Open

This publication was made possible by:

COST European Cooperation in Science & Technology

Funded by the European Union

nai010 publishers

TU Delft

nai010 publishers is an internationally orientated publisher specialized in developing, producing and distributing books in the fields of architecture, urbanism, art and design. www.nai010.com

nai010 books are available internationally at selected bookstores and from the following distribution partners:

North, Central and South America - Artbook | D.A.P., New York, USA, dap@dapinc.com

Rest of the world – Idea Books, Amsterdam, the Netherlands, idea@ideabooks.nl

For general questions, please contact nai010 publishers directly at sales@nai010.com or visit our website www.nai010.com for further information.

NUR 648
BISAC ARC001000
THEMA AMA

9 789462 088030 >